Working in  class
together from ti rtant
science concepts skills
listed above. In a nthly
or bimonthly "d complex scientific and
environmental issues, such as whether oil spills should be
cleaned up or allowed to disperse naturally. Also, there can be
personally relevant discussions, in which students make predictions for their own lives based on what they are learning about
the topic.

Meeting the Challenge

1. Select an elementary or high school grade level and
   develop a series of possible topics on which to base a
   "learning by talking" curriculum. Keep in mind the diversity of backgrounds that will be represented in your classroom, and the different learning issues depending on
   your students' grade level. Be sure to build in to your
   plan the opportunity for students to shift the focus or to
   develop their own topics for discussion.
2. Create some guidelines for language use in your "learning
   by talking" classroom. Who will get to talk, and for how
   long? How will speakers be recognized? Is interruption
   permitted? What will your role be? Devise a way to allow
   your students input into this decision making so they will
   feel comfortable abiding by the guidelines.
3. When you next spend some time with friends, take a step
   back and observe the language pragmatics operating.
   What are the rules everyone seems to be following? What
   can be said or not said, and how are tone of voice and
   body language used? What happens when someone
   breaks a rule? How long does it usually take a newcomer
   to catch on to the rules? What if he or she is unable to
   master the pragmatics?

UNDERSTANDING AND MEETING THE CHALLENGE OF STUDENT CULTURAL DIVERSITY

Eugene García

University of California, Santa Cruz

HOUGHTON MIFFLIN COMPANY
BOSTON   TORONTO
Geneva, Illinois   Palo Alto   Princeton, New Jersey

Sponsoring Editor: Loretta Wolozin
Senior Developmental Editor: Susan Granoff
Senior Project Editor: Janet Young
Production/Design Associate: Caroline Ryan Morgan
Senior Manufacturing Coordinator: Florence Cadran
Marketing Manager: Rebecca Dudley

Cover design by Carol H. Rose.

Photographs on Part Opener pages by: page xviii, Bill Cadge/The Image
Bank; page 102, Stock Boston; page 180, Dennis MacDonald/The
Picture Cube.

Printed in the U.S.A.

Library of Congress Catalog Card Number: 93-78671

123456789-AM-96 95 94 93

ISBN: 0-395-51735-4

BRIEF CONTENTS

CONTENTS

BECOMING A RESPONSIVE TEACHER

FIGURES

TABLES

PREFACE

I remember the day one of my eldest brothers came home from school noticeably disturbed—physically and otherwise. He had been in a nasty fight. Like most younger brothers, I didn't hesitate to ask, "How bad does the other guy look?" After my brother yelled at me for asking such a dumb question, he told me why he had been in that fight.

It seems that some kid had called him a "dirty Mexican." I had heard those words myself. At the age of five, I had already begun to realize that I was different, and that some kids didn't seem to like that. My brother then made it quite clear why, to him, the words "dirty Mexican" were fighting words. He said we should be proud to be Mexicans—should allow no one to call us dirty. My brother said those were bad words aimed at our mother. She worked hard to keep us clean, he continued, and we should always be proud of that.

Since that day, I recognized that to be different—by culture and by language—was not a negative. My brother was absolutely clear about his conclusion. Sadly, many in our society have not yet arrived at this same conclusion.

This book is written in recognition of those children who are considered "dirty" by many other children, because of the color of their skin, their language, or their culture. Some of these children are my own, others are children of my brothers and sisters, but most are just children marked by society because they are outside the "preferred" boundaries. Diversity is a wonderful gift to our society, but often it's an unrecognized gift—at times easily discarded or even scorned. Just as the motto of our nation is stated to be "e pluribus unum," meaning "out of many, one," the motto of this book is best articulated by its variation "e *diversitate* unum"—out of many groups bonded by their humanity, yet distinct from one another, we form one nation.

It has always been the challenge of humankind to get along cooperatively and peacefully in the world. That challenge remains substantive and grows daily as our own existence becomes more and more dependent on

our near and far neighbors' well-being. We know so much more today
about meeting this challenge, especially in the domain of education.
Educating all of our children to meet our highest expectation is possible.
Like the fear of diversity, ignorance of how to meet the challenge is no
excuse. This book's aim is to help eliminate both of these excuses.

Audience and Approach

Understanding and Meeting the Challenge of Student Cultural Diversity
is an introductory core text for courses on teaching culturally
diverse students. The text is for one-semester, junior, senior,
and fifth-year courses in Multicultural Education. The text can
also be a supplement in a variety of education courses. Teachers
taking such courses increasingly ask, "How can I teach the entire
range of students that I will find in classrooms today?"

The Roots of Diversity

This book provides the basis for responsive teaching by exploring the roots of diversity. This basis consists of the social, the
cognitive, and the communicative roots of diversity; how children of diverse backgrounds learn to think and communicate
within their home, community, and school environments is the
pivotal framework of this book. Language—from its early acquisition to its use to construct and communicate meaning—is
treated fully as a key component of the roots of diversity.

The Responsive Teacher

An understanding of the roots of diversity in context helps
teachers create classroom climates and instruction that are
responsive to diverse students' needs. To connect concepts to
active classroom practice, the theme of responsive teaching is
integrated throughout the text narrative. Additionally, a feature
called "Becoming a Responsive Teacher" presents practical class-
room-oriented interludes in each chapter. Finally, helping
teachers develop responsive pedagogy is the main topic of Part
Three, "The Educational Response." Teachers who are truly
effective learn to adjust their teaching strategies in response to
the learning styles of individual students. The dual point consistently made by this book's approach is that 1) the roots of diver-

sity provide understanding necessary for 2) meeting the challenge of responsive teaching.

Content and Organization

The text consists of eight chapters divided into three parts. *Part One*, "Student Diversity in Context," assesses the breadth and complexity of America's culturally diverse student population. Chapter 1 explores demographics and immigration trends, identifying more clearly the students we will be teaching today and tomorrow, and the cultural and language backgrounds they bring with them. Chapter 2 provides a conceptual overview of culture: how the term is defined, and what it means to be inside or outside of a particular culture. Chapter 3 examines past and present educational approaches to diversity. Where have we been successful, and where have we fallen short? How far have we come in providing equitable means and opportunities to a multicultural population?

Part Two, "The Roots of Diversity," the core of the book, probes into the communication process itself, and how teachers interact with their culturally diverse students. Chapter 4 shows how language develops in early childhood, and presents research on bilingualism, multilingualism, and the use of non-standard dialects. Chapter 5 examines the effects of social contexts—peers, the family, and the community—on the individual child's learning style and how well he or she performs in school.

Part Three, "The Educational Response," focuses on concrete ways in which educators can address the needs of culturally diverse students. Chapter 6 describes methods of helping students to build bridges between the sometimes incongruous worlds that they experience inside and outside the classroom. Chapter 7 looks at the preparation and characteristics the teacher of culturally diverse students must have, and what assessment methods may be used to determine his or her effectiveness in the classroom. Chapter 8 examines the preparedness of the school itself, describing the qualities of some schools that have experienced success in educating multicultural populations. This chapter also makes recommendations on how other schools can share in this success. Finally, an Epilogue provides additional context—and, I hope, inspiration—for the challenge of providing educational equity to all Americans.

Special Learning Features

Understanding and Meeting the Challenge of Student Cultural Diversity offers a number of valuable features designed to help students to easily grasp and learn the material in the text.

- *Focusing questions* at the opening of each chapter introduce the major topics to be explored.
- *"Becoming a Responsive Teacher"*—a unique feature appearing at least once in each chapter—presents classroom situations drawn from the author's experience and from current studies and research. As a departure point, *"Meeting the Challenge"* questions and activities, a section within this feature, encourage students to reflect, then to respond thoughtfully and creatively to the diversity in real-world classrooms.
- *Marginal notations* draw attention to central points throughout the text and provide helpful landmarks for review.
- *Key terms* appear in boldfaced type so that their meanings are reinforced and can be more easily located.
- *A summary of major ideas* at the end of each chapter helps the student to further understand and clarify what has been read.
- *"Extending Your Experience"* questions prompt students to apply their new understanding of diversity to their own lives and to the outside world. These questions will be especially helpful for students whose experience has primarily been among homogeneous populations.
- A list of *resources for further study* also appears at the end of each chapter, providing students with additional opportunities to read and learn.
- A *glossary* at the end of the book defines important terms.
- A *references* section provides background for books and studies cited in the text, which students may wish to explore further.

Acknowledgments

A number of reviewers made useful suggestions and provided thoughtful reactions at various stages in the development of the manuscript. I wish to thank the following individuals for their conscientiousness and for their contributions to the content of this text:

Mario Baca, California State University, Fresno
Mario Benitez, University of Texas
Leah Engelhardt, Purdue University, Calumet
Dolores Fernandez, Hunter College
Herman García, New Mexico State University
Tonya Huber, Wichita State University
Frank Kazemak, Eastern Washington University
Carmen Mercado, Hunter College
Susan Mintz, University of Virginia
Antoinette Miranda, Ohio State University
Robert Rueda, University of Southern California
George Stone, Arkansas College

I would like to give special thanks to Josephine Velasco, Anne Bauer, and Dagoberto García for their assistance. And a very special thank-you to my wife, Erminda, who served as assistant, critic, and supporter.

Eugene García
Washington, D.C.

Part One describes the scope and complexity of America's population of culturally diverse students. In Chapter 1 we examine how the rapidly changing cultural and ethnic makeup

STUDENT

of the nation as a whole affects our classrooms. Who are the children we will be teaching, and what cultural and language backgrounds will they bring to the classroom?

Before turning to our discussion of

DIVERSITY

cultural diversity in the U.S. schools, we need to define what is meant by the term *culture*. Chapter 2 provides such a conceptual overview. What does it mean to be a member of a particular culture, and how does cultural

IN CONTEXT

membership affect people's interactions both within and outside of that culture?

Chapter 3 supplies a historical survey of American educational approaches to the teaching of culturally diverse students. What has been done? Have we made significant strides in achieving educational equality?

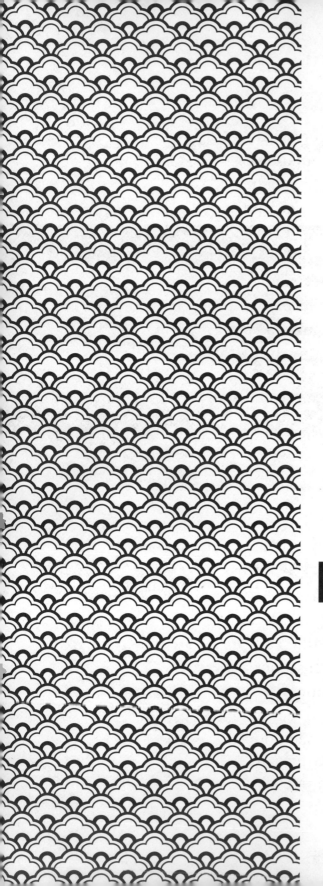

CULTURAL

DIVERSITY

IN AMERICA'S

SCHOOLS

CHAPTER 1

Focus Questions

○ What are some of the trends in immigration to the United States over the last two decades?

○ What are the demographics of the U.S. student population expected to be in 2026?

○ How do indicators of child and family well-being relate to educational achievement?

○ What do the changing demographics of the U.S. student population imply for the training and assessment of teachers?

○ How are language minority students defined, and what types of educational programs are designed to serve them?

"Not the best or worst of times, but times of challenge." —TOMÁS ARCINIEGA

A Portrait of Change and Challenge

Mrs. Margaret Tanner's classroom in a sunny, southern California elementary school looks much like any other fifth-grade room. The walls are brightly adorned with the children's work, and an aura of busy concentration prevails. The playgrounds outside the windows and the cafeteria down the hall complete a picture repeated countlessly in communities all over the United States. Mrs. Tanner's school was built in the 1950s, and the number of students it serves has remained around 600 since its opening. This changed briefly for a five-year stretch during the enrollment boom of the late 1970s, when it served over 900 students and operated "split" morning and afternoon sessions. Mrs. Tanner has had as few as 19 students in her classroom and as many as 35, but on the average her daily attendance has remained at between 26 and 28 students.

Mrs. Tanner has taught fifth grade in this very classroom, in this school, in a suburb of Los Angeles, for twenty-one years. She is a dedicated and committed teacher. When she accepted her initial teaching assignment, her students and most of the other people in her community shared many demographic characteristics: they were almost all middle class, white, and English speaking—the descendants of people who had emigrated to the United States from Europe during the nineteenth and early twentieth centuries. In short, they were all very much like herself.

In that first decade of her professional career, however, demographic shifts began in the population of her state. Los Angeles expanded and its suburbs multiplied, and her community became a haven for recently arrived Mexican immigrants and for other Spanish-speaking people flooding into California from towns and cities in the southwestern United States. In that decade, the demographic makeup of Mrs. Tanner's fifth-grade class also began to change. Her white, middle-class students were joined by African American children whose parents had relocated from the southern United States, and by children who spoke Spanish in their working-class homes and commuted regularly between the United States and Mexico. The parents of

Demographic
Shifts

these children, like the grandparents of her earlier students, had come to the United States to find employment and to achieve a higher standard of living for their families. Although these new students were not like her in some ways, Mrs. Tanner recognized their needs and abilities and felt just as committed to them as she had felt toward her first students.

In the second decade of Mrs. Tanner's tenure, further shifts in the population have continued to dramatically alter the nature of the student body in her classroom. More and more, she teaches students who speak a variety of languages in their homes and communities: Spanish, Vietnamese, Russian, Hmong, Chinese, and Farsi. The communities from which these students originate are made up of first and second generation Mexican immigrants, and first generation Vietnamese, Hmong, Chinese, Iranian, Russian, and Central American refugees. Many of these families have traveled to the United States to seek a better standard of living, but some have come because they were forced to escape politically volatile and dangerous circumstances in their nations of origin.

| **Different** |
| **Languages** |
| **and Cultures** |

Mrs. Tanner is quick to point out that her commitment and determination to serve these students is no less, and may be even greater, than ever before. But she is also the first to admit that the diversification of her student body has challenged, to the very core, her own concept of her role as a teacher and her grasp of the skills necessary to teach effectively. As she sees it, the greatest challenge to her commitment as a teaching professional is the challenge of cultural diversity in her student body. Her students come from different cultures, language backgrounds, and economic levels. Effectively teaching a classroom of over two dozen fifth-graders who come from radically different cultures and who speak different languages is not the job Mrs. Tanner was originally hired to do. Back in her first years as a teacher, she could fairly safely assume that all her students would respond similarly to a lesson, and in ways that were familiar to her. Now, however, she can assume very little. In order to reach her diverse students while creating a cohesive learning environment, considerations of cultural and language differences must enter into her teaching strategies.

| **Teachers in** |
| **the Next** |
| **Century** |

The changes and challenges Mrs. Tanner faces in her role as a teacher are being played out in classrooms all over the United States. Schools characterized by a culturally and linguistically diverse student population are soon to be the norm rather than the exception for new teachers of the twenty-first century. We need no crystal ball to see that the future for U.S. schools will mirror the changes that have occurred in Mrs. Tanner's class-room. The demographic shifts in our country's population are thoroughgoing and well documented. Groups of students once labeled minorities will become majorities, particularly in highly populated metropolitan areas where most of the student popula-tion is concentrated—areas where most of this country's stu-dents will either succeed or fail. Mrs. Tanner is a pioneer, a representative of things to come. And much like her own expe-rience of self-examination regarding the practice of her profes-sion, all of us will be required to take a fresh look at the assumptions underlying our current methods of teaching, learn-ing, and schooling. Also, like her, our commitment to an increasingly diverse student population must never waiver.

This book is dedicated to all the Mrs. Tanners of this country. Moreover, it is an attempt to address the many complex forces and issues that are likely to demand the attention of teachers for years to come. I hope the insights it offers and the discussions it engenders will be of service to the dedicated individuals who devote themselves to children within a variety of educational settings.

In this chapter, we focus on the demographic attributes of culturally diverse students in the United States. Clearly identify-ing and defining this population has not been an easy task for educators, and most of the categories of definition reveal more about the definer than the defined. The educational initiatives targeted at culturally diverse students have been variously syn-onymous with programs for "poor," "lower class," "immigrant," "at-risk," "underachieving," and "dropout" students. As Gonzalez (1990) has documented, the children thus categorized are usu-ally perceived as "foreigners," "intruders," or "immigrants" who speak a different language or dialect or who hold values signifi-cantly different from those of the American mainstream. These perceptions have led policymakers (including the U.S. Supreme Court) to highlight the most obvious demographic characteris-tic—a racial or language difference—in their attempts to address widespread academic underachievement in a population.

In this chapter we will see that there are many more demo-graphic characteristics that help us understand academic under-achievement in this population. Specifically, this chapter will provide:

1. An overall demographic assessment of factors related to the schooling of culturally diverse populations, including issues of poverty, family stability, and immigrant status.

Perceptions

of Culturally

Diverse

Students

2. An in-depth discussion of the issue of academic performance, including comparative data with regard to high school dropouts, academic achievement, and funding for education.
3. A particular analysis of the challenges associated with the growing number of language minority students—that is, students who come to school with no proficiency or with limited proficiency in English.

In all this discussion of demographic information, it is easy to lose sight of the actual significance of these figures and numbers. Keep in mind that as cultural and linguistic diversity in our schools increases arithmetically, the challenge to education increases geometrically and possibly exponentially. The schools of tomorrow will be transformed by our response today to a number of pressing variables and agendas. One of the most significant of these variables is the demographic reality of our school-age population.

The Extent of Cultural Diversity Among U.S. Students Today

Immigration: The Historical Basis of Diversity

From 1981 through 1990, more than 7.3 million people immigrated to the United States, which was a 63 percent increase in immigration over the previous decade. Table 1.1 shows a detailed breakdown of immigration to the United States by country of origin. Apart from the sheer magnitude of numbers, what are the characteristics of this immigrant population? In relative terms, which are the significant countries of origin? Perhaps more importantly, what are the greatest changes in immigration patterns and emerging immigration trends?

Over the past two decades, Mexico has remained the country of origin for the majority of U.S. immigrants. As Table 1.1

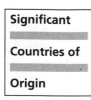

Significant Countries of Origin

shows, an estimated 1,655,843 Mexican citizens have emigrated here since 1981. This figure far exceeds that for any other nation of origin by over a million for the same period of time. The Philippines is ranked second with 548,764, and China (346,747), Korea (333,746), and Vietnam (280,782) follow close behind. In terms of numbers, this ranking of countries of origin has remained relatively stable since 1971, with the exception of

Table 1.1 Immigration to the United States by Region, 1820–1990, with Special Emphasis on 1971–1980 and 1981–1990

REGION AND COUNTRY OF ORIGIN	1820–1990 (TOTAL 171 YEARS)	1971–1980	1981–1990
All Countries	56,994,014	4,493,314	7,338,062
Europe	37,101,060	800,368	761,550
Austria-Hungary	4,342,782	16,028	24,885
Austria	1,828,946	9,478	18,340
Hungary	1,667,760	6,550	6,545
Belgium	210,556	5,329	7,066
Czechoslovakia	145,801	6,023	7,227
Denmark	370,412	4,439	5,370
France	787,587	25,069	32,353
Germany	7,083,465	74,414	91,961
Greece	703,904	92,369	38,377
Ireland	4,725,133	11,490	31,969
Italy	5,373,108	129,368	67,254
Netherlands	374,232	10,492	12,238
Norway-Sweden	2,145,954	10,472	15,182
Norway	801,224	3,941	4,164
Sweden	1,284,475	6,531	11,018
Poland	606,336	37,234	83,252
Portugal	501,261	101,710	40,431
Romania	204,841	12,393	30,857
Soviet Union	3,443,706	38,961	57,677
Spain	285,148	39,141	20,433
Switzerland	359,439	8,235	8,849
United Kingdom	5,119,150	137,374	159,173
Yugoslavia	136,271	30,540	18,762
Other Europe	181,974	9,287	8,234
Asia	5,019,180	1,588,178	2,738,157
China	914,376	124,326	346,747
Hong Kong	302,230	113,467	98,215
India	455,716	164,134	250,786
Iran	176,851	45,136	116,172

REGION AND COUNTRY OF ORIGIN	1820–1990 (TOTAL 171 YEARS)	1971–1980	1981–1990
Asia *(continued)*			
Israel	137,540	37,713	44,273
Japan	462,244	49,775	47,085
Korea	642,248	267,638	333,746
Philippines	1,026,653	354,987	548,764
Turkey	412,327	13,399	23,233
Vietnam	458,277	172,820	280,782
Other Asia	1,030,718	244,783	648,354
America	**13,067,548**	**1,982,735**	**3,615,255**
Canada & Newfoundland	4,295,585	169,939	156,938
Mexico	3,888,729	640,294	1,655,843
Caribbean	2,703,177	741,126	872,051
Cuba	748,710	264,863	144,578
Dominican Republic	510,136	148,135	252,035
Haiti	234,757	56,335	138,379
Jamaica	429,500	137,577	208,148
Other Carribean	780,074	134,216	128,911
Central America	**819,628**	**134,640**	**468,088**
El Salvador	274,667	34,436	213,539
Other Central America	544,961	100,204	254,549
South America	**1,250,303**	**295,741**	**461,847**
Argentina	131,118	29,897	27,327
Colombia	295,353	77,347	122,849
Ecuador	155,767	50,077	56,315
Other South America	668,065	138,420	255,356
Other America	110,126	995	458
Africa	**334,145**	**80,779**	**176,893**
Oceania	**204,622**	**41,242**	**45,205**
Not specified	**267,459**	**12**	**1,032**

Source: U.S. Bureau of the Census, *Historical Statistics of the United States, Colonial Times to 1970* (1975). U.S. Bureau of the Census, *Statistical Abstract of the United States, 1991* (1990). Washington, D.C.

Cuba. Immigration to the United States from Cuba declined from 264,863 in the 1970s to 144,578 in the 1980s.

Comparing the past two decades, which countries of origin exhibit the greatest rate of growth in immigration to the United States? In the last ten years, more than six times as many Salvadorans have fled here from war-torn El Salvador than in the previous decade. Irish immigrants have increased 178 percent. The numbers of Iranian and Haitian immigrants have more than doubled, as have immigration figures for Eastern European countries such as Poland and Romania. The Vietnamese immigrant community in this country grew at a rate of 62 percent between 1971 and 1990. Mexico, however, shows the most significant growth trend. Immigration from Mexico has almost tripled since 1980, and this combined with the fact that Mexico ranks first in actual numbers of immigrants translates into perhaps the greatest impact on the U.S. population.

| Growth |
| Rates in |
| Immigration |

These statistics describe a U.S. immigrant population composed of vastly different peoples, which is both rapidly growing and rapidly diverging. We always have been and continue to be a nation of immigrants. As we will see, this feature of our national identity holds much significance for education.

Measuring Racial and Ethnic Diversity in the Population

In order to document the racial and ethnic heterogeneity of our country's population, the U.S. Bureau of the Census uses a set of terms that place individuals in separate exclusionary categories: white, white non-Hispanic, black, and Hispanic (the latter with some five subcategories). Unfortunately, these terms are simplistic and for the most part highly ambiguous and nonrepresentative of the true heterogeneity of the U.S. population. It is therefore important to note at the outset of this discussion that these categories are useful only as the most superficial reflection of our nation's true diversity. Given the forced-choice responses allowed them in census questionnaires, many U.S. citizens whose racial or ethnic identity crosses categories are constrained and are forced to answer inaccurately. Racially and culturally we are not "pure" stock, and any such measurement by the Census Bureau, by the Center for Educational Statistics, or by other social institutions that attempt to address the complexity of our diverse population is likely to result in only a vague sketch.

However, once we grant the inherent restrictions on efforts to document population diversity in the United States, we must note that an examination of the available data does provide a suggestive portrait of our society. We can discern a sketchy outline of the specific circumstances of various groups within our nation's boundaries. That sketch depicts consummate social and economic vulnerability for nonwhite and Hispanic families, children, and students. On almost every indicator, nonwhite and Hispanic families, children, and students are "at-risk," meaning they are likely to fall into the lowest quartile on indicators of "well-being": family stability, family violence, family income, child health and development, and educational achievement. The census data also show that this specific population (usually referred to as the "minority" population) has grown significantly in the last two decades and will grow substantially in the decades to come. Teachers in the U.S. schools will see increasing numbers of at-risk children in their classrooms in the years ahead.

Vulnerability for Some Populations

Projected Trends for U.S. Schools

The most comprehensive report on the growing diversity of the student body in U.S. schools was published in 1991 by The College Board and the Western Interstate Commission for Higher Education. Called *The Road to College: Educational Progress by Race and Ethnicity,* this report indicates that the U.S. nonwhite and Hispanic student population will increase from 10.4 million in 1985–86 to 13.7 million in 1994–95. These pupils will constitute 34 percent of public elementary and secondary school enrollment in 1994–95, up from 29 percent in 1985–86. Enrollment of white students, meanwhile, will rise by only 5 percent, from 25.8 million to 27 million, and its share of the student population will drop from 71 percent to 66 percent in 1994–95.

Figures 1.1 and 1.2 graphically display this astounding shift in student demographics. Figure 1.1 presents actual nonwhite and Hispanic K–12 public school enrollments from 1976 to 1986 and projected enrollments based on changes in enrollment from 1976 to 1986 by decade through 2026. Figure 1.2 presents similar data but focuses on nonwhite and Hispanic student enrollments as a percentage of total enrollment. Each figure depicts a dramatic transformation projected for our nation's student body. Nonwhite and Hispanic student enrollment will grow from 10 million in 1976 to nearly 50 million in 2026. The percentage of

Projections for 2026

Figure 1.1   **K–12 Public School Enrollment Projections:
Total versus Nonwhite and Hispanic Enrollment**

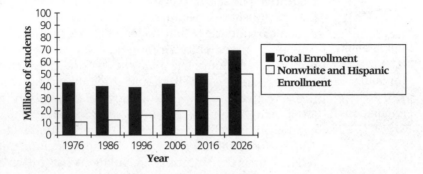

Source: U.S. Department of Education, Office for Civil Rights, *Directory of Elementary and Secondary School Districts and Schools in Selected Districts:* 1976–1977; and 1984 and 1986 Elementary and Secondary School Civil Rights Survey. As cited in U.S. Department of Education, National Center for Education Statistics, *The Condition of Education,* 1991, Vol. 1, p. 68, Elementary and Secondary Education. Washington, D.C.: 1991.

Figure 1.2   **K–12 Public School Enrollment Projections:
Percentage of Nonwhite and Hispanic Enrollment**

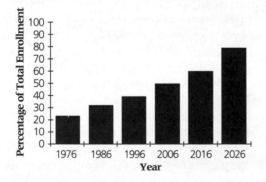

Source: U.S. Department of Education, Office for Civil Rights, *Directory of Elementary and Secondary School Districts and Schools in Selected Districts:* 1976–1977; and 1984–1986 Elementary and Secondary School Civil Rights Survey. As cited in *The Condition of Education, 1991,* Vol. 1, p. 68, Elementary and Secondary Education. Washington, D.C.: 1991.

those enrollments will rise from 23 percent to 70 percent of the total during this same time. Projections show that in 2026, student representation in our schools will be the exact inverse of what it was in 1990, when white students made up 70 percent of the enrolled K–12 student body.

It is of distinct educational significance that in 1986, 30 to 35 percent (3 million) of nonwhite and Hispanic students were identified as residing in homes in which English was not the primary language (August and García, 1988). Using these figures and extrapolating from the projections displayed in the preceding graphs, we find that by the year 2000 our schools will be educating 6 million students who have limited proficiency in English. By the year 2026 that number will conservatively approximate 15 million students, or somewhere in the vicinity of 25 percent of total elementary and secondary school enrollments. In the next few decades, it will be virtually impossible for a professional educator to serve in a public school setting, or even in any private school context, in which the students are not racially, culturally, or linguistically diverse.

Indicators of Child and Family Well-Being

As many researchers have discovered, educational concerns cannot be appropriately addressed without attending to related indicators of child and family well-being. Children who are healthy and who live in safe and secure social and economic environments generally do very well in today's schools. Poor students, on the other hand, are three times more likely to become dropouts than are students from more economically advantaged homes (Children in Need, 1990). Students who reside in economically disadvantaged and socially dangerous environments are at risk for academic underachievement in today's and tomorrow's schools. Our earlier discussion of expected demographic shifts and projected trends in student enrollments is sharpened by a consideration of some economic and social realities. As noted above, family income is correlated with academic performance. Family dislocations, uncertainty, and stress associated with poverty often undermine a child's ability to concentrate and to learn. Culturally and linguistically diverse students tend to live in situations that are not always compatible with a stable educational experience. Unfortunately, on a number of related measures of child and family well-being, the circumstances are bleak for this growing body of students.

Table 1.2 Children and Youth 18 Years Old and Younger in Poverty, Projected to 2026

RACE OR ETHNICITY	1975	1986	1996	2006	2016	2026
Total students in millions	**12.3**	**14.2**	**16.4**	**19.4**	**23.1**	**27.9**
White, non-Hispanic	6.7	7.8	8.8	10.1	11.6	13.2
Total Minority	**5.6**	**6.4**	**7.6**	**9.3**	**11.5**	**14.7**
Black	3.8	4.0	4.2	4.4	4.5	4.7
Hispanic	1.7	2.4	3.4	4.9	7.0	10.0
Total percent of poor children	**100**	**100**	**100**	**100**	**100**	**100**
White, non-Hispanic	54.8	54.4	53.6	52.1	50.0	47.2
Total Minority	**45.2**	**45.6**	**46.4**	**47.9**	**50.0**	**52.8**
Black	31.5	28.5	25.5	22.5	19.7	16.9
Hispanic	13.7	17.1	20.9	25.4	30.3	35.9

Source: U.S. Department of Commerce, Bureau of the Census, Current Population Reports, series P-60, "Poverty in the United States...," various years. As cited in the U.S. Department of Education, National Center for Educational Statistics, *The Condition of Education, 1991,* Vol. 1, pp. 200–201, Elementary and Secondary Education. Washington, D.C.: 1991.

According to the National Center for the Study of Children in Poverty in its 1990 report, *Five Million Children,* 14 million U.S. children and youth under the age of 18 resided in circumstances of poverty in 1986. This represents approximately 20 percent of the total population in this age group and was an increase of some 2 million since 1975. Of the children counted, 6.5 million, or 45 percent, were nonwhite and Hispanic. Table 1.2 presents exact numbers and percentages of children and youth in poverty for 1975 and 1986 and related projections through 2026. Projections in this table indicate that unless poverty is checked in very direct ways, the number of children and youth in poverty will more than double by the year 2026. More than half of these children and youth living in poverty will be nonwhite and Hispanic.

The overall family circumstances expected for these children over the next decades are also alarming. Most children of elementary school age presently reside in families headed by persons under the age of 30. Figure 1.3 provides evidence that these families will be economically disadvantaged. The figure shows median income from 1973 to 1986 and projected income through 2026 for families headed by persons under the age

Children

Living in

Poverty

Economically

Vulnerable

Families

Figure 1.3 **Median Annual Income for Families Headed by Persons Under Age 30 (in 1986 Dollars), Projected to 2026**

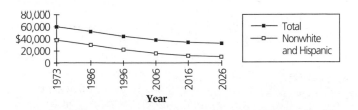

Source: Johnson, C. M.; Sum, A. M.; and Weill, J. D. (1988), Appendix: Table 3. As cited in *Five Million Children: A Statistical Profile of Our Poorest Young Citizens*, National Center for Children in Poverty, School of Public Health, p. 47. New York: Columbia University, 1990.

of 30. All families in this category have experienced and are projected to experience a decrease in economic capability. Again, particularly vulnerable will be families headed by persons who are nonwhite and Hispanic. By 2026 the median family income for nonwhite and Hispanic families will drop to $10,000 per year.

What are the implications for education? Children in families with income below the poverty level are nearly twice as likely to be held back a grade level as their more advantaged classmates. Young people from low-income families also tend to leave school early and enter the labor force to earn additional income for themselves or their families. While work experience during adolescence can have positive effects, recent research indicates that working more than half-time during the high school years can undermine academic performance (Beyond Rhetoric, 1991). As for those students from home environments in which English is not the primary language, over 90 percent in 1984 met poverty guidelines that allowed them to receive free or reduced-price lunches (Development Associates, 1984).

Much more eloquent than any quantitative analyses of this situation are the more intensive case studies that dramatically tell the disheartening educational stories of these underserved populations (Kozol, 1991; Rose, 1989; Wong-Filmore, 1991). Numerous expository in-depth studies have found that serious disruptions of individual, family, and community functioning occur when young children from nonmainstream backgrounds encounter the schooling process. There is much evidence, both in hard figures and in personal testimony, that members of culturally and linguistically diverse populations in the United States face problems socially, economically, and educationally.

Student Diversity and Educational Vulnerability

The inevitable conclusion to draw from patterns evident in the preceding indicators of child and family well-being is that school-age children and their families, particularly those who are non-white and Hispanic, will be placed in economic and social situations that increase their social, economic, and educational vulnerability. Today's educators and educators of the future will be challenged by a student body of increasing cultural and linguistic diversity. Many of our students will come to school from situations that are already identified as educationally disadvantageous. Even though as educators we have little power to ameliorate those situations, we must heed their effects in the academic setting.

Three important and much-debated variables are key to understanding the real human consequences of educational vulnerability: the dropout rate, measures of academic achievement, and educational funding policies.

Dropout Rate. A major indicator of academic success in the United States is completion of high school. One of the national educational goals adopted by the 1990 Educational Summit in Charlottesville, Virginia, aims to increase the U.S. high school completion rate to 90 percent by the year 2000. The dynamics of school completion are not well understood, and the cause and effect relationships involved are unclear (Fernandez and Shu, 1988). Much of the confusion stems from the variety of methods researchers have used to define what is meant by completion. Fortunately, the National Center for Educational Statistics (NCES) has begun to address this confusion. NCES issued two reports (Frase, 1989; Kaufman and Frase, 1990) that attempt to systematize our understanding of high school completion by defining the following set of dropout rates:

| Types of |
| Dropout |
| Rates Reports |

Event rates report—Compiled within a single year, this report gives the percentage of students who left high school without finishing work toward a diploma. This is a measure of the actual event of dropping out.

Status rates report—Compiled at any point in time, this report gives the percentage of the population of a given age range who either (a) have not finished high school or (b) are not enrolled. This measure reflects the current status of a group in the whole population, including adults.

Cohort rates report—Compiled over a given time period, this report describes what happens to a single group of students. This measure reflects changes in any given group over time.

Status and cohort reports provide a useful view of high school completion, since they take into consideration what happens to students after they leave school. These reports indicate that high school completion rates for all persons aged 16 to 24 have generally declined in the last twenty years. In this age group, the status rate declined from 16 percent in 1968 to less than 13 percent in 1989 (Kaufman and Frase, 1990). In 1989, about 4 million persons in the United States aged 16 to 24 were high school dropouts. On average, 87 percent of all U.S. students receive their high school diploma or its equivalent by the age of 24.

Unfortunately, this is not the case for subsets of students. Both event and status reports show that nonwhite and Hispanic students drop out of high school at two to three times the rate of white students. Hispanic youth have the highest national dropout rate, African Americans the second highest, and whites the lowest. During the period of 1987 to 1989, about 8 percent of Hispanic students dropped out of school each year, an event rate almost twice as high as that for white students; 7 percent of African American students dropped out during that same period. More revealing is the status report data. In 1989, among the population aged 16 to 24, only 67 percent of Hispanics had completed high school or its equivalency, versus 86 percent of African Americans and 88 percent of whites (Kaufman and Frase, 1990). This same data indicate that high school completion rates are lowest in central cities and metropolitan areas, which have the highest concentration of nonwhite and Hispanic populations. Completion rates are highest in suburban areas.

Comparative

Dropout

Rates

Academic Achievement. Now that we've determined that high school completion is problematic for nonwhite and Hispanic students, how do these students do while they are in school? The NCES also has generated a set of data that addresses this question (NCES, 1991). The most revealing data concern grade-level achievement as measured by standardized tests of academic achievement over the years 1983 to 1989. This measure attempts to assess the relative number of students who are not achieving at the academic level considered normal for their age, which is called the **modal grade level**. Table 1.3 summarizes this data by showing the percentage of 8-year-olds and 13-year-olds who are performing one or more years below the expected grade level. The data are presented by gender, race, and ethnicity.

As you can see, this table indicates that the percentage of students one or more years below modal grade level has increased overall for boys and girls and for whites, blacks, and Hispanics at each age level over the period reported. For 8-year-olds, the percentage of students below modal grade level increased from 21.0 percent to 24.5 percent; for 13-year-olds, the increase was from 28.1 percent to 31.4 percent. However, an interesting pattern emerges for white students as compared to black and Hispanic students. At the age of 8, there is little difference in below-level performance for whites (24.5 percent), blacks (25.1 percent), and Hispanics (25.0 percent). But by the age of 13, the discrepancy is quite significant. Whereas 28.8 percent of white 13-year-olds performed below grade level in 1989, the figure for blacks was 44.7 percent and for Hispanics was 40.3 percent. From roughly third grade to eighth grade, academic achievement drops off significantly for blacks and Hispanics as compared to whites. Moreover, this effect is most pronounced for black males and for Hispanic males and females.

The unfortunate result is that 40 percent or more of black and Hispanic students are one grade level or more below expected and normal achievement levels by the eighth grade. These findings, in concert with the previously discussed high school completion and dropout data, raise substantive educational concerns. Clearly, as the population of nonwhite and Hispanic students increases to an estimated 70 percent of the total U.S. student population in 2026, this underachievement will be an extreme waste of intellectual potential, which we cannot afford in the least. Intervention of some sort will be necessary to avoid squandering our nation's valuable human resources.

Funding for Education. Educational financing in the United States is not without its national, state, and local complications. On the average, 90 percent of any educational expenditure consists of tax dollars flowing directly from local or state sources. Less than 10 percent of these expenditures come from federal sources. Although funding for education has increased substantially in the United States during the 1980s, education spending actually declined slightly as a proportion of the gross national product to just over 3.5 percent, which is the lowest for all "developed" countries. In real terms, overall state and local spending rose 26 percent between 1980 and 1988, but the

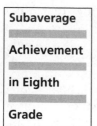

Performance below Modal Grade

Subaverage Achievement in Eighth Grade

Table 1.3 Academic Performance of U.S. Students According to Modal Grade Level

PERCENT OF 8-YEAR-OLDS PERFORMING ONE OR MORE YEARS BELOW MODAL GRADE, BY RACE/ETHNICITY: 1984–1988

Year	All Students			White			Black			Hispanic		
	Male	Female	Average	Male	Female	Average	Male	Female	Average	Male	Female	Average
1984	24.4	17.7	21.0	24.3	17.4	20.1	26.6	18.9	22.7	*	*	*
1985	24.9	18.4	21.7	24.0	18.3	21.1	32.4	19.9	26.1	24.7	28.6	26.6
1986	25.7	19.4	22.5	25.6	18.5	22.0	29.7	23.2	26.4	24.1	21.5	22.8
1987	26.9	19.8	23.3	26.9	19.0	23.0	29.7	24.0	26.8	29.1	19.3	24.2
1988	28.1	21.0	24.5	28.6	20.5	24.5	26.3	23.9	25.1	30.5	19.5	25.0

PERCENT OF 13-YEAR-OLDS PERFORMING ONE OR MORE YEARS BELOW MODAL GRADE, BY RACE/ETHNICITY: 1983–1989

Year	All Students			White			Black			Hispanic		
	Male	Female	Average	Male	Female	Average	Male	Female	Average	Male	Female	Average
1983	35.1	21.2	28.1	32.7	20.8	26.7	52.5	26.0	39.2	*	*	
1984	30.9	22.5	26.7	28.5	20.5	24.5	44.4	32.0	38.2	45.0	48.8	46.9
1985	31.7	24.0	27.8	29.3	20.2	24.7	44.1	40.0	42.0	48.5	30.5	39.5
1986	31.8	24.1	28.0	29.6	22.2	25.9	44.0	33.1	38.5	46.8	41.2	44.0
1987	35.6	24.7	30.1	34.5	22.7	28.6	43.2	33.2	38.2	55.1	32.5	43.8
1988	33.6	23.7	28.6	31.8	21.8	26.8	41.7	35.3	38.5	44.9	34.3	39.6
1989	36.7	26.1	31.4	34.0	23.6	28.8	51.5	38.0	44.7	40.0	40.6	40.3

*Not Available

Source: U.S. Department of Commerce, Bureau of the Census, Current Population Reports, series P-20, "School Enrollment...", various years; October Current Population Survey. As cited in the U.S. Department of Education, National Center for Educational Statistics, *The Condition of Education, 1991,* Vol. ", p. 123, Elementary and Secondary Education. Washington, D.C.: 1991.

federal share has actually decreased by 2 percent (The Unfinished Agenda, 1991).

Keep in mind that nonwhite and Hispanic children primarily reside in central city and metropolitan areas, in densely populated pockets of racial and ethnic segregation, and are immersed in neighborhoods of concentrated poverty (Kozol, 1991). These children are likely to attend troubled schools with fewer resources and larger classes (Beyond Rhetoric, 1991). Moreover, these children have been more negatively affected than others by recent changes in educational funding policies. The reduction of federal assistance to education, including funds for compensatory education and desegregating school districts, has reduced the fiscal resources directly available for the education of these children (Levin, 1986). Districts that cannot be integrated because they lack white students are not eligible for enhanced funding available to establish science and math magnet schools, an emerging federal funding priority (Oakes, 1991). The educational personnel of such schools are not so concerned with the educational buzzwords of the eighties—"restructuring," "reform," "teacher empowerment," "site-based management," "teacher competencies," "outcome accountability," "national goals," and so on. Instead, they are preoccupied with the bare necessities: windows, books, typewriters, classrooms with heat, working bathrooms, sufficient lighting, repairs and renovations long overdue (Kozol, 1991; Rose, 1989).

| Loss of |
| Federal |
| Support |

These schools have been transformed into institutions that must spend valuable time seeking the resources for basic survival. Much like developing countries, they seek alliances and petition for grants and loans from one source after another. These schools "beg" from city, state, federal, business, and charity sources. They do so only because the basic resources are not provided by present funding structures and formulas. In fact, those structures and formulas are working to their disadvantage. These students attend schools in cities in which competition for tax dollars is great. These communities have high unemployment and underemployment and are pressed to provide a higher level of related social services. These communities are also competing to retain businesses. These variables directly affect the resources that can be directed to education.

Most directly, students in these schools are underfunded, even in times that argue for "fairness" in school financing. As a society, we make it quite clear that we abhor the notion of social privilege. We strongly believe that an individual's financial background should not be a deterrent to educational success. Yet, such beliefs do not seem consistent with the ways in which we allocate educational resources. These fiscal disparities were identified over two decades ago. In 1968, in a now famous legal case, Demetrio Rodriguez, a parent in the Edgewood School District in San Antonio, Texas, argued that his children were underfunded relative to children in an adjacent school district only a few miles away. In the Edgewood School District (which was 96 percent nonwhite) residents paid a higher tax rate than did residents of the nearby district, which was predominantly white. Edgewood was able to generate only $37 for each pupil, and with additional resources provided by the state, spent $231 yearly per student. The neighboring school district generated $412 per student on its own, and with state resources spent $543 yearly per student. This amounted to a differential of over 100 percent.

Underfunding and "Fairness"

Coons, Clune, and Sugarman (1970) documented the distinct differential funding between "rich white" districts and "poor minority" districts identified in this legal action as a national phenomenon. They argued that there is in such funding discrepancies something incongruous with the American ideology of fairness: "a differential of any magnitude the sole justification for which is an imaginary school district line." These boundaries and funding inequalities combined to make the public schools the institution that educated the rich and kept the poor uneducated (Coons, Clune, and Sugarman, 1970).

Comparative Per-Student Spending

Preferential education for the rich and denial of the poor continues today. Table 1.4 provides an analysis of more recent educational funding differentials for school districts in New Jersey, New York, and Chicago (source of these figures in Kozol, 1991). These data are arranged in order of per-pupil yearly expenditure, showing that school districts with the greatest proportion of nonwhite and Hispanic populations consistently spend the least amount per student.

Twenty years after research documented patterns in funding that were creating a "class" structure in education, with nonwhites and Hispanic students at the lower end, we have achieved no substantive remedy. Court actions seeking such remedies are being revisited by the Edgewood School District as well as by school districts in California, Illinois, New Jersey, and New York. Kozol (1991) sums up this situation best:

Table 1.4 Selected Per-Student Yearly Expenditures

SCHOOL FUNDING IN THE CHICAGO AREA (1988–89 SCHOOL YEAR)		SCHOOL FUNDING IN NEW JERSEY (1988–89 SCHOOL YEAR)		SCHOOL FUNDING IN SIX DISTRICTS IN THE NEW YORK CITY AREA (THREE-YEAR PERIOD)		
School or District	Spending Per Pupil	District	Spending Per Pupil	District	1986–87	1989–90
Niles Township H. S.	$9,371	Princeton	$7,725	Manhasset	$11,372	$15,084
New Trier H. S.	$8,823	Summit	$7,275	Jericho	$11,325	$14,355
Glencoe (Elem. & Junior H. S.)	$7,363	West Orange	$6,505	Great Neck	$11,265	$15,594
Winnetka (Elem. & Junior H. S.)	$7,059	Cherry Hill	$5,981	Mount Vernon	$6,433	$9,112
		Jersey City	$4,566	Roosevelt	$6,339	$8,349
Wilmette (Elem. & Junior H. S.)	$6,009	East Orange	$4,457	New York City	$5,585	$7,299
		Paterson	$4,422			
Chicago (average all grade levels)	$5,265	Camden	$3,538			

Source: Chicago Panel on School Policy and Finance; Educational Law Center, Newark, New Jersey; *Statistical Profiles of School Districts,* New York State Board of Education; The New York Times. As cited in Kozol, J. (1991). *Savage Inequalities: Children in America's Schools,* pp. 236–237. New York: Crown.

These are Americans. Why do we reduce them to this beggary—and why, particularly, in public education? Why not spend on children here [in schools underfunded] at least what we would be investing in their education if they lived within a wealthy district like Winnetka, Illinois, or Cherry Hill, New Jersey, or Manhasset, Rye, or Great Neck in New York? Wouldn't this be a natural behavior in an affluent society that seems to value fairness in so many other areas of life? Is fairness less important to Americans today than in earlier times? Is it viewed as slightly tiresome and incompatible with hardnosed values? What do Americans believe about equality? (Kozol, 1991, p. 41)

A Wasted Resource

The most pressing argument for our attention to the above signposts of educational vulnerability is the prospect of losing a significant body of our country's human resources at a time when we need all the resources we can muster. Added to this is the fact that young people lost from productive membership in our society often become a substantial resource liability. Estimates of fiscal resources diverted to high school dropouts throughout the United States in areas such as health services, unemployment, employment training, and social welfare reach billions of dollars yearly (National Commission on Children, 1991). Close to 85 percent of people incarcerated in the U.S. prison system are high school dropouts. Why can't our educational system invest in children so they become assets instead of liabilities? The irony of our predicament is most telling. The cost for a one-year stay in most state and federal prisons is nearly $30,000—the approximate cost, including tuition, fees, books, room and board, and miscellaneous, of sending a student to Harvard University for one year.

Costs of Low Educational Achievement

Recent efforts such as the Taylor Plan recognize the debilitating effect of educational vulnerability and work to find solutions. Patrick Taylor, a Louisiana state legislator and the author of the plan, has begun a campaign to revolutionize U.S. education. The plan calls for guaranteed free college tuition and fees for any student who completes a high school education with a C-plus average and scores well on college entrance exams. In 1992 Taylor convinced the state legislature to adopt the plan, which recognizes that keeping students in high school makes economic sense. In Louisiana, the long-term cost associated with individuals who drop out of high school is estimated at $250,000. This estimate does not include the extra cost associated with high school dropouts who become involved in the criminal justice system, which is an additional $25,000 to $35,000 per year. In short, in terms of education the old adage seems to apply: pay now or pay later. We will pay a lot more later.

Besides the monetary costs to our society are the more intangible human costs. In my own family of ten siblings, the children of migrant farm workers, only four graduated from high school and only one—this one—had the opportunity to attend college. Like so many families, its members had the native intelligence, motivation, and work ethic to succeed in high school and beyond. Yet the circumstances of poverty, cultural and linguistic difference, and the absence of a responsive educational system led to the direct underdevelopment of this family's potential. This underdevelopment pertains not only to each family member's individual educational, economic, and personal growth, but to his or her potential contribution to the family itself, to the community in which it is embedded, and to society at large. Considering the overall challenges faced by our country and our planet, continued neglect of this raw native potential is spit in the wind.

> **Loss of Contribution to Society**

The Implications for Educators

The demographic information we have been discussing indicates that the diversity in our schools is a recent but an explosive and long-term phenomenon. Teachers, administrators, and other educational professionals who received their training over a decade ago were not encumbered by the challenges facing pre-service teaching candidates today. A readiness to respond to the challenge presented by a highly diverse student body was not a recognized part of their training. Indeed, relatively few individuals of minority status themselves succeeded academically a decade ago, with the result that even now the makeup of the teaching profession does not match the demographics of the students it serves. For the 1987–88 school year, of 2.6 million public and private school teachers and 103,000 school administrators, over 88 percent were white. Less than 12 percent were nonwhite and Hispanic: 8 percent were African American,

3 percent were Hispanic, and less than 1 percent were American Indian, Alaskan Native, or Asian or Pacific Islander. In this same academic year, however, nonwhite and Hispanic academic enrollment was at 30 percent (NCES, 1991).

Effective Teaching

It appears that in the near future the vast majority of schoolteachers and administrators will be white while the proportion of nonwhite and Hispanic students will continue to increase rapidly (NCES, 1991). What significance does this hold for the training of teachers? Although it is difficult to pinpoint specific attributes of teachers that have served a diverse student body effectively, recent research efforts have attempted to identify some. Unlike earlier reports that identified and described effective programs only, recent reports have sought out effective programs and/or schools and then attempted to describe the specific instructional and attitudinal character of the teacher (Carter and Chatfield, 1986; Pease-Alvarez, Espinoza, and García, 1991; Tikunoff, 1983; Villegas, 1991).

Skills of "Good" Teachers

Dwyer (1991) identifies four domains of instruction at which "good" teachers excel: (1) content knowledge, (2) teaching for student learning, (3) creating a classroom community for student learning, and (4) teacher professionalism. Villegas (1991) has extended these four domains for teachers who serve a student population that is culturally and linguistically diverse. She suggests that "good" teachers in these classroom contexts incorporate culturally responsive pedagogy, meaning that they adjust their teaching strategies in response to the learning styles of individual students.

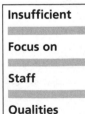
Insufficient Focus on Staff Qualities

A concern for the effectiveness of teachers is not new. From the earliest days of education program evaluation, the quality of the instructional staff has been considered a significant feature (Heath, 1982). Unfortunately, for programs serving students of minority status, the evaluation of "effectiveness" has lately been consumed by an empirical concern for multicultural representation in the content of curriculum, at the expense of examining teaching strategies themselves. For students with limited English proficiency, concern has centered only on the use or nonuse of the students' native language and academic attention on developing English language skills (August and García, 1988). Very little attention is given to considering the attributes desired in the professional and paraprofessional staff members who

Becoming a Responsive Teacher

1.1   Educational Backgrounds of Today's Immigrant Students

Over the past two decades, America's classrooms have undergone a dramatic change. Anyone coming into contact with the school system—whether educator, student, parent, policymaker, or service provider—cannot help but notice the profound and continuous diversification of every facet of the student population: racial, ethnic, religious, and social. This trend is hardly new, but its accelerated pace is having a tremendous impact on our educational system.

Each year, thousands of school-aged immigrant childen arrive in the United States seeking a better life. Each enters school with his or her own unique educational history and life experiences.

Somxai and Souphanh   Somxai and Souphanh Noum, a teenaged brother and sister, spent the last seven years in a refugee camp in Laos waiting for resettlement in another country. After six years with no schooling in the refugee camp, Somxai and Souphanh were provided with a few months of "survival" English to prepare them for life in a new land and a new culture.

Swetlana   Swetlana Borishkevich, a teenaged Ukrainian, attended regular classes in the Soviet Union through the eighth grade, but she was not able to fulfill her wish to enroll in vocational training in the Soviet Union because her family fled to Italy. From there, she and her family came to America. She is enrolled in a large secondary school in New York City.

José   José Cardenas, a Mexican immigrant who came to the United States with his uncle, attended school in Mexico only occasionally, since he had to spend most of his time helping on the family farm. Although José is a very mature 16-year-old, he has completed only the third grade. He now finds himself in a Los

Angeles ESL program with children who are much younger. He is embarrassed to be there and is quite bored with the endless drill. He can hardly wait to drop out of school and go to work in a fast-food restaturant.

Soo Jung Chu   Last year, Soo Jung Chu transferred from a presitigious Korean school to an American public school. Soo Jung Chu was at the top of his class in Korea. Now he feels intense frustration whenever he can't understand his schoolwork in English, but he is afraid to ask for help because it makes him feel dumb. He knows that the math class the school counselor placed him in is a "bonehead" class far below his mathematical abilities.

Meeting the Challenge

1. Imagine you are one of the school-aged children described above. Write a journal entry expressing your thoughts and feelings about your first day of school in the United States. Which areas of the educational experience seem the most difficult? Which seem most exciting?
2. Select one of the young people described and suggest two alternative ways in which a classroom teacher might introduce the student to his or her new school peers. Remember the importance of first impressions.
3. If you were the classroom teacher for one of more of these students, what would you want to know about their family backgrounds? What would you want to know about their languages and the cultures of their countries of origin?
4. What are the implications for these students' lives if their educational needs are not met by our schools? List the job opportunities available to each one of them if they drop out of high school.

implement the myriad of program types that serve students in compensatory education. Typically, attention to the characteristics of staff represents merely a notation as to the years of service and the extent of formal educational training received (Olsen, 1988). Yet most educational researchers will grant that the effect of any instructional intervention is directly related to the quality of implementation by the instructor. A recent report issued by the California Commission on Teacher Credentialing verified that because of high teacher turnover, large numbers of misassigned teachers, and classrooms staffed by teachers holding only emergency (temporary and not state approved) credentials, a disproportionate number of poor and minority students are taught during their entire school career by the least-qualified personnel.

Problems in Training and Assessment

It is important to note that professional teaching organizations such as the National Education Association (NEA), the American Federation of Teachers (AFT), and the National Association for the Education of Young Children (NAEYC), to name a few of the largest, have specifically addressed the need for teachers to receive special training in teaching a culturally diverse student body. Certification agencies, such as The National Council for Accreditation of Teacher Educators (NCATE) and the California Commission on Teaching Credentialing, have included particular provisions related to "multicultural" education that institutions of higher education must implement in order to be accredited as teacher-training institutions and to ensure their graduates will be considered viable candidates for state teacher credentialing.

Special

Training

Recommended

Unfortunately, even though the need to train and assess teachers for competence in teaching culturally diverse students is a widely accepted idea, present modes of training and assessment remain highly problematic. The data quite clearly portray the problems in assessing individual professional competence. Present assessment practices can be criticized on several levels (McGahie, 1991; Shinberg, 1983; Sternberg and Wagner, 1986).

1. Professional competence evaluations usually address only a narrow range of practice situations. Teaching professionals engage in very complex planning, development, implementation, problem solving, and crisis management. These

endeavors usually require technical skills and knowledge that is not easily measured.

2. Professional competence evaluations are biased toward assessing formally acquired knowledge, likely as a result of similar assessment of student academic achievement. We assess teachers the same way we assess students, even though we have differing expectations regarding these populations.

| Criticisms of |

| Current |

| Assessment |

| Practices |

3. Despite the presumed importance of "practice" skills, professional competence assessments devote little attention to the assessment of enunciated practice skills. With regard to teachers of culturally diverse students, we do have some understanding of specific skills that might be necessary. Even so, because of the lack of specific research in this area, it remains difficult to articulate the exact skills to recommend for assessment.

4. Almost no attention is given to what has earlier been identified as the "disposition" and "affective" domains of the teacher, identified later more specifically in Chapter 8. In recent analyses of "effective" teachers, these attributes were identified as being as significant for student learning, as are content knowledge and practice skills (Pease-Alvarez, Espinoza, García, and Villegas, 1991).

In addition to the preceding concerns, professional assessment instruments are subject to severe violations of reliability and validity. Feldt and Brennan (1989) have demonstrated that components of measurement error are highly inconsistent in the arena of professional teacher assessment. Test validity is also a fundamental problem (Berk, 1986).

Keep in mind that inferences about a teacher's professional competence or ability to practice are actually inferences about what the researcher has decided is important to measure. We construct an assessment, and soon we are willing to say that whoever scores at "such and such" on that assessment is competent. Underlying the assessment, however, is the often questionable legitimacy of the constructs the test makers defined. What if their list of "most important teacher attributes" is not, in fact, particularly pertinent to classroom realities? We presently lack any definitive body of research and knowledge regarding the constructs that define good teachers in general, and good teachers of culturally diverse students in specific. That knowledge base is developing, but it is presently not substantive in nature (García, 1991).

| Questionable |

| Basis for |

| Assessment |

The Connoisseur Model

What are we left with? According to McGahie (1991), despite the appearance of objectivity in assessment instruments, teacher assessment actually is presently operating according to the **connoisseur model**. This model of professional assessment carries certain presuppositions that are relevant to the education of our diverse student body:

Not all features of professional practice can be quantified.

There is no "one best answer" to a professional problem or question.

Connoisseurs are unbiased, are fair in rendering judgments, and due to their demonstrated professional competence and commitment, are the most effective evaluators of teaching professionals.

> **Relevant**
>
> **Assumptions**

The connoisseur model is routinely and explicitly used in a number of professional assessment endeavors such as in the visual and performing arts. We would never imagine using a "test" to determine the motion picture Academy Awards. In fact, to determine "Teacher of the Year" honors at local, state, and national levels, connoisseurs are regularly called upon to serve as judges. They are asked to use their varying experience and expertise to identify the "best" teacher among the candidates nominated. Close examination of present methods of evaluating teacher-training programs indicates that the connoisseur model is the primary model in operation. In an NCATE accreditation review, "experts" are sent to a teacher-training program to evaluate the program's effectiveness. In turn, instructors in those local programs, also acting in the role of connoisseur, evaluate individual teacher candidates.

Might the connoisseur model be an acceptable way to train and assess the competencies of teachers who will face the challenges of an increasingly diverse student population? Unfortunately, due to the explosion of this diverse population and our own professional unpreparedness, we are learning how to apply the connoisseur model at the same time that we are doing it. Because of the limited number of experts or connoisseurs available, and the diversity of students and the myriad programs that serve them, training and assessment of teachers remains highly problematic. Over time, as we develop a large corps of connoisseurs with special knowledge and experience regarding student cultural diversity, it will be possible to utilize this model—and it will likely be the only model appropriate. At present, however, it is not possible to implement the connoisseur model of evaluation on any large scale with the hope that it will be either reliable or valid.

We know now from both case-study observations and educational research data that the teaching expertise of professionals charged with meeting the challenges of diversity is not sufficient. The individual teachers held responsible for this gargantuan task have not been well prepared and we are beginning to address that fact. Many of you are reading this book because of your interest, concern, and specific professional obligations in teaching or related educational professions. It is important to recognize that we are struggling together in this enterprise. We are far from achieving the instructional expertise that will effectively meet the growing challenges of diversity. Those challenges will not dissipate, and you will likely be called upon to assist directly in developing and implementing educational initiatives to meet them. You will not be just an actor on this stage. You will be strategically involved in writing the script.

| Challenge |
| to New |
| Teachers |

The Language Minority Student

In our demographic discussion of student diversity, one distinctive subpopulation will receive selective attention due to its growing size, both relatively and absolutely, and its precarious situation within our educational institutions. These students come to the schooling process without the language skills through which that process is communicated. As the previous demographic data have indicated, in the next two decades in the United States, language minority students will comprise some 15 percent of K–12 enrollment. By 2026, these students are projected to make up nearly a quarter of our student body.

Language minority students present a special challenge to our educational institutions because of their linguistic diversity. So much of what we do in the formal teaching and learning enterprise requires effective communication of specific facts, concepts, ideas, and problem solving strategies. Students with linguistic diversity encounter this teaching and learning enterprise not absent of abilities but rich in communication skills that do not match those required in the classroom. If it is ineptly handled, this scenario is a formula for failure, despite the intellectual gifts such students might possess.

| Language |
| Diversity |

Becoming a Responsive Teacher

1.2   California: The "Minority Majority" State

Over the last five years, student enrollment in California has changed significantly. Enrollment in California's 7,400 public elementary and secondary schools increased by 554,181 students between October 1986 and October 1990. This was an overall increase of 13.2 percent, but the number of minority students—defined as American Indians, Alaskan Natives, Asians, Pacific Islanders, Filipinos, Hispanics, and blacks—increased by 26 percent during this decade. And the number of students identified as limited-English-proficient (LEP) increased by a startling 65 percent. (See Figure 1.4.)

In fact, a major milestone was reached in this period: by 1988, the *majority* of students in California's public schools

Figure 1.4   **Composition of the Student Population in California, 1986–1990**

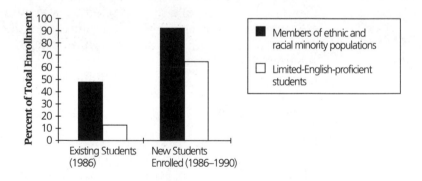

were from ethnic and racial "minorities." Non-Hispanic white students now constitute the minority of students in the schools and, based on demographic projections, will continue to do so.

The extent of the changes in the composition of California's student population can be best appreciated by comparing the composition of existing students in 1986 with the composition of "new" students who entered school between 1986 and 1990 (actually, new students who entered minus existing students who left). The accompanying graph illustrates these differences. In 1986, 48 percent of all existing students were from ethnic and racial minority populations, and 13 percent were LEP. But of the new students who entered the schools in the last five years, 92 percent were from ethnic and racial minority populations and 65 percent were LEP. Clearly, the new students entering California's schools are much different from previous students.

Enrollment projections by the California Department of Finance suggest that these trends will continue in the 1990s. Total elementary and secondary enrollment is projected to increase by 47 percent during the next decade, or by 200,000 students per year, which is about three times the rate of enrollment growth in the 1980s. The proportion of students from minority populations is projected to increase from 54 percent to 63 percent during the same period.

Meeting the Challenge

1. Research the comparable elementary and secondary school enrollment data for your own state or city for the period 1986 to 1990. Are the trends similar to or different from those described for California schools? Construct a graph from the data if you can.
2. If you were a teacher in the California schools during this dramatic shift in student demographics, what types of in-service training would have been helpful to you?
3. How might the social life of a school be affected by a significant increase in limited-English-proficient students? As a teacher, what classroom methods would you use to encourage communication among students with different language backgrounds?

Who Are These Students?

We would search long and hard for a comprehensive definition of *language minority student*. At one end of the spectrum are general definitions such as "students who come from homes in which a language other than English is spoken." At the other end are highly operationalized definitions used in educational research, such as "students who scored in the first quartile on a standardized test of English language proficiency." Regardless of the definition we adopt, it is apparent that language minority students come in a variety of linguistic shapes.

Some

Definitions

The language minority population in the United States is linguistically heterogeneous, with over one hundred distinct language groups identified. There is also heterogeneity within groups. For example, within the largest language minority group, labeled "Hispanic," some members are monolingual Spanish speakers, and others are to some degree bilingual. Such individual variation persists throughout other non-English-speaking groups in the United States. Also of consequence are the related cultural attributes of language minority students, making this population distinct not only linguistically but also in terms of values and beliefs.

Describing the "typical" **language minority student**, as you may have surmised by now, is highly problematic. Put simply, though, we might propose that such a student is one who (a) is characterized by substantive participation in a non-English-speaking environment, (b) has acquired the normal communicative abilities of that social environment, and (c) is exposed to an English-speaking environment on a regular basis only during the formal schooling process.

Common

Attributes

Estimates of the number of language minority students have been compiled by the federal government on several occasions (O'Malley, 1981; Development Associates, 1984; Waggoner, 1991). These estimates differ because of the definition adopted for identifying these students, the particular measure used to obtain the estimate, and the statistical treatment utilized to generalize beyond the actual sample obtained. For example, O'Malley (1981) defined the language minority student population by using a specific cutoff score on an English language proficiency test administered to a stratified sample of students. Development Associates (1984) estimated the population by analyzing reports from a stratified sample of local school districts. Estimates of the population of language minority students have thus ranged from 1,300,000 (Development Associates, 1984) to 3,600,000 (O'Malley, 1981).

The population of language minority students, whatever its "true" size, has been described as having the following attributes:

1. The total number of language minority children aged 5–14 in 1976 approximated 2.52 million; this number dropped to 2.39 million in 1980 and will gradually increase to a projected 3.40 million in the year 2000 (Waggoner, 1984). In 1983, this population was more conservatively estimated to be 1.29 million (Development Associates, 1984). Recall that this divergence in population estimates reflects definitions and procedures used to obtain language minority "counts."
2. The majority of language minority children reside throughout the United States, but there is distinct geographical clustering. For example, about 75 percent of language minority children live in one of these states: Arizona, Colorado, California, Florida, New Jersey, New Mexico, New York, and Texas (O'Malley, 1981; Development Associates, 1984; Waggoner, 1991).

| Percentage |
| of Spanish |
| Speakers |

3. Of the estimated number of language minority children in 1978, the language background of 72 percent was Spanish, 2 percent was other European, 5 percent was Asian, and 1 percent was American Indian. These distributions are expected to change as a result of differential growth rates, until by the year 2000 the proportion of children with Spanish language background is projected to be about 77 percent of the total (O'Malley, 1981). Estimates by Development Associates (1984) of language background for students in grades K–6 indicate 76 percent Spanish, 8 percent Southeast Asian (e.g., Vietnamese, Cambodian, Hmong), 5 percent other European, 5 percent East Asian (e.g., Chinese, Korean), and 5 percent other (e.g., Arabic, Navaho).
4. In the stratified sample of local school districts in the nineteen most highly affected states analyzed by Development Associates (1984), 17 percent of the total K–6 student population was estimated as language minority.

Regardless of differences in estimates, it is plain that a significant number of students from language backgrounds other than English are served by U.S. schools. Moreover, this population is expected to increase steadily in the future. The challenge these students present to U.S. educational institutions will continue to increase concomitantly.

Which Educational Programs Serve Them?

School districts presently serve language minority students by choosing from a variety of possible program options: "transitional bilingual education," "maintenance bilingual education," "English as a second language," "immersion," "sheltered English," and "submersion," to name a few (U.S. General Accounting Office, 1987). Ultimately, school district staffs will reject program labels and instead address their own particular needs and resources with the following questions:

> What are the native language (L1) and second language (L2) characteristics of the students, families, and communities we serve?

> What model of instruction is desired? Specifically, (a) how do we choose to utilize L1 and L2 *as mediums of instruction*? and (b) how do we choose to handle the instruction of L1 and L2?

> What is the nature of staff and resources necessary to implement the desired instruction?

These program initiatives can be differentiated by the way they utilize the native language and English during instruction. Development Associates (1984) surveyed 333 school districts in the nineteen states that serve over 80 percent of language minority students in the United States. For grades K–5, they report the following salient features regarding the instruction of language minority students:

| Features of |
| Current |
| Programs |

1. Ninety-three percent of the schools reported that the use of English predominated in their programs, and 7 percent indicated that the use of the native language predominated.
2. Sixty percent of the sampled schools reported that both the native language and English were utilized during instruction.
3. Thirty percent of the sampled schools reported minimal or no use of the native language during instruction.

As this report shows, two-thirds of the schools studied have chosen to utilize some form of bilingual curriculum to serve their population of language minority students. However, some one-third of these schools minimize or altogether ignore native language use in their instructional practices.

We have seen that some two-thirds to three-fourths of language minority students in this country are of Spanish-speaking backgrounds. The programs that serve these students have been characterized primarily as **transitional bilingual education.** These programs provide students with a transition from early-grade instruction with Spanish emphasis to later-grade instruction with English emphasis and eventually to English-only instruction. For the one-third of language minority students who receive little or no instruction in the native language, two alternative types of instructional approaches likely predominate: English as a Second Language (ESL) and Sheltered English. Each of these program types emphasizes the use of English during instruction but does not ignore the fact that the students served are limited in English proficiency. Importantly, however, these programs do not require instructional personnel who speak the native language of the student. Moreover, these programs are best suited to classrooms in which students are from many different language backgrounds and in which no substantial number of students from one non-English-speaking group predominate (Ovando and Collier, 1985).

Local
Initiatives

School district staffs across the country have been creative in developing a range of programs for language minority students. They have determined their own program needs and resources differentially for (a) different language groups (Spanish, Vietnamese, Chinese, etc.), (b) different grade levels within a school, (c) different subgroups of language minority students within a classroom, and even (d) different levels of language proficiency. The result is a wide and at times perplexing variety of program models. Such variety in program types demonstrates the breadth of professional expertise that is presently available to serve the growing number of students who are both culturally and linguistically diverse. It is best understood as a response to "diversity within diversity."

Conclusion

Sometimes, making sense of demographic data from the realm of education is like trying to make sense out of baseball by picking through the vast array of statistics printed in tiny type at the back of the sports pages. No one can develop a "feel" for the game merely by examining the statistics, no matter how comprehensive, strategic, or ingenious those numbers are. Numbers may indicate but will never fully convey the excitement in the stands or on the field. Think for a moment about how you would describe your own experience in formal schooling activities if you could answer only the statistical questions, how many? how much? for how long? These questions allow you no room to tell the story of your educational experience or to describe what it was like.

We utilize demographic statistics in education, much as we use baseball statistics, to help us summarize the nature of the enterprise through the description of the status or well-being of the teams and individual players. The demographic analysis in this chapter has presented specific status indicators for specific groups and individuals with the provision that such description can add some depth, but not total understanding, to the challenge that today's and tomorrow's educators face. To understand the quality of the educational experience lived through by most culturally and linguistically diverse children, you will have to go beyond the numbers. For that you will need imagination—and a feel for the game.

Where do we start? What can these descriptive data tell us about the challenge to us? It is unmistakable that the students who will populate our schools, who will play the "game," will soon radically differ with regard to race, culture, and language. In less than two decades, one-half of the students in the U.S. schools will be nonwhite and Hispanic—and half of these students will speak a language other than English on their first day of school. Teachers who receive their credentials today will likely be responsible for the education of a student body that is more diverse than at any other time in the history of U.S. formal education. This will be true at all levels of education.

The growing population of diverse students will undertake their schooling with several strikes against them. They are and will be coming to bat from social and economic circumstances that will leave them most vulnerable to the various pitches that they will be asked to hit. Those pitches carry two powerful spins: a globally competitive climate in which educational success is an absolute must and a world in which our fundamental knowledge base is growing exponentially.

These students are likely to be equipped not with the best that money can buy but probably with the least that society is willing to allow them. They are likely to be "coached" by individuals who do not meet the highest standards or who themselves are learning the game as their own responsibilities and commitments increase. Many of these players will require coaching in a language not their own. They will need to acquire knowledge of the game along with facility in the language and culture in which the game is immersed.

Yet despite the immensity of their task and the difficulties stacked against these students, the data unequivocally indicate that the future of education rests with them. As they grow to represent the majority, their success is our success and their failure is our failure. They must succeed. We have no other alternative short of disbanding the game. But education, unlike baseball, is not an endeavor we can call off when the weather looks bad. The U.S. educational system must rise to the challenge and accommodate students it has historically underserved.

Mrs. Tanner believes so. She is living this challenge and is not about to give up. There is no doubt that as a nation we have the resourcefulness we need. The remainder of this book will address ways of identifying those resources and applying them to the task at hand.

SUMMARY OF MAJOR IDEAS

1. Educators in the U.S. schools face the challenge of teaching increasing numbers of children who are culturally and linguistically diverse. The education of these children must take into account demographic factors, issues of academic performance, language background, and child and family well-being.
2. In the last ten years, immigration to the United States has increased 63 percent over the previous decade. Mexico is the most typical country of origin, with the Philippines, China, Korea, and Vietnam close behind. The rate of immigration from such countries as El Salvador, Ireland, Iran, and Haiti has dramatically increased, but immigration from Mexico has nearly tripled since 1980.
3. The racial and ethnic makeup of the United States is more diverse than census data indicate. The nonwhite and Hispanic population, which is growing, is most at risk on indicators of child and family well-being: family stability, family violence, family income, child health and development, and educational achievement.
4. Reports on student demographics show that nonwhite and Hispanic enrollment is projected to grow to represent 70

percent of total school enrollment by 2026. Nearly 25 percent of students in 2026 are projected to come from homes in which English is not the primary language spoken.

5. Students living in poverty are three times more likely to drop out of school than are students with economic advantages. The number of children and youth in poverty is projected to greatly increase by 2026.

6. The dropout rate is one indicator of educational vulnerability. The 1990 Education Summit proposed as one goal the aim of increasing the U.S. high school completion rate to 90 percent by 2000.

7. An event rates report gives the percentage of students who leave high school without finishing work toward a diploma. A status rates report gives the percentage who have not finished high school or are not enrolled. A cohort rates report describes what happens to a single group of students. Event and status rates reports show that nonwhite and Hispanic students drop out of high school two to three times more often than white students.

8. The percentage of all 8-year-old and 13-year-old students performing below modal grade level increased between 1983 and 1989. Forty percent or more of black and Hispanic students were one or more levels below expected performance by eighth grade.

9. Most nonwhite and Hispanic children are likely to attend schools with fewer financial resources and larger classes. Funding discrepancies between "rich" and "poor" school districts raise questions of "fairness" in education.

10. Effective teachers of students who are culturally and linguistically diverse excel in five domains: (1) content knowledge, (2) teaching for student learning, (3) creating a classroom community for student learning, (4) teacher professionalism, and (5) incorporating culturally responsive pedagogy.

11. Professional teaching organizations, such as the National Education Association and the American Federation of Teachers, and some certification agencies have addressed the need to train educators to teach culturally diverse students. Nevertheless, the training and assessment of teachers of culturally diverse students remain problematical.

12. The connoisseur model is a method of teacher assessment whereby experienced and knowledgeable educators train and judge other educators. This method may be the best way to improve the teaching of culturally diverse students.

13. The language minority student is characterized by substantive participation in a non-English-speaking social environment, has acquired the normal communicative abilities of that social environment, and is exposed to an English-speaking environment on a regular basis only during the formal school process. Between two-thirds and three-fourths of language minority children in the United States are from Spanish-speaking backgrounds.

EXTENDING YOUR EXPERIENCE

1. Describe the high school you attended, in terms of its physical facilities and the programs it offers to students. Describe the demographics of the student body during your attendance. What special materials were available for student use, such as computers, art and music supplies, and sports equipment? Research the school district expenditures for your state. How does your high school rank statewide in terms of per-student spending?

2. Design an elementary school whose sole purpose would be to respond to a student body of maximum cultural and linguistic diversity. As creator of this school, what are your requirements for staff credentials and experience, for educational materials, and for curriculum? Describe a typical classroom in your dream school.

3. Reflect on the personal interactions you have regularly with people who are fluent in languages other than English. Is language diversity part of your daily experience? If not, how might you prepare yourself to teach in a linguistically diverse classroom?

4. Your best student has just informed you that she has to drop out of high school and get a job to help support her family. Part of her earnings will go to support her brother, who is in college. Her parents seem unconcerned and claim that since she will be getting married, it is not so important that she finish high school. What will you say to this student and her parents? What will you need to know about them before offering them helpful counsel?

5. You have 26 students in your fourth-grade language arts class, but there are only 20 texts available and your school has no budget for more. How will you make sure all of your students have the necessary materials for learning?

RESOURCES FOR FURTHER STUDY

August, D., and García, E. (1988). *Language minority education in the United States: Research, policy and practice.* Chicago, Ill. Charles C. Thomas.

This publication advances the discussion of issues pertaining to language minority students and how researchers, practitioners, and policymakers can utilize this dialogue to address the issues that affect minority students. The authors present and analyze legal precedents that have affected the education of language minority students.

Frase, M. (1989) *Dropout rates in the United States: 1988* (Analysis Report). Washington, D.C.: Superintendent of Documents, U.S. Government Printing Office.

As mandated by law, this report presents data on high school dropout and retention rates for 1988 and time series data since 1968. The dropout rates are divided into two areas: (1) event dropout, or the proportion of students who leave school in one year; and (2) status dropout, or the proportion of individuals who are not in school and who have not completed high school. Overall, high school dropout rates have declined. Rates for blacks show improvement in these two areas, but rates for Hispanics have increased each year.

National Commission on Children (1991). *Beyond rhetoric. A new American agenda for children and families: Final report of the National Commission on Children.* Washington, D.C.

The commission took over 2 years to investigate, analyze, and recommend national, state, and local changes. The agenda calls for action to reinvest and reinforce the care, education, and protection of children in the United States. The commission estimates that it would take about $60 billion to bring its recommendations to reality. The point is clearly made that if our nation is to compete, succeed, and grow, it needs citizens who are capable. Particular attention is given to students who are poor, who are from minority groups, who are limited English speakers, and who have single parents.

Wong-Fillmore, L. (1991). When learning a second language means losing a first. *Early Childhood Research Quarterly, 6,* 323–346.

The author argues that children's loss of a primary language, particularly when it is the only language spoken by the parents, can be very costly to the children, their families, and society at large. There is no question about the benefits children from diverse backgrounds receive when they learn English. The problems arise in how students come into contact with English and the impact English language learning has on family consciousness. Wong-Fillmore argues that the goal of education for new immigrants should not be limited only to learning English.

VIEWS

OF CULTURE

AND

EDUCATION

CHAPTER 2

Focus Questions

○ What are some of the social and economic changes that have resulted in new contexts for education in the United States?

○ What are the group-oriented and the individual-oriented concepts of culture?

○ How does the concept of culture prevalent in U.S. schools affect which practices are deemed appropriate for teaching culturally diverse children?

○ What are some of the cultural demands of U.S. schools, and how might students respond if the demands of the home culture are different?

○ What are the three ingredients for teaching effectively in a context of student cultural diversity?

"A text without a context is a pretext."

The subjects of this book are the increasing numbers of young people all over the United States whom I have referred to as culturally or linguistically diverse. In all our coming discussions of educational theories and practices, we must keep these children firmly in mind. They are our subjects and, in a sense, they are our "text"—we will open the book of their educational experiences and read the signs of change that we as educators must follow. We will consider both the stories of individuals and the broader trends that generalize to groups of individuals. We will approach our "text" informed of a full range of social and educational issues that will help us be better readers of what is in store for schools in the United States.

This chapter lays out some of the contexts for education in the years to come. Social, economic, and cultural changes in the United States have raised questions about the proper role for our schools. The answers to these questions require a clearer understanding of our assumptions regarding culture and the individual and the part our schools play in transmitting culture to children. We also take a look at the culture of school itself and examine the qualities that will be important for teachers of culturally diverse students.

New Contexts for Education

The accomplishments of all societies rest on the fundamental educational capabilities of their individual members. We must examine our past educational practices for successes and failures and use the present to rework and reenvision our goals for teaching and learning. We must look ahead and prepare our nation's children for the future. We will talk much in this book about change. Fortunately, continuing attention to educational reform in this country provides us with some solid information about changing social and economic circumstances that affect education. Between ten and twenty national reports are produced yearly about our country's schools, ranging from preschool to higher education. The reforms these reports suggest have focused our attention on many significant variables that currently influence our educational institutions and others that will affect our future schooling endeavors. The following list highlights several of these new contexts for education.

Global Marketplace

- Economically, the United States finds itself at a significant competitive disadvantage relative to the growing emphasis on what is termed the "global marketplace." International trade will be the arena for economic growth in the next century. At the present, only one in ten U.S. jobs is related directly to international trade. It is estimated that over the next two decades, more than 50 percent of U.S. jobs will relate to international trade. As activity in the global marketplace heats up, we will no longer "make and sell" to ourselves. The economic stability of our country depends on how well we prepare the next generation for participation in this global context.
- Education has become a major activity of institutions that are not primarily educational in nature. An example of this is education provided to employees by the business sector. Only one-third of formal educational endeavors occur within primary, secondary, and postsecondary educational institutions.

Career Flexibility

- Today's sixth-graders will likely average seven to ten job changes in their working lifetime, along with two to three changes in career. My father was an agricultural worker and died an agricultural worker. I have had four jobs but only one profession: teaching. My daughters may change jobs ten times and experience two or three shifts in profession.
- Only 8 percent of tomorrow's jobs will require less than a high school education. Thirty-five percent will require at least a high school education, and a whopping 60 percent of jobs will require three or more years of postsecondary education.
- Eighty percent of new jobs will be in the information and service sector of the economy. This has been the fastest-growing area of our economy for the last decade. Employees in these sectors must be flexible, computer literate, creative, and highly skilled at communication (preferably in more than one language), with good "people" skills.

Opportunities

for Girls

- Major shifts in values over the last three decades have broad-ened the educational prospects for girls in the United States. No longer limited to traditionally "female" professions such as teaching or nursing, young women are training in high num-bers for a whole spectrum of careers in business, law, and technical fields. Along with the demise of gender-based barri-ers to economic participation have come a host of other issues regarding changes in sexual behavior, health and environ-mental concerns, and family priorities.

The Role of Schools

Considering these new and developing circumstances, what is the role of the school? It seems evident that schools cannot pro-vide adequate job training skills. The job market described above will be much too volatile, and employers themselves already find it necessary to provide their employees with job training that is highly tailored to specific tasks and functions. It appears that the schools must take on several responsibilities, some simi-lar to and some significantly different from the ones they have now.

1. Schools must serve children well with regard to the develop-ment of academic skills: "readin', writin', and 'rithmetic." Our society needs all its members to be able to communicate well and to be linguistically, mathematically, and technologically literate.
2. Schools must focus their emphasis on the development of what I call "living" processes, involving students in curricula that enhance human relationships, critical thinking, and civic responsibility. An emphasis on process means attending to means as well as ends—that is, examining *how* individuals think through their ideas and actions and make decisions in addition to examining the ideas and decisions themselves.

Schooling

for 2000

In essence, in the new curriculum of 2000 and beyond, school-ing must become collaborative, highly social in nature, and pro-cess oriented. The lives of the young people now in school, even more than our own, will be characterized by continuous and dramatic social, economic, and technological change. As adults, these students must be able to react flexibly to these changing situations. They must be equipped with enough understanding, knowledge, and skill to act as well-informed individuals. They must be able to reflect on and analyze the perplexing array of social and individual problems that are part of modern life.

Cultural Change and Disruption

Change is never easy. The cultural shifts our nation is now undergoing take their toll on individuals and on our collective experience. Disruptions in the social fabric often lead to misunderstanding, miscommunication, and tension among people. In the most stressful situations, especially ones that involve economic hardships, people can feel pitted against one another, and old hatreds and old ignorances may rise to block progress and growth. We will see more growing pains as the demographics of the U.S. population are transformed. In fewer than twenty years, 70 percent of California's students will be nonwhite and Hispanic, and one half will speak a language other than English on their first day of school. As we saw in Chapter 1, this same scenario is transforming schools in fifteen other states, including New York, New Jersey, Florida, Michigan, Illinois, and Texas. Such states will represent over 50 percent of the U.S. population in the near future.

| Growing |
| Pains |

We are a country of incredible cultural and linguistic diversity. We are singularly nationalistic—"American" to the core—but still unaccepting of the diversity among us. Recent data gathered on sociological perception suggest that over the last three decades, the white majority of the U.S. population has not changed its stereotyped view of minority groups. The data showed that the majority continues to perceive minorities as less intelligent, as lazy, and of lower moral character. These findings are absolutely frustrating considering that within these same three decades our country has undergone a civil rights movement, a women's movement, and an equal educational opportunity initiative. Millions of dollars and, more significantly, millions of person-hours have been dedicated to addressing the inequalities and human injustices of our age.

Sometimes it is hard to see whether so much passion and lifetime commitment on the part of so many people has had any effect at all. Even the university system in which I teach, the University of California at Berkeley, now has revised its commitment to intellectual excellence by limiting the number of Asian students accepted. The concern is that high present entrance standards would lead to an entering freshman class that is 50 percent Asian. There are many, many issues involved here, but this suggests that the U.S. majority may be similarly unaccepting of populations that it perceives as *more* intelligent and *more* hardworking—a realization that makes many educators stop in their tracks and begin to consider the larger picture.

The context of "us versus them" is exemplified at many educational levels by the experience of language minority children. In a nationwide survey of families, Wong-Fillmore (1991) found evidence of serious disruptions of family relations when young children learn English in school and lose the use of the language spoken at home. The study revealed that parents of language minority students fully recognize the importance of English and want their children to learn it at school, but they do not want it to be at the expense of the home language. Many such parents expressed concern that their children will lose their language and become estranged from their families and cultural heritage. Others reported that their children had already lost or were losing the home language.

An interviewer quoted in this study told the story of a Korean immigrant family whose children had all but lost the ability to speak their native language after just a few years in American schools. The parents could speak English only with difficulty, and the grandmother who lived with the family could neither speak nor understand English. She felt isolated and unappreciated by her grandchildren. The adults spoke to the children exclusively in Korean, refusing to believe that their children could not understand them. They interpreted the children's unresponsiveness as disrespect and rejection. It was only when the interviewer, a bilingual Korean-English speaker, tried to question the children in both languages that the parents finally realized that the children were no longer able to speak or understand Korean. The father wept as he spoke of not being able to talk to his children. One of the children commented that she had never understood why her parents always seemed to be angry.

Keep in mind that the family difficulties caused by the inability to communicate do not manifest only in the home. On the contrary, family problems form the basis of children's problems, and those problems follow them back into school, into the streets, and into their work lives. We know that when enough individuals have problems, our whole society has problems. Systematic lack of support for students' home language has been pervasive in U.S. schools during most of the twentieth century.

It may take years before the harm done to families can be fully assessed. The experience of one family that had been in the United States for nearly twenty years described how breakdowns in communication can lead to the alienation of children from parents. The four children, now teenagers, had completely

Language at Home and School

Children's Loss of Home Language

lost their ability to speak or understand Spanish. The children reportedly were ashamed of Spanish. They did not acknowledge it when their parents spoke it, even though it was the only language their parents knew. The mother indicated that her 17-year-old son was having problems in school. He was often truant and was in danger of dropping out. She had tried to talk with him, but he didn't understand her. Their attempts at discussion ended in physical violence, with mother and son "coming to blows" when words failed them (Wong-Fillmore, 1991).

This would be a disturbing story all on its own. But when we begin to appreciate the numbers of families in this condition, our predicament as a nation sinks in. To prosper, we must find a way out of "us versus them" and embrace the great diversity of our culture. The next section discusses two different theories of culture and their implications for education in the United States.

What Is Culture?

When we speak of the **culture** to which an individual belongs, we generally refer to the system of understanding characteristic of that individual's society, or of some subgroup within that society. This system of understanding includes values, beliefs, notions about acceptable and unacceptable behavior, and other socially constructed ideas that members of the culture are taught are "true." This is the common definition of culture employed by many anthropologists, who analyze the behavioral patterns and customs of groups of people. The word *culture*, however, can have a variety of different connotations in general usage.

An Experiment in Definition

Recently I taught a class in which I asked a group of university juniors and seniors preparing for careers in education to break into small groups and identify, very specifically, attributes of their individual cultures. It was no surprise to me that one student responded, "I'm White. I have no culture." Such responses occur all too frequently. "Of course you have a culture," I answered as the other students scrutinized our interaction. "Everyone has culture." They all went off, some a bit reluctantly, to complete the assignment.

At the end of the exercise, each group reported their findings and analysis. Yes, they all had culture, but with a diverse set of students it was not easy to discuss individual cultural characteristics. These students, like most of us, usually do not sit down and expose their culture. They live it. They can recognize it when they see it. And they can determine when they are not in it, and that usually distresses them. These students also seemed distressed in speaking openly about culture to one another, as if exposing their culture would leave them vulnerable to criticism and negative feelings of attribution regarding who they were or what they might represent.

My students all survived their initial distress and discovered in a few minutes the basic tenets of the science of anthropology. To define a culture by its attributes might be a start, but this in itself is not particularly useful. The students did identify cultural attributes. They indicated that their cultures were made up of many distinguishable attributes: familial, linguistic, religious and spiritual, aesthetic, socioeconomic, educational, diet, gender roles, and so on. The list was quite long. But what seemed quite evident was that they all came to the conclusion that this thing—culture—was not easy to define because it meant (1) defining these attributes in relation to specific individuals who live in distinct physical and social contexts and (2) taking into consideration the previous histories of those individuals and those social contexts. In short, they determined culture to be not only complex but dynamic, yet for individuals living their cultures, quite recognizable.

| Problems of |
| Definitions |

Having begun with the ideas of novice educators and their conceptualizations of culture, it seems appropriate to turn now to the "experts." I must warn you that even professional anthropologists struggle with the same questions as bedeviled my students. Their thinking is more systematic, though, and that will help us.

The Group-Oriented Concept of Culture

The **culture concept,** with its technical anthropological meaning, was first defined by Edward Tylor in 1871 as "that complex whole which includes knowledge, belief, art, law, morals, custom, and other capabilities and habits acquired by man as a member of society" (Kroeber and Kluckhohn, 1963, p. 81). Since Tylor's time, many other definitions of culture have been advanced by anthropologists. These definitions, like Tylor's, commonly attempt to encompass the totality (or some subset of the totality) of humanity's achievements, dispositions, and capabilities. Virtually every anthropologist considers culture to be something that is learned and transmitted from generation to generation.

| Culture Is |
| Learned |

Most definitions of culture include another dimension, the notion that culture is something that members of a group share in common. A recently published textbook on anthropology states, for example, that behaviors and ideas may be considered cultural only insofar as they are shared among members of a social group (Nanda, 1990). This formulation is useful for anthropological comparisons between societies or subgroups within societies. Its basic assumption, however, is that of uniformity in the cultural attributes of individual members of societies and subgroupings of societies. In this formulation, the primary focus of culture is some kind of group.

Culture Is
Shared

Anthropologists do acknowledge that members of all societies display individual differences in their behaviors and ways of thinking. That is to say, societies are characterized to some extent by intercultural heterogeneity. But these differences are not significant for anthropologists and usually are noted only insofar as they determine the "looseness" or "tightness" of a society's cultural system. When researchers in anthropology proceed to write their ethnographies, their deep descriptions and analyses of any group, they tend to ignore individual variations and to abstract what they apparently consider "an essential homogeneity from the background noise of insignificant diversity" (Schwartz, 1978, p. 419).

Along these lines, anthropologist Ralph Linton defined culture as "the sum total of ideas, conditioned emotional responses and patterns of habitual behavior which the members of a society have acquired through instruction or imitation and which they share to a greater or less degree" (quoted in Kroeber and Kluckhohn, 1963, p. 82). Although ideas or learned behavioral habits need not be totally shared by everyone in a group, it is nevertheless this property of sharing, the commonality of attributes, that defines the domain of culture.

Educational Considerations. Some emphasis on shared traits is basic to any conceptual understanding of the role of culture in education. However, such an emphasis leaves little if any room for the recognition of each student's individuality within the framework of the culture concept. Individuality becomes the domain of psychology, relevant only to discussions of personality, while "culture" is used to refer to ideas and behaviors that prevail in the individual's group. Using the culture concept as a basis for theories of education might be appropriate if the goal is to educate (or reeducate) a group, as in modernization programs applied by developing countries to their peasant populations.

But the focus of most education, as all who have taught for any time know, is the education of the individual student, not the education of his or her ethnic group.

The relevance of this problem lies in the possible consequences of the group-oriented concept of culture for the perceptions and expectations of teachers in their interactions with culturally diverse children. A group-oriented concept may serve to distract the teacher's attention from the student's particular experience of culture-generating processes, in and outside of school. The culture concept adopted by the teacher greatly affects teacher-student interaction. The assumptions a teacher makes about the student's "culture," whether right or wrong, may stereotype the student and thus preclude the flexible, realistic, and open-minded quality of teacher-student interaction needed for effective instruction. The effect of this stereotyping on students is significant, since the educational process is fundamentally a process of social interaction, with socialization as a primary goal.

> **Consequences for Teacher-Student Interaction**

Let's consider an example of how the group culture concept might operate in a teacher-student interaction. Picture a situation where the teacher is perplexed by some action or response by a student of minority status. A teacher who has studied some anthropological descriptions of the student's ethnic culture may leap to an interpretation of the student's behavior based on idealized characteristics anthropologists have attributed to that culture. The teacher may mean well, but to construe an individual's behavior solely on the basis of generalization about group traits is to stereotype the individual, no matter how valid the generalizations or how well meaning one's intentions.

> **Stereotyping of Students**

It would be better for the teacher to encounter the student in the way anthropologists most often come to understand the people they study. Though they write about cultures in collective terms, anthropologists build their understandings through observations of individuals. The teacher's efforts to understand the individual student could (and should) be supplemented by knowledge of cultural attributes widely held in the student's ethnic community. But this fund of knowledge should be viewed only as background information. The question of its applicability to the particular student should be treated as inherently problematical. Many studies (for example, Rodriguez, 1989; Tharp and Gallimore, 1989) also caution educational personnel against hasty "ethnographic/cultural" generalizations on the grounds that all linguistic-cultural groups are continuously undergoing significant cultural changes.

The student-teacher interaction is a powerful phenomenon. Thomas Carter's research (1968) into the effects of teacher's expectations on student learning and classroom behavior are particularly pertinent. Carter showed that Chicano students may sometimes actualize in their behavior the negative expectations held for them by teachers. It may be expected, of course, that a pattern of negative expectation would be less likely among teachers who have elected to teach in bilingual and bicultural settings in which both Spanish and English are used for instruction. We have to remember, though, that many teachers teach in bilingual and bicultural settings that have not been so formally designated and for which these teachers received little preparation.

| **Power of** |
| **Teacher** |
| **Expectations** |

Even teachers of the same minority status as their students may be considered in some ways culturally different from the children of their own ethnic group. This observation is not recent. Guerra (1979) points to linguistic and other cultural variations both within (student-student) and between (student-teacher) generations of bilingual populations. Cuellar (1980, p. 198) argues that one's understanding of the meaning and value of culture and language must take into account the fact that "a community's characteristics reflect the composition of the different generational cohorts in the different age strata." What this adds up to is individual variation within cultures, of particular importance to educators.

The Individual-Oriented Concept of Culture

The group culture concept is not the only instrument available for understanding individuals and groups. Fortunately, anthropological theory contains an individual-oriented concept of culture developed and used by a number of anthropologists with interests in psychology. As Ted Schwartz notes, these theorists criticized the group culture concept for the way it can "lead one to imagine culture as floating somehow disembodied in the noösphere or, at best, carried by human beings as a conductor might carry an electric current containing information" (Schwartz, 1978, p. 434). Rather than work with an abstract idea of culture, these theorists were interested more in how culture was manifested in the lives of individual human beings.

An early expression of the individual-oriented concept of culture is seen in the work of anthropologist J. O. Dorsey. U.S. anthropologist Edward Sapir (quoted in Pelto and Pelto, 1975, p. 1) wrote the following of Dorsey's orientation:

Living as long as he did in close touch with the Omaha Indians, [Dorsey] knew that he was dealing, not with a society nor with a specimen of primitive man but with a finite, though indefinite, number of human beings who gave themselves the privilege of differing from each other not only in matters generally considered as "One's own business" but even on questions which clearly transcended the private individual's concerns.

Advocates of the individual-oriented concept of culture frequently describe a society's culture as a "pool" of constructs (rules, beliefs, values, etc.) by which the society's members conceptually order the objects and events of their lives. The participation of individuals in this pool is seen as variable. Spiro (1951), for example, distinguished between the cultural "heritage" of all members of a society (that which has been made available to them by their predecessors) and each individual's particular cultural "inheritance" (that portion of the group's heritage that the individual has effectively received, or "internalized," from the past). Ted Schwartz adds that the individual also manipulates, recombines, and otherwise transforms these inherited constructs. This process of transformation, together with the outright creation of new constructs, is a major source of culture change (Schwartz, 1978). The individual's own portion of a society's culture is termed by Goodenough as a "propriocept" (1981), by Wallace as a "mazeway" (1970), and by Schwartz as an "idioverse" (1978). All of these specialized terms are variations on a core nature of culture: each individual assembles his or her own version of the larger culture.

| Culture as Variable |

For some of the anthropologists who employ an individual-oriented concept of culture, "the private system of ideas of individuals is culture" (Pelto and Pelto, 1975, pp. 12–13). Other anthropologists of like mind reject the implication in such a notion of individual cultures. As they see it, the contents of one subjective system alone cannot be considered a culture. Like Schwartz, these theorists consider a cultural system to consist of all the constructs available to a society's members. Nevertheless, the society is itself not the locus of culture; its individual members are. The culture thus is a **distributive** phenomenon in that its elements are widely distributed among the individual members of a society. A major implication of this **distributive**

| Individual Is Locus of Culture |

model of culture is a rejection of the traditional assumption of cultural homogeneity—that is, the idea that all members of a culture share all that culture's attributes. The distributive model instead implies that each individual's portion of the culture differs in some ways from that of any other.

According to Schwartz, Wallace's antidote to the homogeneous view of culture is an overdose, leading to the opposite malady of ignoring the degree of cultural sharing that does occur between individuals. Schwartz's own model of culture takes into account both the sharing and nonsharing of cultural constructs between members of a society, and he argues that both are fundamentally essential to a society's viability. Diversity, he argues, increases a society's cultural inventory, whereas what any individual could contain within his or her head would make up a very small culture pool. Commonality then permits communication and coordination in social life. In Schwartz's own words, "It makes as little sense to depict the distribution of a culture among the members of a society as totally heterogeneous and unique in each individual as it did to argue for complete homogeneity. We must dispense with the *a priori* assumption of homogeneity, but, similarly, we are not served by an *a priori* assumption of heterogeneity" (Schwartz, 1978, p. 438).

Educational Considerations. I view Schwartz's formulation of the distributive model of culture as the most appropriate for addressing issues of cultural diversity in the schools. This formulation permits, within the framework of culture, simultaneous recognition of a student's "ethnic" culture and those characteristics that define the student as a unique individual. Students share with their ethnic peers constructs they do not share with others, but all individuals are in some ways different from their ethnic peers. The distributive model also permits recognition of traits that members of subgroups share with members of the larger culture, such as those acquired through acculturation.

Schooling is a major variable in **acculturation,** which is the process by which the members of a society are taught the elements of the society's culture. The acculturation process is a crucial consideration in the analysis of ethnic minorities in plural societies. Variety in acculturation also contributes significantly to the heterogeneity of ethnic cultures. Writing about the U.S. cultural subgroup labeled "Hispanic," Bell, Kasschau, and Zellman (1976) note that among Chicanos, "many have ancestors who

Acculturation

Is Variable

Becoming a Responsive Teacher

2.1 Influential Teachers, Influential Students

These students will change American society.

American society is not the same as it was a century ago, or even a decade ago, partly because of the different peoples who have come to our shores. Without the contributions of individual groups, we would not have such American icons as the Christmas tree, the log cabin, labor unions, and jazz. Jewish immigrants in the early part of this century made a key contribution—they demanded entry to college in such numbers that they transformed what had been a finishing school for the wealthy into an opportunity for individual advancement.

Those college-bound students were fortunate to have teachers dedicated to their success, even if the teachers never anticipated that their efforts would have the far-reaching effect of helping to democratize higher education. Teachers of that era were selected not only for their formal credentials, but for their suitability as role models for the young. The impact of teachers on the life of young people can hardly be overestimated. Teachers represent a link to the adult world of educated, successful professionals. Especially for children from a different culture and language, teachers have a tremendous impact; they are their link to American society. Without the caring guidance of teachers, the immigrant and minority youth of today will readily learn how to eat at McDonald's, play video games, and watch MTV. But they will have great difficulty getting to college and becoming engineers, playwrights, or teachers themselves.

1. Write a letter to a young relative or friend. In this letter, describe some of the changes that have occurred in the world since you were his or her age. You might mention specific political or social events or trends and your thoughts about them. Feel free to refer to any types of changes you have encountered that you feel have affected your life. Then, given your perspective as an older mentor for this young person, provide some suggestions about which aspects of schooling might help prepare him or her to confront change constructively. If you decide to send this letter, consider sharing any response from the addressee with your classmates.

2. Find out what student cultural centers are on your college or university campus and then visit each one. If possible, also visit cultural centers in the local community outside your campus. Gather leaflets and flyers and take some notes about the activities these cultural groups are planning. In class, compile a master list of events to attend over the semester and decide which ones interest you the most. Volunteer to attend an event and review it for your classmates.

3. You have been granted the opportunity to spend an entire day with a 10-year-old child doing anything you want, wherever you want. This child is from an ethnic and linguistic background that is radically different from yours. In fact, you may not even have a shared language. What would you want this child to teach you about his or her world?

came to North America several centuries ago, but others are themselves recent immigrants. Hence, a simple cultural characterization of [this] ethnic group should be avoided" (p. 7). These authors also caution against a simplistic view of the process of acculturation, noting that it "may not be linear, in the sense that one simply loses certain Mexican attributes and replaces them with Anglo attributes" (1976, pp. 31–32). Acculturation may be characterized by more complex patterns of combination and by ongoing recombination than by simple substitution. Thus, language minority children who hear some English spoken at home experience a different process of acculturation than children who hear only the home language. These children may all belong to the same ethnic subgroup, but their different acculturation makes them each unique.

Some people are likely to respond to the individual-oriented concept of culture with the question "What about customs?" Chicanos, for example, might point out that all the members of their group are alike in that they recognize certain *costumbres* that distinguish them from the larger society. Customs occupy a realm of culture that is highly shared and is more likely to belong to the public sphere than to form a specific part of an individual's subjective orientation. Referring to the "layered" nature of culture, anthropologist Benjamin Paul (1965, p. 200) has observed:

Customs

and Culture

> What we call customs rest on top and are most apparent. Deepest and
>
> least apparent are the cultural values that give meaning and direction
>
> to life. Values influence people's perceptions of needs and their choice
>
> between perceived alternative courses of action.

I purposely emphasize the problematic nature of cultural variability and sharing. The variable nature of acculturation and the individual uniqueness that it engenders are, I believe, no less important for the education of culturally diverse students than are the "real" cultural differences between ethnic groups. Education must deal with both the individual and the culture.

I hasten to add that teachers who work with children from linguistically or culturally diverse populations must be not only keenly aware of the instructional objectives of education but also knowledgeable about and sensitive to the impact that culture and language have on the student. We will see more of these two issues in Chapters 4 and 5.

The Culture of School

The classroom has many, if not all, of the characteristics that anthropologists and sociologists tell us belong to culture. There are tacit rules, patterns, formal structures of organization, and an ecological component. Most important are the tacit dimensions. We tend to think that school is all about learning "the Three R's." Parents and children, and sometimes teachers themselves, do not recognize that the school makes cultural demands on students in addition to the intellectual ones.

Competing

Concepts

As in our earlier discussion of culture, we need to distinguish between competing concepts of the nature and purpose of school. Recent research acknowledges that schools are social situations which are constructed through the interactions between individuals (Feldman, 1986; Gardner, 1983) More traditional views represent schools as institutions with stable traits generally impervious to individual influence. It is important for educators to understand how our society views the concept of school. This concept underlies how we approach the teaching of students in schools. If we see teaching and learning as embedded within a cultural context, we are more likely to recognize that performance will vary as a function of that context.

Student Response to School Culture

Some examples from research into the cultural demands of school will demonstrate this point. Philips (1982, 1984) examined the classroom performance of Native American students. Observed in the schools, Native American students appeared to conform exactly to the stereotype of "the silent Indian child."

Observations

of Students

Philips was puzzled, however, since her observations also indicated that outside the classroom these children were certainly not silent. She identified what is now considered an important aspect of school culture: **participant-structured demand,** or the demands of instruction that are imposed by the organization of the learning environment itself. She was able to make this discovery only because she observed the children across a number of situations—in community settings, in their homes, and in the school.

Philips found that classroom lessons imposed varying demands on the children. The classrooms were organized in an individualistic, competitive way. Children were expected to stand up alone in front of the classroom and to respond competitively to the teacher's questions. The Native American children were not doing well in this arrangement. Philips contrasted the demands of the school with the demands of the home. There were definite demands in each culture. In the homes of the Native American children, she found a culture in which children were working cooperatively in groups, not competitively. For an individual to stand out, to act on his or her own, independent of the group, was to violate the norm of the home. Conversely, it was to violate the norm of the classroom not to stand out. The children were caught in a bind between the competing demands of home and school.

| Contrasting Demands of Home and School |

Other studies have compared home and school cultures. Shirley Brice Heath's work, conducted in a number of different areas, contributes a good deal to our knowledge base. Heath (1982) noted in her study of low-income black and white Appalachian children that their teachers, who came from different economic and cultural backgrounds, talked to children differently than did the children's parents. Heath described a difference in language used between home and school. The school placed a great demand on children to display their knowledge. Children would often be asked a question for which the teacher already had the answer. If, for example, a child correctly answered the question "What time is it?" the teacher would not respond "Thank you" but "Very good," indicating that the child's knowledge had been tested. The teacher did not need the information. At home, however, when a child was asked "What time is it?" the underlying assumption was that the child had information needed by another member of the family. Interestingly, middle-income parents often use a questioning strategy similar to the teacher's. They play games such as peek-a-boo that also have a dimension of information. But Heath found that in low-income families, there was little imitation of the conversational demands of school. These children were not gaining practice at home with a linguistic device essential to their school performance.

| Language Use |

The Schools' Response to Children

Both Heath's work and Philips's study portray ways in which a school culture may deviate from a student's home culture. This and other research demonstrate quite clearly that a school culture truly does exist and can directly or indirectly influence children's performance and teacher perceptions. Since we cannot ask children to leave their cultures at the door, we must ask, how can schools allow for a better balance of these disparate demands?

One recommendation is to allow cultural elements that are relevant to the children to enter the classroom freely. Some refer to this practice as **scaffolding.** The school provides a set of supports that utilize the child's home language, discourse style, participation orientation, and so on, enabling the child to move through relevant experiences from the home toward the demands of the school as representative of the society. It is not a subtraction of culture, and it is not an attempt to reproduce home environments in the context of the school. The idea is to encourage the child to respect the demands of the school culture while preserving the integrity of the home culture.

Primarily, we must first comprehend the fact that children— all children—come to school motivated to enlarge their culture. But we must start with their culture. We need not regard them, certainly not initially, as organisms to be molded and regu- lated.We look first to determine how they seek to know them- selves and others and how their expertise and experience can be used as the fuel to fire their interests, knowledge, and skills. We do not look first at their deficits: what they do not know but need to know. Far from having deficits, they are rich in assets. As teachers, we enter their world in order to aid them and to build bridges between two cultures (Sarason, 1990).

Teaching in a Cultural Context

If by understanding culture and cultural diversity and respecting individuality, educators can better serve culturally diverse stu- dents, have they fulfilled their obligations as teachers? I believe they have not. Our culturally diverse populations continue to be highly vulnerable in today's society and in our schools. We examined this social, economic, and educational vulnerability in the previous chapter. It is in all our very best interests for cultur- ally diverse students to succeed. They will carry us all to either a bright or a beleaguered future.

| Respect Is |
| Not Enough |

Recognizing the present circumstances and the magnitude of this challenge, what is called for? What must we do? Sensitivity toward "culture," while necessary, will not be sufficient. Ear- lier we saw how even well-meaning teachers may stereotype students when trying to allow for cultural differences. There are three additional ingredients for effective teaching in a context of student cultural diversity:

- Personal commitment
- Knowledge of what makes a difference
- Educational leadership

Let's look more closely at these elements and take an inventory of them in our schools today.

Personal Commitment

We need not be fooled by liberal or conservative rhetoric. We have not achieved educational equality for our culturally diverse populations, and substantive progress requires further resolve. It is often trumpeted that Head Start, school choice, restructuring, site-based management, cooperative learning, the whole language approach, educational technology (computer-assisted instruction), and so forth have already or will soon reverse the pattern of underachievement among linguistically and culturally diverse populations. Doubtlessly these contributions are important, but our own part in the U.S. educational system suggests that we as teachers should resist the notion of a miracle cure. No new methodologies, reorganizations, or curricula will satisfactorily address the problem of underachievement unless the individuals who implement these initiatives are deeply committed to the enterprise. The change that is necessary must be fueled by the type of social energy that our nation has tapped in the past. As in the eras of Kennedy's "New Frontier" or Johnson's "War on Poverty," we must grasp the spiritual importance of this new educational challenge.

No Miracle Cures

More than a decade after Jimmy Carter warned of a crisis of spirit in America—a warning that proved politically disastrous for him and a boon to rival Ronald Reagan—a broad spectrum of the nation's social and intellectual leadership is concluding that Carter was right. In fact, they say, the crisis has deepened. It was heresy when Carter declared, "we've always had a faith that the days of our children would be better than our own." We are losing that faith, and it is no longer possible to conceal it from ourselves.

A consensus has emerged that a lack of confidence among Americans, in the future and in one another, lies at the heart of the nation's ills. A nation that passed much of the 1970s, in the aftermath of Vietnam, in search of its soul and self spent the 1980s in what many see as a self-consuming materialism. We now enter the 1990s in a cynical, dispirited mood. "There is disturbing evidence to suggest that most forms of responsibility toward others have eroded in recent decades," asserts Derek Bok, former president of Harvard University, in his 1990 book, *Universities and the Future of America.* The percentage of people who feel that most individuals in power try to take advantage of others has doubled over the last two decades and now exceeds 60 percent.

One source of information about prevailing attitudes in the United States is the book *The Cynical Americans* (1989), by Donald L. Kanter and Philip H. Mirvis. Based on a national survey of attitudes, Kanter concludes that "the tendency to behave cynically is being reinforced to an unprecedented degree by a social environment that seems to have abandoned idealism and increasingly celebrates the virtue of being 'realistic' in an impersonal, acquisitive, tough-guy world. In citizen and country alike, there seems to be a loss of faith in people and in the very concept of community. A recent national survey found that 43 percent of Americans—and more than half of those under age 24—believe selfishness and fakery are at the core of human nature." Large majorities of those sampled say they feel most people lie if they can gain by it, sacrifice ethical standards when money is at stake, and pretend to care about others more than they really do.

| **Temptations** |
| **of Cynicism** |

It is difficult to believe that the picture is truly bleak. Most of us know people who are generous and creative in their interactions with others—even heroic in small ways, considering the multiple stresses and strains of modern life. They work hard, tend to their families, and contribute to their communities. There are many people who care deeply about individual and collective welfare in the United States. It is possible that our current cynicism is simply a measure of disappointed idealism, of surprise and dismay that our work as a nation is not done and may never be "done," and that we must continue to call upon the inspiration, resolve, commitment, and passion of everyone.

| **Importance** |
| **of Inspiration** |

Some have argued that we have lost the ability to inspire our children. Others say we have lost the ability to inspire ourselves. But inspiration is the spark that leads to resolve and commitment, and we cannot afford to be without it. Borrowing from Jaime Escalante, the noted California educator characterized in the popular 1988 film *Stand and Deliver,* we will need *ganas*—the desire that fires the will to overcome great challenges.

Knowledge of What Makes a Difference

We will also need a new knowledge base. Recent research has pinpointed the problem of educational vulnerability. It has destroyed stereotypes and myths about the educational needs of culturally diverse students and laid a foundation upon which to reconceptualize present educational practices and to launch new initiatives. As we saw earlier in this chapter, the basis for change is a new understanding of individual uniqueness within a cultural context. No one set of descriptions or prescriptions will suffice for all students of a given cultural background.

| Individual |
| Uniqueness |

We should pay attention to what seems to work. Recent research summarized by García (1992) has documented educationally effective practices with linguistically and culturally diverse students in selected sites throughout the United States. These descriptive studies identified specific schools and classrooms that serve students of minority status and that were particularly successful academically. The case study approach adopted by these studies included examination of preschool, elementary, and high school classrooms. The researchers interviewed teachers, principals, parents, and students and conducted specific classroom observations that assessed the "dynamics" of the instructional process.

| Attributes of |
| Successful |
| Schools |

The results of these studies for elementary schools provide important insights into general instructional organization, literacy development, and academic achievement in such content areas as math and science. The results also yield enlightening information on the perspectives of students, teachers, administrators, and parents. The interviews showed that these classroom teachers were highly committed to the educational success of their students. They perceived themselves as instructional innovators utilizing "new" learning theories and instructional philosophies to guide their practice. Most of these teachers were involved in professional development activities such as participating in small-group support networks with other educators. They had a strong, demonstrated belief in the importance of communication between the school and the home (several teachers were interacting weekly with parents) and felt they had the autonomy to create or change the instruction and curriculum in their classrooms, even if it did not exactly meet district guidelines. They had high academic expectations for all their students ("Everyone will learn to read in my classroom") and served as advocates for their students. They rejected any conclusion that their students were intellectually or academically disadvantaged.

This and other research shows that curriculum, instructional strategies, and teaching staffs that are effective are rooted in sharing "expertise" and experiences through multiple processes of communication. Abundant and diverse opportunities for speaking, listening, reading, and writing, along with home-to-school bridges that help guide students through the learning process, constitute an effective curriculum. Effective schools also encourage culturally diverse students to take risks, construct meaning, and reinterpret the knowledge they acquire as it applies to their lives. Within this curriculum, skills are taught as tools for acquiring further knowledge. Research into such effective programs should continue. The more we know about what makes them effective, the more equipped we will be to educate diverse student groups.

Educational Leadership

The leadership necessary to mobilize this growing commitment and knowledge will recognize four interlocking domains that pertain especially to teachers.

Retraining

Teachers

Knowledge Dissemination. We will need to disseminate knowledge about effective practices to those who can utilize it. This requires training, retraining, and more retraining. Individually and institutionally, new knowledge must be appropriated by people working in the field of education. It is of no use to students if researchers share their knowledge only among themselves. New avenues for knowledge dissemination and appropriation are required. Leadership in this domain is required.

Professional Development. New knowledge alone does not automatically lead to a new set of pedagogical or curricular skills ready for use by practitioners. Knowledge must be transferred to teachers and adapted for use in specific instructional contexts. Time and energy must be devoted to the collaboration required between teachers and researchers to develop new skills. Moreover, these new pedagogical and curricular skills must be evaluated "in the field"—they must prove themselves effective for students. We will need to hold ourselves and others "automatically" accountable. This requires leadership in both knowledge dissemination and professional skill development.

Disposition for Leadership. Many are called, but few will self-select. We need a generation of educational leaders who are willing to sacrifice, work very hard and very long, take risks, learn from failure, rise above frustration, rethink existing paradigms, and support and collaborate with their colleagues. Those who do not possess this set of dispositions must step aside, minimize obstruction, and otherwise admit that if they cannot be part of the solution, they will not be part of the problem.

Risk and
Collaboration

Affective Engagement. We will need leadership that welcomes, adopts, nurtures, celebrates, and challenges our culturally diverse students. "They" must become "we." Anything short of raw advocacy every minute of every day will not suffice. Too many of these students have given up hope in themselves. We must not give up hope.

Mostly, educators need to act. Presidents and governors "proclaim" and set national educational goals. Educators need to move beyond such proclamations. The task at hand is not only to see the future but to enable it. With commitment, knowledge, and leadership, educators can enable the future for our culturally diverse society.

Conclusion

In this chapter, I have tried to set the context for a more thorough discussion of the educational challenges facing this country's educators. The challenge stands for all students and specifically for those who are culturally diverse. This country's educational future will be much different from our educational past. We will have to be capable of responding to transformations in social structures and institutions, in global organization, and in values. Historically, our schools' efforts to merge diverse groups into a homogenized "American" culture have not resulted in academic success for culturally diverse students. However, new insights into educational concepts, new research, and new educational practices suggest that we can meet this challenge successfully.

In the chapters that follow, I will more clearly define the notions of culture outlined here and describe the interrelationships among social, cultural, and linguistic contexts for education. We must continue to build a knowledge base regarding children, families, communities, and schools. Research studies that add dimension to what we already know about culturally diverse students will be valuable pieces of the puzzle. However, as the discussion in the preceding pages has indicated, merely building this knowledge base is not enough.

I want to point out, before you turn another page, that the information in this book will not make a critical difference in the lives of many of our most educationally needy students. Even with all its theoretical underpinnings and its comments on research, pedagogy, curriculum, and educational philosophy, it is still only a book. It is a forum through which knowledge can be developed, examined, and transmitted. But this knowledge must be combined with action on the part of educators if the challenges I have articulated are to be met head on and successfully overcome.

SUMMARY OF MAJOR IDEAS

1. Ongoing social and economic changes, in this country and worldwide, have produced new contexts for education in the United States. We need to prepare students for participation in the global marketplace and for flexibility in their future careers. Projections show that in the near future, 60 percent of all jobs will require some postsecondary education and 80 percent of new jobs will be in the information and service sector.

2. It is not the role of the schools to prepare students for specific jobs. Rather, schools must teach academic skills that develop students' intellectual abilities and that involve students in learning activities that enhance human relationships, critical thinking, and civic responsibility.

3. Despite its undeniable cultural and linguistic diversity, U.S. society still demonstrates an "us versus them" relationship between the white majority and minority populations. This pattern of thinking is reflected in schooling practices, with negative results especially for language minority students.

4. Culture is a system of values, beliefs, notions about acceptable and unacceptable behavior, and other socially constructed ideas characteristic of a society or of a subgroup within a society. The group-oriented concept of culture describes culture as a set of attributes that are shared by all the members of a group. The individual-oriented concept of culture describes culture as a set of attributes made available to members of a group but which may not be shared by all

members. The group concept of culture emphasizes cultural homogeneity, and the individual concept of culture emphasizes cultural heterogeneity.

5. Criticism of the group-oriented concept of culture as a basis for educational theory centers on the assumption of cultural homogeneity. It may lead to stereotyping children in terms of their cultural group identification, rather than addressing children as unique individuals.

6. The distributive model of culture, which is based on the notion of cultural heterogeneity, implies that each individual's portion of a culture differs from that of any other individual. Because it recognizes the uniqueness of the individual, who is the focus of educational efforts, this concept may serve as a useful basis for educational theory.

7. Acculturation is the process by which the members of a society are taught the elements of the society's culture. There is much variety in the acculturation process within all societies. Variety in acculturation contributes to cultural heterogeneity.

8. Educational theory must be founded on the acknowledgment that individuals of similar cultural backgrounds may share some attributes but are also unique from one another. Educational practices must respond to the individual student first, within the context of the student's culture.

9. An important aspect of school culture is participant structured demand, a term that describes the demands of instruction that are imposed on children by the organization of the learning environment. Students for whom the cultural demands of home do not mesh with the cultural demands of school may not perform well academically. Different attitudes toward cooperation and competition and different use of language between home and school are two possible cultural variables.

10. Scaffolding is an educational practice that provides support for children as they move between disparate home and school cultures. The goal is to keep the home culture intact while the child learns to function within the demands of school.

11. Children enter school motivated to enlarge their culture. Building on what they already know instead of focusing on what they do not know is the goal of effective teaching.

12. Effective teaching in a context of student cultural diversity requires personal commitment, knowledge of what makes a difference, and educational leadership. Initiatives proposed

by the educational leaders of tomorrow will focus on transmitting knowledge to teachers and developing new teaching skills. These leaders will be risk takers who support one another's ideas and who celebrate student diversity in the schools.

EXTENDING YOUR EXPERIENCE

1. The text suggests that future job markets will require workers who are flexible and creative, skilled at communicating, and technologically literate. Outline some curricula that you think would develop these attributes in young people. As a further step, design a course for any grade level that focuses on developing children's awareness of three things: human relationships, critical thinking, and civic responsibility.

2. In your own words, and referring back to the chapter if necessary, explain the concepts of cultural homogeneity and cultural heterogeneity. Now list all your group memberships, both formal and informal: sets of friends and acquaintances, clubs, teams, and organizations in which you participate. Select one of these groups and describe what all its members have in common. Then describe how members of the group differ from one another. Write out a few sentences introducing yourself to a new member of the group. Do you emphasize what you share with others, what makes you different, or both?

3. Using the categories listed in the text (familial, linguistic, religious and spiritual, aesthetic, socioeconomic, educational, diet, gender roles) and any others you can think of, characterize your cultural heritage—the systems of belief and thought in which you were raised. What portion of this heritage have you actually "inherited," or consciously incorporated into your own life? What portion, if any, have you rejected? Why?

4. Define *participant-structured demand* in your own words and describe how it operates in two of the courses you are taking. How do the cultural demands of these two class environments differ? Characterize your learning experience in each one. Write three serious recommendations to your instructor for altering the class culture to benefit your own particular style of learning.

5. Review the comments on cynicism by Derek Bok and Kanter and Mirvis quoted in the chapter. Realize that if you

are younger than 24, these comments refer to you. Do you feel that they accurately portray your vision of human nature? Interview five friends and compile their opinions on this passage in the text. Using verbatim quotes from your friends, who may remain anonymous if they wish, present your findings to the class.

RESOURCES FOR FURTHER STUDY

Goodenough, W. H. (1981). *Culture, language, and society* (2nd ed.). Menlo Park, Calif.: Benjamin/Cummins.

The essay looks at how humans expand their linguistic knowledge and cultural base. The study is based on research conducted in South America in a remote area of the Amazon River. The author points out that language and culture are a direct result of what individuals and groups do collectively, for their own benefit and knowledge. All their decisions are made within the boundaries of what they have, think they might have, or based on previous experiences. This microscopic view of language and culture expands the lens on how we can clarify the relationship between culture and society and to begin grappling with a general theory of cultural stability, essentially by looking and observing our commonalties, gains, and knowledge as a unifying force.

Kroeber, A. L., and Kluckhohn, C. (1963). *Culture: A critical review of concepts and definitions.* New York: Vintage Books.

The authors argue that culture is a general descriptive category of human nature. This definition allows cultures to have similar distinctive designs; however, the only changes culture can have are initiated by individuals because individuals create organisms that operate in groups. These groups or cultures are a direct result of individuals interacting at the concrete level. In short, cultures begin, continue, or change as the result of individual action.

Rodriguez, C. E. (1989). *Puerto Ricans born in the U.S.A.* Winchester, Mass.: Unwin Hyman, Inc.

This book is an extensive discussion of American citizens of Puerto Rican descent. The discussion primarily supports the theory that their individual and group contributions have not brought prosperity to the Puerto Rican community. The theory is well supported by detailed census data and socioeconomic trends. One area of particular interest is education. Puerto Ricans, like most Hispanic students in the United States, lag behind academically, are rapidly dropping out, are segregated, and overall have low academic achievement. The author presents some of the arguments traditionally used to validate the low educational attainment of Hispanic students and gives recommendations to improve the educational situation of Puerto Rican students.

Schwartz, T. (1978). Where is the culture? Personality as the distributive locus of culture. In G. Spinder (Ed.), *The Making of Psychological Anthropology*. Berkeley, Calif.: University of California Press.

The author presents a model of culture as neither homogeneous nor heterogeneous but instead as a conglomeration of similarities and differences. Both culture and individual are constantly changing, but it is essential to recognize that even while changing, both are still stable and inherent. The author argues that individuals are the driving force behind cultural change, yet that change affects other individuals and creates and re-creates culture.

EDUCATIONAL

APPROACHES TO

STUDENT CULTURAL

DIVERSITY

CHAPTER 3

Focus Questions

○ What is Americanization, and what concept of culture underlies it?

○ How have legal reforms in educational equity and the movement toward multicultural education in the U.S. schools affected the education of culturally and linguistically diverse children?

○ What are the shortcomings of educational equity and multicultural education as approaches to understanding the educational needs of diverse populations?

○ What are two new theoretical perspectives that attempt to explain why culturally diverse children often fail academically?

○ How does the constructivist approach to knowledge provide the basis for a new pedagogy?

"Equity and pluralism in schools does not address diversity."

In our efforts to understand the effects of cultural diversity in the schools, we use theories of language, learning, thinking, teaching, socialization, and culture (August and García, 1988). Research pertinent to education has expanded its scope in recent decades. What was once considered the study of values and behavior (Mead, 1939; Skinner, 1957) has become today an interlocking study of elements from linguistics, psychology, and sociology. Findings in each of these areas are independently significant, but together they help us understand the nature of the cultural experience at both micro and macro levels. Educators, for example, can focus on smaller units of social analysis, such as a speech event, for insight into a student's experience. We can also broaden the view to a larger unit of social analysis, such as social class, for vital contextual information. For teachers of culturally and linguistically diverse students, the issue of culture—what it is and how it directly and indirectly influences academic learning—is the crux of research interest.

This chapter concentrates on the schooling initiatives that have been targeted at culturally diverse students in the United States. In so doing, it discusses the way in which educational research, theory, policy, and practice of significance to these students converge. We will look underneath the variety of action plans and programs that have been devised for culturally diverse students and reveal the educational concepts and theories used as a foundation. We will find that definitions of culture and assumptions about cultural differences largely determine past and present educational practices.

A Historical Survey

Within the last few years, educational approaches related to culture and education have shifted from an early focus on "Americanization" (Dewey, 1921) to concerns about educational equity (Ramirez and Castaneda, 1974) and then to multicultural education (Banks, 1981; Grant and Sleeter, 1988). More recent approaches center on the "effective" instruction of children from culturally and linguistically diverse groups (García, 1991; Purkey and Smith, 1983; Tharp, 1989). This section introduces these earlier educational approaches and explains how they developed from past theory and data on culture and education. Later sections will discuss newer approaches based on a broader understanding of cultural diversity as it relates to schooling. You will see that linguistic, cognitive, social, and educational research and theory developed over the last two decades have reshaped in a dramatic way our view of cultural "difference" in education.

Americanization

Historically, "Americanization" has been a prime institutional education objective for culturally diverse children (Elam, 1972; Gonzalez, 1990). Based on a sociological theory of **assimilation,** Americanization has traditionally been recognized as a solution to the problem of immigrants and ethnicity in the modern industrialized United States. **Americanization** is an approach to acculturation that seeks to merge small ethnic and linguistically diverse communities into a single dominant national institutional structure and culture. It is the "melting pot" solution.

Americanization schooling practices were adopted whenever the population of culturally and linguistically diverse students rose to significant numbers in a community. The government established special programs and applied them to both children and adults in urban and rural schools and communities. The desired effect of "Americanizing" students was to socialize and acculturate the diverse community. In essence, the reasoning went, if schools could teach these students to speak standard English and to accept "American" values, then educational failure could be averted. Ironically, social economists have argued, efforts to assimilate immigrant populations were coupled with systematic efforts to maintain disparate social and economic conditions between them and majority populations. Indeed, more than anything else, past attempts at addressing the educational problems of minority populations have actually preserved the political and economic subordination of these communities (Spencer, 1988).

Many immigrant populations have come to the United States in the last century. Thomas and Park (1921) argued that the "Old World" consciousness of immigrants would eventually be overcome by modern American values. Recent analysis by Gonzalez (1990) and Spencer (1988) shows, however, that Americanization did not evenly affect all immigrant groups. There are a number of reasons for this. According to Gonzalez (1990), there were important distinctions between the experience of European immigrants and that of other immigrant groups.

| **Different** |
| **Experiences** |
| **of Immigrant** |
| **Groups** |

1. The Americanization of the non-European community has been attempted in a social context that continues to be highly segregated. Black, Hispanic, and other nonwhite students are more segregated today than three decades ago.
2. Assimilation of these groups had both rural and urban aspects, whereas the European immigrant experience was overwhelmingly urban.
3. Assimilation was heavily influenced by the regional agricultural economy, which retarded a "natural" assimilation process.
4. Slaves and immigrants from Africa, Mexico, Puerto Rico, and other Latin and Asian countries could not escape the economic and political stigma assigned by the United States, an advanced industrialized nation, to their semi-industrialized, semifeudal nations and territories of origin. Many such immigrants came from countries under U.S. sway. This relationship led to a very constrained immigration pool, with only farm and low-skilled labor immigrating continuously to this country. None of the European nations had such a relationship with the United States, and thus their national cultures tended to be judged more on an equal footing. This factor alone would have significantly affected the manner in which Americanization was applied to immigrants of non-European background.

| **American** |
| **Indians:** |
| **An Example** |

Although many immigrant groups have been subjected to the Americanization phenomenon, the effects of this process can be seen most dramatically on the indigenous population of the United States during the late 1800s and early twentieth century. In the aftermath of segregating the American Indian population on a variety of federal reservations, boarding schools were established for American Indian children. At an early age, sometimes as young as 4 or 5 years old, children were required to be removed from their families and were placed in schools hundreds or thousands of miles away. The clear intent of such removal was to wash these children clean of native and tribal influences regarded as negative by the majority of U.S. society.

As they became students in hundreds of boarding schools, these children were forbidden to speak their native languages, to practice their native religions or traditions, or to wear their usual dress. They were often forbidden to return to the reservation for visits. At the same time, they were taught English, "standard" manners of behavior, other standard school content, and were subjected to Christian missionary efforts. In short, this major national effort at education, requiring significant economic and social resources, was built on a policy that accepted the need to rid these children of "negative" cultural attributes while instilling new "positive" cultural attributes—"American" attributes. The intended goal was rehabilitation of a problematic cultural group over time through the use of the U.S. schools. The focus was on the young. The actual result, many American Indians have argued, was the anguish of young children and their families at separation, the loss of tribal responsibility and authority over the young, and the accelerated loss of culture and language of indigenous peoples (Banks, 1986).

It can be argued that Americanization is still at the bottom of many programs aimed at culturally diverse students (Rodriguez, 1989; Weis, 1988). Americanization for these students unfortunately still means the elimination not only of linguistic and cultural differences but of an "undesirable" culture. Americanization programs seem to ride on the incorrect assumption that in the United States a single homogeneous ethnic culture is in contact with a single homogeneous nonethnic one, and the relationship between the two is not that of equals. The dominant community, enjoying greater wealth and privileges, claims its position by virtue of cultural superiority (Ogbu, 1987). In one way or another, nearly every culturally diverse child, whether born in the United States or elsewhere, is likely to be treated as a foreigner, an alien, or an intruder.

In 1923 the superintendent of the Los Angeles schools voiced an eerily familiar complaint in an address to district principals: "We have the [Mexican] immigrants to live with, and if we Americanize them, we can live with them." Unfortunately, even today the objective is to transform the diversity in our communities into a monolithic English-speaking and American-thinking-and-acting community. This attitude was recently articulated by Dr. Ken Hill, a superintendent in the California schools who has received national and state distinction for his efforts to serve a large number of African American, Mexican American, and Asian American students: "We've got to attend to the idea of assimilation and to make sure that we teach

Elimination

of

Differences

English and our values as quickly as we can so these kids can get in the mainstream of American life (Walsh, *San Francisco Examiner*, 1990, B14). Dr. Hill is echoing the Americanization solution articulated again and again over the last century. It is important to note that the dropout rate for nonwhite students in Dr. Hill's school district was recently reported as over 40 percent (Matute-Bianchi, 1990).

The Americanization solution has not worked. Moreover, it depends on the group-oriented concept of culture, which as we saw in the previous chapter leads to mistaken notions about cultural difference. The Americanization solution presumes that culturally different children are as a group culturally flawed. To "fix" them individually, we must act on the individual as a member of a cultural group. By changing the values and language of the group, we will have the solution to the educational underachievement of students who represent these groups. In essence, the groups should "melt" into one large and more beneficial so-called American culture. Research has shown that this "melting" does not in fact occur.

| Children as |
| Culturally |
| Flawed |

Our educational efforts have been responding quite ignorantly with regard to the processes in which individuals and groups actually come together to form culture. The challenge facing educators with regard to culturally diverse students is not to "Americanize" them. Instead, it is to understand them and to act responsively to their specific diversity, with the educational goal of academic success for all students. In recent decades, this realization has led directly to issues of educational equity.

Educational Equity

No one argues about the significance of education in this country. We are all quite convinced that an educated society is beneficial for enhancing individual well-being and our standard of living, and for maintaining a democratic society (Dewey, 1921). Moreover, education is perceived as a vehicle for achieving the "American Dream." It is not surprising that many organizations in the United States, from large businesses to small community groups, have attempted to initiate and maintain their educational endeavors in conjunction with efforts in the public schools. In fact, what with the many courses, workshops, seminars, conferences, and other structured learning opportunities available today, people are exposed to more formal educational experiences outside of the typical K–12 system than within it.

Education in this society, from cradle to grave, is important to our citizens.

If so, then equal access to educational opportunities must be a corollary to this basic value. This was clearly brought home by the U.S. Supreme Court decision of 1954 in *Brown v. Board of Education.* This landmark case concluded that separate, segregated education provided for black Americans was unequal to education provided for white Americans. In essence, the court argued that every effort must be made to address equal access to education regardless of race. The Court's decision was reinforced for Hispanic Americans, Asian Americans, and Native Americans, and for women, in significant U.S. congressional activity during the 1960s and 1970s. The major legislative piece was the 1964 Civil Rights Act. Title IV of that act banned discrimination on the grounds of race, color, or national origin in any program receiving federal financial assistance (Title VII of that act addressed educational equity across gender). Not coincidentally, the Elementary and Secondary Act of 1965 began to provide millions of federal dollars in assistance to state and local school systems. If these school systems were to make use of federal funds, they were to be held accountable to the standard of nondiscrimination.

Directly, this legislation banned recipients of federal resources from "restricting an individual in any way in the enjoyment of any advantage or privilege enjoyed by others receiving any service, financial aid or benefit under the [federally] funded program." Importantly, the recipient of federal funds was also prohibited from utilizing criteria or methods that would have the effect of undermining the objectives of the federally funded program for individuals of a particular race, color, or national origin. Other provisions of this legislation provided the possibility of a private cause of action (a lawsuit) against the federally funded institution to rectify issues of discrimination. This meant that students and their parents were not required to wait until the federal government noted that a funded program was out of compliance. They could independently move the courts to seek relief. And they did. A barrage of legal action aimed at addressing educational inequities soon followed.

| Legal Redress Allowed |

In addition to legal action, further administrative and legislative activity also flowed from attention to equal educational opportunity. In 1970 the U.S. Department of Health, Education and Welfare issued a memorandum, later referred to as the **May 25 Memorandum,** which clarified the mandate of the 1964 Civil Rights Act with respect to the non-English-speaking

| Language Barriers Must Be Overcome |

populations of students: "Where a liability to speak and understand the English language excludes national origin minority group children from effective participation in the educational program offered by a school district, the district must take affirmative steps to rectify the language deficiency in order to open instructional programs to these students." The 1974 Equal Educational Opportunities and Transportation Act placed this administrative protection for language minority students into formal law. The act makes "the failure by an educational agency to take appropriate action to overcome language barriers that impede equal participation by its students in its educational programs" an unlawful denial of equal educational opportunities.

Taken together, these legal and legislative initiatives directly related the value placed on education in U.S. society to the educational needs of culturally diverse populations. Every child, regardless of race, color, national origin, or language, is legally entitled to the benefits of equal educational opportunity. This movement toward equal educational opportunity pervaded our schools for over a decade and still drives many initiatives designed for culturally diverse students. In 1990 the *Phi Delta Kappan,* a respected publication for this country's community of professional educators, dedicated its entire September issue to concerns still being addressed by programs in school desegregation and equal educational opportunity. But equal access to education has not been the only stimulus behind our attention to culturally diverse students.

Multicultural Education

During the late 1970s and early 1980s, the educational establishment and representatives of minority groups themselves began to confront another important educational issue of particular consequence to culturally diverse students. Mostly aimed at curriculum reform, this debate suggested that the content of curriculum taught in U.S. classrooms should reflect the diverse character of the nation's population. A **multicultural education** was recommended for several reasons. First, advocates argued that the curriculum should better represent the actual contributions by various cultural groups to this country's society. They criticized prevailing curriculum for its unbalanced perspectives emphasizing only Western European values, history, literature, and general world-view (Banks, 1982). The United States was not one monolithic culture, these critics claimed, and the curriculum should reflect its true cultural diversity. Second, a multi-

Unbalanced
Curriculum

cultural curriculum would educate children of majority status as to the many accomplishments and contributions to U.S. society by individuals of minority status. This would at the same time reaffirm the significance of the minority group to the larger society and help develop positive self-esteem in children of minority status (Ethnic Cultural Education Program, 1977). Third, multicultural education was perceived as a school reform movement aimed at changing the content and process of education within schools. Its goal was not to stop at merely providing equal educational opportunity but to go further and enhance the schooling experience for all students (Grant and Sleeter, 1987).

Enhanced
Education
for All

The concept of multicultural education gave rise to several distinct approaches to the instruction of students in general and of culturally diverse students in particular. However, the major impact of this reform movement has been in the area of **curriculum**—that is, the area of schooling that addresses the content of instruction. In essence, this major reform attempted to address what students should be learning. This reform made it quite clear that we needed to know more about this country's diverse cultural groups and that after we had uncovered such knowledge we needed to dispense it in our everyday schooling endeavors.

Disparate Goals of Multicultural Education. The overall agreement about the importance of including curriculum that addressed diversity was quite significant, since there was some disagreement about the goals of curriculum reform. Sleeter and Grant (1987) have provided an excellent review of the varied goals and the overall limited consequences of the multicultural education reform movement on American education.

Within a model described as "Teaching the Multiculturally Different," one goal was to assist educators charged with helping culturally different students succeed in mainstream schooling. Although this model did not directly cite the need to assimilate children of different backgrounds into the mainstream, this seemed to serve as its main end. The prescription for success was usually subtractive in nature. That is, children with different cultures and languages were asked to leave behind these attributes through the assistance of bridgelike educational programs that promised access and success in academics and later in other societal domains. This type of multicultural education was regarded as a temporary, highly directed educational endeavor that would lead to a melting pot of a successful and more homogeneous student population.

A Bridge to
Success

Becoming a Responsive Teacher

3.1 Assimilation Doesn't Equal Success

How can schools cope with the diversity presented by their students? Should they harken back to the model of education developed in the early decades of this century to deal with the huge influx of immigrant youngsters? At that time, educators responded to increasing cultural and linguistic diversity among their students by attempting to accelerate their assimilation into the American mainstream. Their mission was to Americanize immigrants by replacing their native language and culture with those of the United States Educators confidently sought to fit newcomers into the American mold by teaching them the English language and literature, a sugar-coated version of American history, and a respect for the U.S.'s political system and civic life.

Although some recommend a similar approach today, it is no longer possible even to describe American culture with confidence; to what mold should educators seek to fit all children? There is no single definition of American culture; multiple definitions have been informed by ethnic minority voices.

We also have never counted the cost of Americanization philosophy. How many children were estranged from their family and culture; how many grandparents of today's teachers lost their native langugage; how many worked a lifetime on the assembly line when they should have gone to college; how many became ashamed of who they were?

When immigrant students become shining academic stars, their success is often attributed to the values and habits of their native culture rather than their Americanization. There is some evidence that assimilation may actually inhibit academic success. Studies of Mexican immigrants, Indian immigrants, and children who escaped from Vietnam by boat all suggest that those who maintain a strong identification with their native language and culture are more likely to succeed in school than those who readily adopt American ways.

Meeting the Challenge:

1. Research seems to indicate that assimilation does not serve culturally diverse students. Since it nevertheless persists as a response to cultural difference, who or what might it serve?

2. How would you define the culture in which you live? Develop a list of at least ten highlights of this culture that characterize it best, in your opinion. Your list items may include values, events, people, places, or things both past and present that you consider culturally significant. Compare your list with those of your classmates. Make a separate list of all the items others selected that are surprising or unknown to you. Why, do you think, were these items not on your list?

3. Consider these three Filipino children:
   (a) Renaldo has recently arrived in the United States from the Philippines with his parents and three brothers.
   (b) Carlo and his three brothers were born in the United States, as were both of their parents. Carlo's grandparents emigrated from the Philippines when they were in their twenties.
   (c) Joshua was born in the Philippines but was adopted at birth by Anglo-American parents. His three adoptive brothers are also Anglo-American.

   Explain the variety in acculturation these three children have experienced. Describe how an approach to education based on assimilation might affect each child. Alternatively, if you had all three of these children in class, how would you build on each one's specific relationship to language and culture?

Early vestiges of Head Start can be seen to reflect this multicultural approach. For preschool children aged 3 to 4, Head Start, and its extension for the early elementary student, Follow Through, were perceived as bridges to the mainstream academic environment. Other compensatory education programs, such as Title I and now Chapter I programs that address under-achievement directly, are in this same category of programs that are meant to provide underachieving students with bridges to achievement. They are temporary and their goal is to transition unsuccessful students to success through a process likened to natural cultural assimilation. In such assimilation, immigrants with very diverse cultures and languages come to embrace mainstream American values and to acquire English as their main mode of communication. Schools were asked to serve, positively, as an organized vehicle to hasten this natural process.

> **Schools to Serve in Assimilation**

It is important to note that this perspective on multicultural education did stress the importance of cultural diversity among the students, families, and communities served. In this way, it was definitely distinct from earlier educational strategies of Americanization. The practice of taking American Indian youngsters from their families and placing them in boarding schools far from their homes was not meant primarily to serve as a bridge to American society. It was devised to be a direct break with a child's original but negatively perceived language and culture (Philips, 1983).

The bridging goal of some multicultural education efforts was sometimes combined with the goal of enhancing human relations (Colangelo, Foxley, and Dustin, 1982; Perry, 1975). Such a goal was seen as best achieved by learning about and with each other. In so doing, the members of diverse populations would be able to understand one another, and the corollary of this better understanding would be enhanced communication and social relations. Distinct from programs of assimilation and bridging, educational programs reflecting this approach to multicultural education asked students to add knowledge about other groups not like their own and to utilize it in ways that would enhance social accommodation of diversity—"Let's learn to get along better."

The most dramatic example of a large scale program of this type comes from Canadian educational history. In the province of Quebec, French-speaking populations (Francofones) were in constant social and economic dispute with English-speaking populations (Anglofones). The solution to this problem in social relations was Bilingual-Bicultural Immersion Education (Lambert, 1962). Anglofone children were placed in French-only schooling programs for the first three years of their educational experience. The goal of the program was for children to acquire knowledge of both the language and the culture of Francofones, with the expected product of better human relations. Evaluation of these programs indicate that these expectations were achieved without any loss in academic achievement on the part of children learning in a language other than their own home language (Swain, 1987). Swain (1987) points out that in Canada, the status of French speakers and English speakers is socially equal. Such equal status is not shared by language-diverse groups in the United States.

Yet another approach to multicultural education has been much more activist in nature. Its goals serve to promote respect for diversity. In addition to acquiring and disseminating information about the cultural diversity of the U.S. population, this approach is aimed at developing intellectual and societal acceptance of cultural diversity as a goal in and of itself (Banks, 1981, 1984; Fishman, 1990; García, 1979; Gay, 1975; Golnick and Chinn, 1986; Grant, 1977).

| Respecting |
| Diversity |

Most popular and influential in the last decade, work in this area has attempted to bring together issues of race, ethnicity, gender, and social class. The thrust of such initiatives has been to permeate the curriculum with issues of diversity—in literature, social thought, scientific approaches, historical construction, and so on—while at the same time serving up criticism of "standardized" curriculums, particularly those which reflect Western European contributions as the standard. A corollary of this approach is the overall multicultural and social reconstructionist perspective that is also espoused (Appleton, 1983; Suzuki, 1984). In essence, students are asked to become social critics, particularly as it relates to issues of social injustice. Proponents argue that adoption of this multicultural educational approach would rid society of pervasive social injustices inflicted on the basis of race, ethnicity, and gender.

| A Focus |
| on Social |
| Injustice |

Such a proactive stance toward multicultural education is exemplified by programs in U.S. bilingual education. In the last five years, double immersion programs have begun to be introduced into large Latino school districts in California, New York, Texas, Illinois, and Florida. The goal of a **double immersion** program is to produce a student population that is bilingual and bicultural. For non-Latino, English-speaking students, the goal is English and Spanish language and literacy. Beginning in kindergarten, these students are exposed to Spanish language instruction in classrooms with Spanish-speaking students and to a curriculum that addresses bicultural concerns. For Latino students in the programs, the goals are the same. These goals are in concert with the notion of actively promoting cultural diversity, with a healthy academic respect for the linguistic and cultural attributes of the diverse students involved (Lindholm and Christiansen, 1990). Similar programs in the public schools of San Francisco, San Diego, Detroit, New York, and Chicago are housed in magnet schools. The purpose of a **magnet school** is to attract a highly diverse set of students around a thematically designated curriculum that is multilingual and multicultural. Such programs attempt to integrate African American, Latino, Asian, and other culturally diverse student populations by recognizing diversity as a positive ingredient in addressing the agendas of equal educational opportunity and multicultural education (Grant, 1991).

An Appraisal of Progress. Attention to multicultural education in this country over the last two decades has fired numerous debates and resulted in substantive accomplishments. New curriculum efforts by publishing companies have been launched to address claims by proponents of multicultural education of bias in publishing (Golnick and Chinn, 1986). Teacher-training programs have been required to provide specific training in student cultural diversity at the preservice level (California Commission on Teacher Credential, 1991). School-based programs such as the magnet and double immersion bilingual education programs described above find their roots, at least partially, in the values and goals of multicultural education.

The above discussion has attempted to locate multicultural education in three broad categories based on distinct but not necessarily exclusive goal agendas. We have seen that these goals range from bridging and assimilation for culturally diverse students, to enhancement of human relations, to active promotion of cultural diversity as a societywide goal. Keep in mind that all the goals of multicultural education build upon previous and ongoing initiatives that address equal educational opportunity: no child should be denied the benefits of education. These two educational approaches have provided an alternative to the traditional response of Americanization to the growing presence of cultural diversity in our schools.

Beyond Multicultural Education

As much as they have contributed to changing demands in U.S. schools, efforts at equal educational opportunity and multicultural education have failed to address a number of important educational concerns. For the most part they have lacked a strong theoretical foundation. They have addressed curriculum only—not instructional methods or pedagogy. They have produced many single case studies of ethnic groups but little empirical data to substantiate the positive effects of implementation.

As described in Chapter 1, academic achievement in many culturally diverse populations has not been enhanced significantly over the past decades. Action for equal educational opportunity has generated legislative and legal policy along with concomitant resources to address this core societal value. But such action has not addressed, in any comprehensive manner, how educational equity should be achieved. Educational attention in and around multicultural education has espoused important societal values and has led to advances in a number of educational fronts. But neither has it produced a set of comprehensive strategies that address the educational concerns it has raised (Sleeter and Grant, 1987). Essentially, the result of these initiatives in educational equity and multicultural reform has been to raise issues. This is no small feat, considering the many-headed character of the U.S. schools.

The era of equal educational opportunity and multicultural education has left us a legacy of clearly identifiable nature. Educational endeavors related to culturally diverse students have been pragmatically oriented. That is, they have focused on a set of problems—discrimination, segregation, underachievement, low self-esteem, non-English proficiency, to name a few—and have forwarded programs to address these problems. These pragmatic efforts tended to lack any substantive theoretical underpinnings. The proposed solutions were driven by somewhat ambiguous social values associated with educational equity and pluralism. Conversely, a more theoretical approach would still consider the problems of discrimination, underachievement, and segregation but would attempt to first understand why such problems exist. We could then develop solutions from a storehouse of understanding (García, 1991; Tharp, 1990).

Another legacy of the last three decades of educational activity, particularly in the area of multicultural education, is the extended case study approach to cultural diversity. The educational

Lack of
Theory

community has produced an extensive research literature of the characteristics of different racial, ethnic, and ethnolinguistic groups. The goal of this work was to document the cultural and linguistic attributes of different groups in the United States so that these attributes could be better understood and utilized to serve students. It was not uncommon to learn from these research studies that American Indian children were nonverbal (Appleton, 1983), that Asian American children were shy (Sue and Okazaki, 1990), that Mexican American children were cooperative (García, 1983), that African American children were aggressive (Boykin, 1983), and that Anglo children were competitive (Kagan, 1983).

> **Stereotypes Promoted**

Although this case study work was meant to further advance our understanding of culturally diverse students, it often had the effect of promoting stereotypes. Moreover, it did not recognize the axiom implicitly understood by social scientists who study culture: there is as much heterogeneity within any cultural group as there is between cultural groups. (See Chapter 2 for an extended discussion of this issue.) Unfortunately, descriptively useful indicators began to take on explanatory values: if that student is Mexican American, she must be cooperative, field sensitive, and speak Spanish. The problem came when educators tried to apply case study information in the classroom. They developed educational programs to address the cultural attributes identified only to discover, for example, that many Mexican American children were not cooperative, were field independent, and did not speak Spanish. If all Mexican Americans are not alike, if all African Americans are not alike, if all American Indians are not alike, then what set of knowledge about those groups is important educationally? What overarching conceptualization of culture is truly useful for understanding the educational framework of culturally diverse groups?

New Theoretical Perspectives

Before addressing the preceding questions directly, it seems appropriate to frame this discussion in terms of a continuum of educationally relevant theory. At one end of this continuum, theorists argue that addressing culturally diverse populations calls for a deeper understanding of the interaction of a student's culture and the prevailing school culture (Tharp, 1989). At the other end, theorists claim that any population of students, no matter what their cultural background, will achieve academically if the appropriate teaching methods are implemented. Next we examine these two perspectives and other ideas that fall in between them.

A Continuum of Theories

The claim that culture plays a role in educational underachievement is supported by a wealth of research suggesting that the educational failure of diverse student populations is related to a "culture clash" between home and school. Evidence for this claim comes from Boykin (1986) for African American students; from Heath (1983) for poor white students; from Wiesner, Gallimore, and Jordan (1988) for Hawaiian students; from Vogt, Jordan, and Tharp (1987) for Navaho students; from García (1988) for Mexican American students; and from Rodriguez (1989) for Puerto Rican students. In essence, these researchers have suggested that educational endeavors that do not attend to the distinctiveness of culture are likely to result in failure for certain students. Theoretically, these students do not succeed because the difference between school culture and home culture creates an educationally harmful dissonance—*there exists a home-to-school "mismatch."* Sue and Padilla (1986) directly enunciate this position by asserting, "The challenge for educators is to identify critical differences between and within ethnic minority groups and to incorporate this information into classroom practice" (p. 62).

At the same time, however, other research supports the theoretical position that the academic failure of any student rests on the failure of instructional personnel to implement what we know "works." In other words, it is not a mismatch of culture that is to blame so much as instructional programs that do not utilize appropriate *general principles of teaching and learning.* Using the now-common research tool of **meta analysis,** which is a method of analyzing and summarizing large numbers of research studies, Walberg (1986) suggests that a synthesis of educational research identifies robust indicators of instructional conditions with academically significant effects across various conditions and for various student groups. Other meta analytic reviews (Baden and Maehr, 1986; Bloom, 1984; Slavin, 1989) agree. Among the specific instructional strategies proposed as candidates for "what works with everyone" are direct instruction (Rosenshine, 1986), tutoring (Bloom, 1984), frequent evaluation of academic progress (Slavin and Madden, 1989), and cooperative learning (Slavin, 1989).

Cultural Dissonance

What "Works" with Students

This research also identifies expectations as significant factors in underachievement. Levin (1989) and Snow (1990) have suggested that students, teachers, and school professionals in general have low academic expectations for culturally and linguistically diverse students. Again, as popularized in the film *Stand and Deliver,* raising student motivation in conjunction with enhanced academic expectations and challenging curriculum is a prescribed solution. The assumption of theorists at this end of the continuum is that the educational failure of culturally diverse populations can be reversed by the systemic and effective implementation of general principles of instruction understood to work with "all" students.

Interspersed within this continuum are other theoretical approaches that attempt to explain the academic underachievement of culturally and linguistically diverse students. Paulo Fiere (1970) has argued that educational initiatives cannot expect academic or intellectual success under social circumstances that are oppressive. He and others (Cummins, 1986; Pearl, 1991) suggest that social oppression experienced by students taints any curriculum or pedagogy, however "successful" it is in general, and that only a pedagogy of empowerment can fulfill the lofty goals of educational equity and achievement. Similarly, Bernstein (1971), Laosa (1982), and Wilson (1987) address underachievement by pointing to socioeconomic factors that influence the way schools and instruction are organized. When a group of people is exposed, over generations, to poverty and debilitating socioeconomic conditions, the teaching and learning process for children at home, in the community, and in the schools will suffer. The result is disastrous, long-term educational failure and social disruption of family and community. Ogbu and Matute-Bianchi (1986) offer a broader sociological perspective. They describe this country's present social approach to several immigrant and minority populations as "caste-like." In this attempt to explain underachievement, these theorists claim that certain populations are perceived as forming a layer of U.S. society that is not expected to excel academically or economically. These social expectations are reinforced until they become self-perceptions adopted by the members of "caste-like" populations, with academic underachievement and social withdrawal as the inevitable result.

So far, we have discussed some of these new theoretical perspectives in only a general way. Throughout the rest of this book we will examine them more comprehensively. Realize that the continuum of theories I have represented as "cultural

| Motivations |
| and |
| Expectations |

| Explanations |
| for |
| Lower |
| Achievement |

mismatch" to "general principles" is not a set of incompatible approaches. This brief introduction should make evident that a wide variety of scholars have seriously attempted to understand why so many culturally and linguistically diverse students are not well served by educational institutions in the United States today. These conceptual contributions are not limited to espousing the principles of multicultural education or recommending policies of educational equity. They go farther, and they dig deeper. The theoretical approaches useful to us address the issues of educating a culturally diverse population by searching out explanations for the present unsatisfactory situation.

These contributions take into consideration the work of Fiere (1970), Bernstein (1971), Cummins (1979, 1986), Brice-Heath (1986), Ogbu (1986), Trueba (1987), Levin (1988), and Tharp and Gallimore (1989). This research suggests that the educational vulnerability of culturally diverse students must be understood within the broader context of the circumstances for children in U.S. society. No quick fix is likely under social and schooling conditions that mark students for special treatment according to a category of cultural difference without consideration for the psychological and social circumstances in which each student—as an individual—resides. These theorists warn us against isolating any single attribute (poverty, language difference, learning potential, etc.) as the only variable of importance. More comprehensive views of the schooling process urge an understanding not only of the relationship between home and school but of the psychological, sociological, and cultural incongruities between the two, and the resulting effects on learning and achievement (Tharp and Gallimore, 1989).

Broader

Approaches

How do we as educators begin to understand such a complex set of interactions? One framework for understanding is founded on the concept of "act psychology." First formulated at the end of the nineteenth century, the notion of **act psychology** proposes a model for human cognitive processes, or how we come to know. It focuses on the assertion that the mental functions of perceiving, remembering, and organizing—ultimately, knowing—are all acts of construction (Barlett, 1932). It also asserts that what we know is closely related to the circumstances in which we come to know it.

The term *construction* really is an apt one. Have you ever watched a large building evolve under construction? Scores of people and tons of material are marshalled and organized, and a structure rises seemingly out of chaos. Remember, though, that the process is not without its glitches. Days of rain may halt or

alter construction, and the entire project is subject to the avail-
ability of supplies, not to mention the willingness of people to
work together. The architects must consider features of the surrounding terrain and adjust their designs accordingly. In short,
construction has a context, a set of local circumstances in which
it happens. These circumstances greatly affect the final form of
what gets built.

The **constructionist perspective** is rooted in the notion
that for humans knowing is a result of continual building and
rebuilding. Our "construction materials" consist of give and take
between the organization and content of old information and
new information, processes of organizing that information, and
the specific physical and social circumstances in which this all
occurs. We come to understand a new concept by applying
knowledge of previous concepts to the new information we are
given. For example, in order to teach negative numbers, a math
teacher can use the analogy of digging a hole—the more dirt

| Construction |
| of |
| Knowledge |

you take out of the hole, the greater the hole becomes; the more
one subtracts from a negative number, the greater the negative
number becomes. But a math teacher cannot use this example
with children who have no experience digging holes. It won't
work. As you can see, this theory of how the mind works
implies that continual revisions (or "renovations," as an archi-
tect might say) are to be expected. Therefore, when we organize
teaching and learning environments, we must recognize the
constructionist nature of those environments. As educators, we
"build" teaching and learning environments out of what we
know and how we come to know it. And we must continue to
build. To ignore that is to discount the relevance of previous
educational environments to the ones we are considering now.
They got us to here, but that does not mean they will get us to
tomorrow.

A New Pedagogy

Embedded in the constructionist approach to education is the
understanding that language and culture, and the values that

| Children's |
| Constructed |
| Knowledge |

accompany them, are constructed in both home and community
environments (Cummins, 1986; Goldman and Trueba, 1987;
Heath, 1981). This approach acknowledges that children come
to school with some constructed knowledge about many things
(Goodman, 1980; Hall, 1987; Smith, 1971) and points out that
children's development and learning is best understood as the
interaction of past and present linguistic, sociocultural, and

cognitive constructions (Trueba, 1988). A more appropriate perspective on learning, then, is one that recognizes that learning is enhanced when it occurs in contexts that are socioculturally, linguistically, and cognitively meaningful for the learner. These meaningful contexts bridge previous "constructions" to present "constructions" (Diaz, Moll, and Mehan, 1986; Heath, 1986; Scribner and Coole, 1981; Wertsch, 1985, 1991).

Such meaningful contexts have been notoriously inaccessible to culturally diverse children. On the contrary, schooling practices often contribute to their educational vulnerability. The monolithic culture transmitted by the U.S. schools in the form of pedagogy, curricula, instruction, classroom configuration, and language (Walker, 1987) dramatizes the lack of fit between the culturally diverse student and the school experience. The culture of the U.S. schools is reflected in such practices as:

1. The systematic exclusion of the histories, languages, experiences, and values of these students from classroom curricula and activities (Giroux and McLaren, 1986; Ogbu, 1982).
2. "Tracking," which limits access to academic courses and which justifies learning environments that do not foster academic development and socialization (Duran, 1986; Eder, 1982; Oakes, 1990) or perception of self as a competent learner and language user.
3. A lack of opportunities to engage in developmentally and culturally appropriate learning in ways other than by teacher-led instruction (García, 1988).

This rethinking of the pedagogy of the U.S. schools has profound implications for the teaching and learning enterprise, especially as it relates to culturally diverse students (García, 1991). The new pedagogy is one that envisions the classroom as a community of learners in which speakers, readers, and writers come together to define and redefine the meaning of the academic experience. Researchers variously describe it as a pedagogy of empowerment (Cummins, 1986), as cultural learning (Heath, 1986; Trueba, 1987), or as a cultural view of providing instructional assistance and guidance (Tharp and Gallimore, 1989). Whatever its designation, it allows for respect and integration of the students' values, beliefs, histories, and experiences and recognizes the active role that students must play in their own learning. This responsive pedagogy utilizes students' present knowledge and experiences as a foundation for appropriating new knowledge. For language minority students, this means

Community

of Learners

using instructional strategies that incorporate the student's native language or bilingual abilities. Language is a substantial part of the social network within which children construct knowledge.

A responsive pedagogy for academic learning also requires a redefinition of the instructor's role. Instructors must become familiar with the cognitive, social, and cultural dimensions of learning. We need to recognize the ways in which instructional, assessment, and evaluation practices affect learning. We should

| Redefining the Teacher's Role |

become more aware of the purpose and degree of implementation of the classroom curriculum and understand its full impact on students. Specifically, we need to be alert to the configuration of the classroom environment and the ways students interact with one another and with teachers. Instructors must also recognize that helping students learn often requires us to allow students to display their knowledge in ways that suggest their competence as learners and language users. Once we begin to rethink all these dimensions of our role as educators, classrooms in U.S. schools will be equipped for the task of ensuring academic success for culturally diverse students.

Finally, teachers must question myths about learning processes and myths about the potentially underprepared student. In particular, we must debunk myths about students who come from households with lower socioeconomic status or who grow up in homes in which English is not the primary language. For educators who embrace the concept of a responsive pedagogy, new educational horizons for themselves and their students are not only possible but inevitable.

Conclusion

A focus on the content of specific cultures, such as that advocated in the multicultural education reform movement, is useful but will not be enough to attain educational equity for culturally diverse students.

Similarly, the search currently under way for general principles of learning that work for all students must be redirected. Educational researchers and teachers themselves need a broader view that provides some explanation for pervasive underachievement among culturally diverse student populations. How do individuals with diverse social, cultural, and linguistic experiences construct knowledge—or "make meaning"? How do they communicate and extend that meaning, particularly in the social contexts we call schools? These are the vital questions for today's and tomorrow's educators, and finding answers will require a solid theoretical framework.

We must develop an in-depth understanding of the "meaning-making" process. We need to couple a grasp of socialization processes in and out of schools with a clear-eyed examination of our present pedagogy. Our mission is first to understand the relationships among language, culture, and the learning process. Only then will we be ready to transform our understanding into recommendations for a responsive pedagogy and curriculum. The rest of this book pursues these two goals.

SUMMARY OF MAJOR IDEAS

1. Approaches to the education of diverse student groups in the United States have shifted from Americanization to a focus on educational equity and multicultural education. More recent approaches are based on broader theoretical frameworks that consider the role of language and culture in education.

2. Americanization, or the "melting pot" solution to cultural diversity, seeks to assimilate, or merge, small ethnic and linguistically diverse communities into a single dominant national culture. It is an approach to acculturation that is based on a group-oriented concept of culture and the notion of cultural homogeneity as a desirable goal.

3. Members of non-European immigrant groups experience the process of Americanization differently than do members of European immigrant groups. This is because, comparatively, non-European immigrant groups (1) are subject to more ongoing segregation in the United States, (2) are concentrated in both urban and rural areas, (3) are more dependent on the U.S. regional agricultural economy, and (4) are stigmatized by the low economic and political status of their countries of origin.

4. Native American children were subjected to Americanization on a large scale early in this century. Americanization remains at the bottom of any educational approach that assumes that some children are culturally flawed and have undesirable cultural attributes that should be eliminated or "fixed."

5. The U.S. Supreme Court decided in 1954 in *Brown* v. *Board of Education* that separate educational facilities for black students were not equal to educational facilities for white students and that U.S. schools must provide equal access to education regardless of race. The 1964 Civil Rights Act, the Elementary and Secondary Act of 1965, the May 25 Memorandum of 1970, and the 1974 Equal Educational Opportunities and Transportation Act together legally require equal educational opportunity for every child in the United States regardless of race, color, national origin, or language.

6. The concept of multicultural education began as a criticism of school curriculum that focused only on Western European values, history, literature, and general world-view. The movement toward multicultural education advocated reform of curriculum so that the content taught in U.S. schools would more accurately reflect the truly diverse nature of the nation's population. Multicultural education was expected to highlight contributions to U.S. culture by individuals of minority status in order to provide alternative perspectives to children of majority status and to improve the self-esteem of children of minority status.

7. As a reform movement, multicultural education had three main emphases, which sometimes were contradictory: (1) It would provide a bridge to success for culturally diverse children. Through programs such as Head Start, children would be assimilated into the U.S. mainstream academic environment. (2) It would enhance human relationships by teaching students from different cultures how to understand one another. (3) It would promote respect for diversity by portraying cultural diversity as a desirable social goal.

8. Two multicultural educational approaches that promote diversity and oppose the notion of assimilation are double immersion programs in bilingual education and magnet schools. Double immersion programs produce students who are bilingual and bicultural. Magnet schools offer a thematically designated curriculum that is multilingual and multicultural.

9. Because they lack a strong theoretical foundation, initiatives in educational equity and multicultural education have only partially addressed educational issues of concern to culturally diverse students. They have focused on developing programs to address educational problems at the expense of

fully understanding why the problems exist. The extended case study approach, favored by researchers who sought to document the attributes of different cultural groups, often had the unintended effect of promoting stereotypes.

10. New theoretical perspectives on the educational needs of culturally diverse populations span a broad continuum. Some researchers claim that educational failure is related to a mismatch between home and school cultures. Other researchers claim that students fail academically because schools do not utilize principles of effective teaching and learning. Other theorists point to social oppression, socioeconomic status, and the expectations U.S. society has for certain groups as keys to understanding educational underachievement.

11. More comprehensive perspectives on education focus on both the psychology of the individual student and the sociocultural context in which the student lives. These theories attempt not only to explain the relationship between home and school but also to reveal how learning and achievement are influenced by psychological, sociological, and cultural variables.

12. The constructionist approach to education is based on a specific model of how humans come to know and to understand. It proposes that humans gain knowledge by constructing it—by comparing and organizing old and new information within a surrounding local context or environment that greatly affects the final form the knowledge will take. This approach acknowledges that children come to school with constructed knowledge about many things.

13. In U.S. schools, culturally diverse children often are confronted with contexts for education that do not allow them to apply and extend their constructed knowledge. Such students are vulnerable to failure when faced with schooling practices that exclude their histories, languages, experiences, and values; that feature tracking; and that limit opportunity to learn in ways other than by teacher-led instruction.

14. A pedagogy that is responsive to culturally diverse students utilizes their constructed knowledge as a foundation for appropriating new knowledge. It also incorporates the students' native languages or bilingual abilities. In order to respond effectively to these students, teachers must become more familiar with the cognitive, social, and cultural dimensions of learning.

EXTENDING YOUR EXPERIENCE

1. Research the history of school desegregation efforts in your state during the 1960s and 1970s. Outline the results of any major state court cases you uncover. Look back through the magazine and newspaper coverage of the time and characterize the nature of the national public debate over educational equity. Prepare a list of three comments to report to the class about your findings.

2. Interview an older friend or relative who immigrated to the United States as a young person. Keeping in mind what you learned in this chapter about Americanization and assimilation, create a list of questions to ask this person about his or her experience in a new culture. What aspects of the original culture did he or she have to give up or change?

3. What role do you think teacher expectations play in students' accomplishments? How have high or low expectations from teachers influenced you? Create a written portrait of a particularly inspiring teacher you have had, exploring the possible sources for the inspiration you felt. Share your portrait with your classmates.

4. Reflect on a time in your own past experience—whether in school or in a particular social situation—when you felt most like a foreigner or an outsider. Describe your feelings. What about the situation, do you think, made you feel this way? Was it the way other people treated you? Was it something you were expected to do that you did not know how to do? What might have made you feel less excluded? As a teacher in a classroom of culturally diverse students, how can you be sensitive to a child's experience of outsiderness?

5. Is school the proper forum in which to discuss social issues centered on race, ethnicity, gender, and social class? Should students be encouraged to develop a critical, analytical perspective on social injustice? What types of questions do you yourself have about the unfairness and inequities you perceive in our society? List as many of your questions as you can, and then be prepared to share them in class.

6. Imagine that you are suddenly immersed in a culture completely different from the one in which you grew up. What aspects of your constructed knowledge about your own culture will be helpful to you as you join this new culture?

RESOURCES FOR FURTHER STUDY

Appleton, C. (1983). *Cultural pluralism in education: Theoretical foundations.* New York: Longmans.

The author argues that the central task is to find an equilibrium between the differences and commonalities of individuals. The author discusses the historical, theoretical, ideological, and legal aspects of pluralism and provides assessments and suggestions to ease the conflict pluralism presents, particularly for the educational system.

Cummins, J. (1986). Empowering minority students: A framework for intervention. *Harvard Educational Review, 56(1),* 18–35.

The author offers a theoretical framework for analyzing the school failure of minority students and the relative lack of success of compensatory education, bilingual education, and LEP programs— arguing that these attempts were unsuccessful because of the inflexibility of teachers, students, schools, and minority communities.

Oakes, J. (1990). *Multiplying inequalities: The effects of race, social class, and tracking on opportunities to learn mathematics and science.* Santa Monica, Calif.: Rand Corp.

This publication assesses the opportunities given to underrepresented and low-achieving groups of students to succeed in scientific and technological domains. Statistical reports and economic trends paint a dismal picture for the future. This deficiency can affect the economic well-being of the nation, since our educational system loses important human capital.

Sleeter, C. E., and Grant, C. A. (1987). An analysis of multicultural education in the U.S. *Harvard Educational Review, 57(4).*

The authors provide a framework to educators who are interested in dealing with misunderstandings about multicultural education. The term *multiculturalism* is examined and described, and various other definitions for it are criticized.

Weis, L., Ed. (1988). *Class, race and gender in American education.* Albany, N.Y.: State University of New York Press.

The volume is a compilation of various authors whose main goal is to bring to the forefront a more concise and interrelated discussion of how race, class, and gender harbor inequality. Some writers document the ways in which schools promote inequality, and others describe how cultures or groups outside the school stay out of school.

PART TWO

How much do we really know about the communication process, specifically in relation to the culturally diverse student? Part Two addresses teaching and learning as they

THE ROOTS

relate to research into children's linguistic, cognitive, and social development.

What do current research findings indicate about the relationship between linguistic and cognitive development? How does the develop-

OF DIVERSITY

ment of a child learning one language differ from that of a child learning two languages simultaneously? Chapter 4 traces the steps in language development and discusses research into multilingualism and use of dialect.

Finally, what role does culture play? Chapter 5 examines the social context of learning and the role of the family, the peer group, and the community in the school achievement and psychology of individual learners. It also describes instructional strategies that can help all students become more effective communicators.

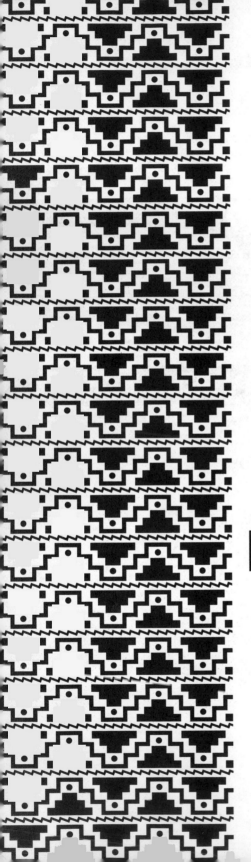

LANGUAGE

AND

COMMUNICATION

CHAPTER 4

Focus Questions

○ What are some of the variables that must interact for communication to occur?

○ What is metalinguistic awareness?

○ How do children develop skills in phonology, vocabulary, grammar, and language pragmatics?

○ What are bilingualism and second-language acquisition? What is code switching?

○ How is language used as a social instrument, and what are two important sociocultural variables that may affect a child's motivation to learn a second language?

○ What is a dialect, and how is classroom use of dialect problematical for students in U.S. schools?

> **"As the test of what the potter molds is in the furnace; so in his conversation is the test of a man. The fruit of a tree shows the care it has had; so too does a man's speech disclose the bent of his mind."**
>
> —THE WISDOM OF BEN SIRA 27:4–7

Place yourself again in Mrs. Tanner's fifth-grade classroom. As we learned in Chapter 1, in the last few years she has begun to teach students who speak a variety of languages in their homes and communities: Spanish, Vietnamese, Russian, Hmong, Chinese, and Farsi. The challenge of effectively communicating—of making meaning—is quite robust in this classroom. Mrs. Tanner has realized that she must understand the cultural context of these students if she is to provide an effective environment for communication. In essence, she must determine the way to communicate that will most serve her in reaching the teaching and learning goals so integral to her classroom.

Teaching and learning do not begin when students walk into her classroom. On the contrary, these processes are omnipresent in children's worlds. This point is so important it cannot be overemphasized. If Mrs. Tanner and other teachers in the U.S. schools do not build on a child's foundation of previous and nonschool learning, then the role of the teacher and the school is merely corrective. At worst the schools would be engaged in trying to subtract the learning experiences a child gains outside of school. As the previous chapters have established, adding to a child's learning experiences is an objective that is much more conducive to the educational success of culturally diverse students. This chapter will establish a firm basis for the worthiness of this objective by focusing on the communicative aspects of human development as they relate to teaching and learning.

The Nature of Communication

Throughout the ages, politicians, theologians, philosophers, poets, playwrights, comedians, teachers, and a variety of social scientists have all relied in their own distinctive ways on the power of the spoken word to convey meaning. Recent interest in **communication** has broadened to a consideration of both verbal and nonverbal systems that enable humans to encode meaning and transmit it to others with some assurance of accurate reception. Scholars who study **language** characterize it as a complex interaction of many variables. These include the verbal signal itself but also include as equally important the signal sender, how and in what environment the signal is sent, signal receiver, and previous experiences the sender and receiver may have with similar signals.

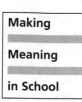

Interaction of Variables

Let's look at an example of communication in progress. To a naive observer, the interaction between a parent and a young child may seem simple and relatively devoid of meaning. Lots of silly sounds, exaggerated facial expression—what kind of "meaning" could this possibly convey? Upon closer examination, however, this scenario of communication proves to be quite rich and meaningful. An infant's cooing, crying, giggling, and other sounds prepare the parent to receive a signal and interpret a meaning. Anyone who has been around babies understands the difference between "a mad cry" and "a pain cry." Parents learn to decipher what an infant is feeling by paying attention to subtle changes in the sound of an infant's cry. This is communication. The infant can be said to influence the reaction of the parent by sending these signals.

Later, as the growing child learns specifically articulated sounds and combinations of sounds, it seems as if a systematic, rule-governed set of communicative symbols is emerging almost magically. What was once for the infant a simple and idiosyncratic vocabulary, with limited grammatical arrangement, becomes for the child in a matter of a few years an unbelievably large vocabulary with varied syntactical arrangements. This is even the case for children who were born with speech or hearing impairments. These children develop alternative, but just as systematic, forms of nonverbal communication.

Making Meaning in School

A naive observer in Mrs. Tanner's classroom may likely note a series of seemingly disconnected communicative acts. In reality, these chunks of communication are so central that they may almost be overlooked. In the course of a day, Mrs. Tanner asks many questions, reads stories, explains science experiments, gives assignments, provides oral and written feedback, and engages in dozens of one-on-one interactions with students. Each time, a complex set of verbal, written, and/or nonverbal transactions is called upon to enhance meaning making—or, in other words, to institute teaching and learning. It is the role of teachers to communicate with students and the role of students to communicate with teachers. Most classroom activity in the U.S. schools is founded on this one principle. At the very root of our teaching and learning activity is the understanding that communication must be a prerequisite.

The Development of Language

Learning to communicate may be a child's most impressive accomplishment. Language is a complex set of systems—phonology, vocabulary, grammar, and pragmatics and discourse rules—and each of these systems has its own rules. We examine these domains of communication more closely below. Each one is acquired relatively unconsciously by children in the course of use. Each also at some point emerges into consciousness and becomes a topic of conversation for children or a focus for play and problem solving. Bringing the various domains of communication into conscious awareness is one of the important achievements of schooling. Becoming aware of distinct communicative systems is a necessary development if people are to understand important aspects of their own culture and the culture of others. Being consciously aware of how we use communication, called **metalinguistic awareness,** is the foundation of distinguishing diversity in the communicative activities going on around us all the time.

| Becoming |
| Aware of |
| Language |

Phonology

Knowing a formal communicative system, a language, involves speaking and understanding words. Those words are made up of specific sounds, called syllables, which are the basic units for language production.

Phonology is the study of speech sounds. Much research has been devoted to the development of speech in humans.

When infants exposed to English language environments are 5 to 8 months old, they start producing spoken syllables (*ba, ma, ga*) in the course of their babbling. Open syllables such as *ba* and *ma* are relatively easy to pronounce and thus form the basis for many "baby talk" words (e.g.,*mama, booboo, peepee*). Words that contain closed syllables (those with a consonant at the end) are harder to pronounce, especially if quite different consonants need to be articulated within one syllable. Thus, young English-speaking children often say "goggie" for "doggie" or "guck" for "truck," because they are not yet able to put such different sounds as /g/ and /d/ or /t/ into one syllable.

Earlier we saw that the United States is home to over one hundred distinct language groups besides English, as well as a variety of dialects. Children exposed to these various languages proceed through similar stages of complex phonological development. Their learning process differs from that of English learners only in the phonological distinctiveness of the language they are learning. For example, Spanish-language learners progress through a distinct process of developmental acquisition marked by early acquisition of vowel sounds (Gonzalez, 1991). In contrast, English learners focus early on consonant sounds.

Stages of Development

Children's pronunciation of words comes increasingly to resemble adult pronunciation around the ages of 3 to 5 years old. However, very young children still do not think of the sounds they are producing in the same ways that adults do. Young children find it difficult to produce rhymes or to segment particular sounds—for example, to say "meat" without the /m/ sound or without the /t/ sound. The reason for this is that when we speak, the articulation of each sound overlaps the articulation of those before and after it. Recognizing an abstract segment of sound such as the letter *m* or *t* requires considerable sophistication in language ability and knowledge about how the phonological system of a language works. Such metalinguistic awareness develops as children grow older.

Rhyming Activities

Three-year-olds can be taught to identify the initial syllables in words fairly consistently. The ability to segment final syllables or to understand the internal structure of words with consonant clusters comes much later. Four-year-olds can judge with very high accuracy whether words rhyme, and many can produce rhymes as well. Many educational activities for young children depend extensively on this rhyming ability. Both children and adults enjoy this metalinguistic activity of rhyming. Preschool children can also distinguish accents and may even incorporate the mimicking of dialect into their play.

Vocabulary

After a rather slow start, a child's knowledge of vocabulary grows very rapidly during the preschool period. **Vocabulary** is the sum of words understood and used by an individual in any language group. Children typically acquire their first word at about 1 year of age. Acquisition of the first fifty words may take several months. Thereafter the process of word acquisition proceeds so blindingly fast that it is impossible to keep accurate records. It has been estimated that children acquire six to ten new words a day between the ages of 2 and 6. Such rapid vocabulary acquisition relies on the child's use of very powerful strategies for guessing what words mean, on his or her considerable willingness to take chances in using new words, and on lots of help from adults and other children in providing information about words and their meanings.

It is important to recognize that the words a child acquires fall into various categories. Words learned early tend to be names for important people (*mama, papa, nana*) or concrete objects (*socks, spoon, bed, teddy, cookie, bottle*) and words used to express important social functions (greetings such as *hi,* or *bye-bye);* forms of requests (such as *wanna, mommy,* or *mine);* and ways of directing attention (such as *there, that,* or *what that?).* Starting a bit later, children begin to acquire verbs that refer to concrete actions: *eat, sleep, read, sing.* As they progress through the preschool period, though, children increasingly come to use verbs that refer to complex and private cognitive or communicative activities (*think, wonder, dream, tell, disagree with, deny*), nouns that refer to abstract, superordinate, or affective entities (*thought, argument, animal, furniture, sadness, glee*), and other words that have roles in structuring discourse (*because, but, however*) or representing one's perspective on matters (*hopefully, doubtfully, despairingly*). For avid readers in languages with a written tradition (English, Chinese, Japanese, and Spanish language cultures, for example), the process of word acquisition continues well into adulthood. In highly oral cultures (Navaho, Zuñi, Hmong, for example), this same process of vocabulary acquisition continues as adolescents and adults encounter complex historical, religious, and personal accounts.

It is crucial in talking about vocabulary to acknowledge that children not only acquire new words as they get older, but also expand their understanding of words they know. Thus, a Spanish-speaking child might first learn and understand a word like *padrinos* (godparents in Spanish) in a relatively restricted context, such as the reliable giver of gifts at each birthday. It could take a child several years to learn exactly how *niño* relates to *padrino* (godfather) and to *madrina* (godmother), and precisely what sorts of characteristics can be attributed to each term outside of gift giving. These individuals, in many cultures, play critical roles for children over a lifetime. This is one reason why

Speed of Word Acquisition

Categories of Words

standard multiple-choice assessments of vocabulary knowledge cannot assess very accurately the full depth of children's vocabulary knowledge.

At some point during the school years, words themselves and their meanings come to be a topic children think, wonder, and talk about. As development of metalinguistic awareness continues to expand, children become able to distinguish between a big word (*building*) and a word referring to a big thing (*building*). They come to understand that words are arbitrary symbols whose forms have no intrinsic connection to their meanings. Regardless of the language or languages to which they are exposed, all children achieve this truly significant understanding of the symbolic nature of language.

Words as

Symbols

Grammar

Grammar is the system of rules implicit in a language that allows words to be arranged with some regularity of structure. Grammar does not necessarily refer to prescriptive grammar (don't say "he don't" or "I ain't"). More broadly, it refers to the system of rules by virtue of which we know whether words are nouns or verbs ("the hit" versus "he hit"). Grammar allows English speakers to interpret which word specifies the subject, object, and indirect object of a sentence ("John gave Mary an apple"), or in such languages as French and Spanish to distinguish the gender of a noun.

Rules for

Interpreting

As soon as children put two words together, they begin to demonstrate what they are learning about the rules of grammar in their native language. Children learning English, for instance, show awareness of word order, or **syntax**, as an important feature of the grammatical system. In English, the sentence pattern subject-verb-object is so common that developing the ability to comprehend and use constructions that deviate from this pattern (passives, such as "The lion was bitten by the flea"; coordinations, such as "I want this and you want that"; and use of relative clauses, such as "The dog bit the cat that chased the rat") is a lengthy process for children that lasts well into the preschool years. In Spanish, gender and number (e.g., *la muchacha*, the girl; and *los muchachos*, the boys) are distinct grammatical features. In Chinese, phonological emphasis—the spoken stress on words—marks the grammar in the language.

From normal communicative interactions with adults, children typically acquire the rules of grammar in their native language with little difficulty. Children also normally develop a metalinguistic capacity, displayed when they comment spontaneously on grammatical correctness or easily respond to questions about sentences being "right" or "wrong." Nonetheless, it is hard even for school-aged children to attend more seriously to grammatical correctness than to meaning. They are likely to accept as "okay" a sentence such as "The boys is jumping in the lake" and to reject a perfectly grammatical but anomalous sentence such as "Ice cream tastes yucky."

Pragmatics and Discourse Rules

Knowing words, how to pronounce them, what they mean, and how to put them into sentences is only a small part of learning to communicate. Each of these skills depends greatly on the language or languages that are available in the child's environment. Children must also learn how to use language appropriately—how to communicate effectively and to be responsive to the needs of listeners. These skills are closely tied to the child's culture. The term **language pragmatics** refers not only to the rules of the language itself but also to generally accepted notions about appropriateness and effectiveness in the use of language. This latter category contains an enormous array of phenomena that are largely cultural in nature. Thus, rules such as "Don't talk with your mouth full" fall under pragmatics, as do rules for politeness that range from saying "please" to avoiding discussion of delicate topics.

> Appropriate
>
> Use of
>
> Language

Metalinguistic awareness in the domain of pragmatics tends to emerge first in rules for politeness, perhaps because parents initiate many transactions with children that are explicitly pragmatic: "What's the magic word?" or "Don't interrupt, I'm talking on the phone." Young children often violate pragmatic rules that have to do with giving their listeners enough information, but by the age of 4 or so they do understand clearly that some adults are likely to need more explanation if names of friends or toys are introduced. Unlike grammar, which is mostly acquired by the time children enter school, pragmatic skills, particularly those associated with understanding how to adjust one's language for different audiences, continue to develop throughout the school years.

Pragmatics for Conversation. Most of the oral communication young children experience involves face-to-face conversation with familiar people. Children of preschool age talk with their parents about events in their own and in others' daily lives, such as doing chores, eating, getting dressed, going for walks, and so on. They talk about experiences they have shared with others. As they get older, they increasingly come to talk about unshared events (what happened yesterday or what will happen tomorrow).

Teachers should realize that children do not often realize when they need to supply more information in conversation. Teachers who are fortunate enough to be informed about the general topic are usually more likely to be able to ask questions that fill in missing information. Those who are not must be willing to work by drawing the child out and interpreting and co-constructing missing information. It is easy to see how, if teacher and student do not share similar experiences or similar cultures, face-to-face communication can be diminished. The concept of conversation, and the pragmatics for how it should "go," are very much culturally determined. In large and authoritarian families (e.g., Mexican American families, Appalachian families, and American Indian families), conversations with adults are usually brief and abrupt. Children learn to listen and to speak very judiciously. A teacher who does not understand this context may mistakenly suspect that such a student is shy or is language delayed.

| Cultural |
| Differences |

Pragmatics for Literacy. As children move through school, they become more familiar with written communication. Written language can differ from oral language not only in purpose, but also in terms of the intended audience and the relationship between the speaker or writer to the audience. Written and oral communication also tend to assign responsibility for effective communication differently. For instance, writers must anticipate the needs of their readers and supply or clarify information up front to avoid confusing the audience. A speaker, on the other hand, may be directly questioned by the audience if something is not clear. The basic pragmatics for literacy are classically demonstrated in the typical newspaper editorial. The task of the essayist is to make a point clearly and completely and in the process to provide the audience with any background information necessary to understand the point on first reading.

| Responsibility |
| for Clarity |

Many instances of oral language use pragmatics similar to that of essayist literacy—public lectures, for example, or telephone conversations with strangers. And some written forms of expression approximate oral communication in their private, personal, or ambiguous nature—diaries or journals, for example, or poetry.

The pragmatic rules governing effective conversational exchange of the type the typical preschooler has mastered are only a first step toward the pragmatics of literacy and must be acquired through much oral classroom discourse.

Pragmatics for Different Discourse Situations. As hinted at earlier, one important dimension distinguishing the pragmatics of different types of communication is the extent of audience collaboration. Can one expect one's listeners to participate actively (asking questions, chiming in with agreements or supportive statements, proposing interpretations and conclusions)? If so, one need not plan ahead so carefully to ensure that the message is completely comprehensible and to make all the implications plain.

Expected audience participation is an element of discourse pragmatics that varies across cultures both for oral and written communication. For example, Hawaiian and Athabaskan children have been described as active audience participants, often interrupting enthusiastically when listening to stories (Boggs and Watson-Gegeo, 1991; Scollon and Scollon, 1981). In contrast, in mainstream U.S. culture the storyteller has full responsibility for plot development and performance, and the audience is supposed to be silent until the end. Japanese novelists tend to demand a considerable amount of work from their readers, rarely providing the tidy, wrapped-up conclusion to the plot often expected by Western readers. In the United States, teenage girls from working-class backgrounds discuss serious topics by sharing comments with other audience members, who audibly echo or even anticipate the speaker's points. Girls from middle-class backgrounds, on the other hand, tend to take long and uninterrupted turns producing—in effect—brief oral editorials on the subject under discussion. Discourse in which responsibility is shared with the audience and discourse in which responsibility rests with the speaker are equally challenging communication skills for children to learn. Practice in the latter skills, in U.S. schools, usually focuses on the types of writing that children are expected to do.

> **Audience**
>
> **Expectation**

The pragmatics of different discourse forms also differ concerning the degree to which background knowledge can be assumed to be shared with the audience. Consider the difference between recounting a harrowing experience to a friend, and remembering the experience with someone who went through it with you. The first account requires considerably more attention to detail and clarity about the participants, the order of events, and the description of the events. These demands are played out linguistically by reduced use of pronouns (saying a name instead of her or them), more elaborated use of grammar ("We lost the paddles, and because of that we went over the falls"), and more explicit background and foreground detail.

An additional dimension of pragmatic complexity is added when the discourse form requires the speaker or writer to presume that background knowledge is not shared when in fact it is. This situation emerges in classroom discourse when teachers ask "known-answer" test questions (questions teachers already know the answer to). Keep in mind that teachers are among the few individuals who ask questions to which they know the answers! It is also at work when at sharing time children are expected to describe objects they are holding and that the whole class can obviously see.

Classroom

Discourse

Giving definitions for common words is a task that taps children's ability to understand that shared knowledge and context must be ignored. When asked, "What is a clock?" children who assume shared knowledge might point at a clock or say something like "They are like watches, but bigger." Children who are sophisticated in the pragmatics of school discourse, however, tend to avoid responses like these that presume shared knowledge and to respond instead with an answer such as "A clock is a machine that tells time" (Snow et al., 1991).

For children to master pragmatics, they must be able to understand the listener's perspective and know the range of expectations the listener might hold. As members of a culture, we all acquire culture-specific expectations as to how interpersonal relationships should be marked linguistically and how information should be packaged for easy communication. Children in the United States have to grasp these culture-specific expectations and move beyond them as they learn to interact in new settings and with different people.

Understand

the Listener

Child or adult, a fundamental challenge for everyone is to understand other people's perspectives and expectations. Part of addressing this challenge is acknowledging that individuals whose cultures are different often have different rules for language use. The specific challenge for any educator is to adapt to diverse communicative needs and expectations in the classroom. This is no easy task. But it is a task that recognizes the crucial importance of effective communication. If it is left undone, the role of the teacher in enhancing the teaching and learning enterprise is substantially compromised.

Bilingualism and Second-Language Acquisition

Let us now contrast what we've learned about the typical pattern of language development among children who speak one language with that of children who speak more than one language. In this section we will examine how bilingualism and second-language acquisition relate to schooling contexts. The next section will focus on the use of dialect in a schooling context. The rest of this chapter will address issues of teaching and learning as they relate to research and theory developed over the last two decades. We will see that studies of children's linguistic, cognitive, and social development have reshaped in a dramatic way our view of language variation, multilingualism, and cultural "difference."

As the revealing demographic information cited in Chapter 1 indicates, bilingualism and second-language learning are fast becoming common attributes of classrooms in U.S. schools. How are these two attributes of language development defined? **Bilingualism,** which is the ability to speak two languages with equal fluency, occurs in settings in which children are exposed to two languages during the early years of their lives, usually before they are 5. (By contrast, monolingual children are exposed to only one language during these years.) **Second-language acquisition** is a process of language development whereby a child acquires first one language and then is exposed to and required to learn a second language.

Compared to the amount of research focusing on monolingual development, little systematic investigation has been available regarding children who are simultaneously acquiring more than one language during the early part of their lives. Recent work in this area, particularly in terms of schooling contexts, has centered separately on the linguistic (García and Gonzalez, 1983), cognitive (Cummins, 1979), and social and communicative aspects (Hakuta, 1986) of language acquisition. In other words, research into the language acquisition of young multilingual populations has concentrated independently in three areas:

| Research |
| Focus |

1. The developmental nature of phonology, (word sounds), morphology, (word formation), and syntax (word order)
2. Related cognitive aspects of language acquisition
3. The social context of language development and its effect on language pragmatics.

The next two sections review research in these areas and high-light similarities and differences in underlying theoretical con-cepts. We also relate these research findings to important school-ing issues.

Patterns of Language Development and Cognitive Aspects

It does seem clear, from evidence in many societies throughout the world, that a child can learn more than one linguistic form. For example, Sorenson (1967) describes the acquisition of three to four languages by young children who live in the northwest region of the Amazon River. The Tukano tribal language serves as the lingua franca (common language of the region), but some twenty-five clearly distinguishable linguistic groups also continue to exist in the region. **Multilingualism** has also been reported within the European community (Baetens and Beardsmore, 1982; Skutnabb-Kangas, 1979) and among school-aged children in the United States (Skrabanek, 1970; Veltran, 1988; Waggoner, 1984).

Spanish-English Bilingualism

Research into bilingual development in U.S. children, and into Spanish-English language acquisition in particular, yields some common findings. Young children 2 to 4 years old do acquire complex morphological, phonological, and syntactic skills for both Spanish and English without any evidence of neg-ative linguistic effects (García, 1983; Padilla and Liebman, 1975). Children also exhibit a significant ability to produce well-formed and communicative mixed-language utterances referred to in bilinguals as **code switching** (García, 1983; Huerta, 1977; Padilla and Liebman, 1975). On the topic of code switching, Padilla and Liebman report:

> The appropriate use of both languages in mixed utterances was evi-dent; that is, correct word order was preserved. For example, there were no occurrences of "raining esta" or "a es baby," [these are inap-propriate grammatical combinations of the two languages] but there was evidence for such utterances as "esta raining" and "es a baby" [these are appropriate grammatical combinations of the two lan-guages]. There was also an absence of the redundancy of unnecessary words which might tend to confuse meaning. (Padilla and Liebman, 1975, p. 51)

These researchers found that learning two languages simultaneously did not prevent children from understanding more abstract language rules such as those for correct word order, or syntax. García, Maez, and Gonzalez (1983), in a study of Spanish-English bilingual children between 4 and 6 years old throughout the United States, found regional differences in the relative occurrence of code switching. Spanish-English bilingual children from Texas, Arizona, Colorado, and New Mexico showed higher incidence of switched language utterances than did children from California or Illinois, especially at prekindergarten levels. These findings suggest that some children may very well pass through an intermediate developmental stage in which the two languages can merge, before they then move to the development of two independent language systems. Research into code switching indicates that it is a highly expected and normal developmental phenomenon in children exposed to multiple languages. It is not to be taken as evidence of a language disability or "confusion."

> **Code Switching in Development**

The mistakes learners make when they are acquiring language have provided researchers with guideposts in understanding the strategies and processes employed during second-language acquisition (Corder, 1967). Dulay and Burt (1974) studied the errors in the natural speech of 179 children 5 to 8 years old (including a sample of Chicano children in California) who were learning English as a second language. They classified errors as either related to first language (interference errors) or related to normal language development (developmental errors). Their analysis indicated that first-language interference accounted for only 4.7 percent of the errors the children made, whereas 87.1 percent of the errors were similar to those made by children learning English as a first language.

Dulay and Burt postulated that a universal "creative construction process" accounts for second-language acquisition. They proposed that the process was creative because no one had modeled the hundreds of types of sentences that children produce when acquiring a second language. The authors suggested that innate mechanisms caused children to use certain strategies to organize linguistic input. Dulay and Burt did not claim that they could define the specific nature of the innate mechanisms. They did claim, however, that these mechanisms have certain definable characteristics that cause children to use a limited set of hypotheses to deal with the knowledge they are acquiring. The strategies parallel those identified for first-language acquisition.

> **Innate Mechanisms**

Krashen (1981; 1985) has developed a concept of second-language acquisition that considers as fundamental this innate process of creative construction. His thinking is based on two hypotheses about how bilingual children learn language. His "natural order" hypothesis indicates that the acquisition of grammatical structures by the second-language learner proceeds in a predictable "natural" order independent of first-language experiences and/or proficiency. Such acquisition occurs unconsciously, without the learner's concern for recognizing or using structural rules. Krashen's "monitor" hypothesis suggests that learning of a second language can occur consciously, however, when the learner has achieved a significant knowledge of structural rules and has the time to apply those rules in a second-language learning situation. The "monitor" hypothesis extends Dulay and Burt's concept of creative construction. Krashen concludes, however, that conscious learning of a second language is not as efficient or functional as the natural acquisition of a second language.

Other research has documented a distinct relationship between first-language and second-language acquisition. Ervin-Tripp (1974) conducted a study of 31 English-speaking children between the ages of 4 and 9 who were living in Geneva, Switzerland, and were attending French schools. She found that the errors these children made in French, their second language, were a result of their application of the same strategies that they had used in acquiring a first language. Erin-Tripp described the application of three strategies: overgeneralization, production simplification, and loss of sentence medial items. In overgeneralization, the American children acquiring French applied the subject-verb-object strategy of English to all sentences in French, and thus systematically misunderstood French passives. In production simplification, the children resisted using two forms if they felt that two forms had the same meaning. Finally, medial pronouns were less often imitated than initial or final pronouns. Ervin-Tripp believed that interference errors occurred only when the second-language learner was forced to generate sentences about semantically difficult material or concepts unfamiliar in the culture of the new language. The strategies children use in acquiring a second language may change as they become more proficient in that language. At the beginning of second-language acquisition, imitation plays an important role in language learning. As children acquire more of the target language, they begin to use first-language acquisition strategies to analyze this input.

Application
of Rules

Hakuta (1974) demonstrated that children, through rote memorization, acquire segments of speech called prefabricated patterns. Examples of these prefabricated patterns are various renditions of the English verb "to be" (such as "I am," "you are," "he is"), the segment "do you" as used in questions, and the segment "how to" as embedded in how questions. These patterns are very useful in communication. Children use them readily without understanding their structure but knowing which particular situations call for which patterns in order to communicate in the target language.

Wong-Fillmore (1976) spent a year observing five Spanish-speaking Chicano children acquiring English naturally, and she noticed the same phenomenon of acquiring segments of speech. The first thing the children did in order to figure out what was being said was to observe the relationship between certain expressions and the situational context. They inferred the meaning of certain words, which they began to use as "formulaic expressions." (They acquired these expressions and used them as analyzed wholes.) The formulaic expressions became the children's raw material used to figure out the structure of the language. Wong-Fillmore provided two examples of how children use first-language acquisition strategies to begin to analyze these expressions: (a) Children notice how parts of expressions used by others vary in accordance with changes in the speech situation in which they occur, and (b) children notice which parts of the formulaic expressions are like other utterances in the speech of others. As the children figured out which formulas in their speech could be varied, they were able to "free" the constituents they contained and use them in productive speech.

Children acquiring a second language may depend initially on transfer from the first language and on imitation and rote memorization of the second language. In more practical terms, the less interaction a second-language learner has with native speakers, the more likely it is that transfer from the first language to the second language will occur. As the second language is acquired, many of the strategies that children use to acquire this language seem to be the same as those used in first-language acquisition. Current research suggests that natural communication situations must be provided for second-language acquisition to occur. Regardless of the different emphases of the theories discussed above, recent theoretical propositions regarding second-language acquisition suggest that through natural conversations the learner receives the necessary input and structures that promote second-language acquisition.

Segments of Speech

Similar Strategies of Acquisition

To summarize, the research findings with regard to patterns in language acquisition suggest three things:

1. The acquisition of one or two languages seems to follow similar developmental processes. Language learners utilize a consistent set of cognitive hypothesis along with previous experiences with language.
2. The acquisition of more than one language may result in an intermediate phase of language convergence, called code switching, that incorporates the attributes of several languages.
3. The acquisition of two languages does not hamper the acquisition of either language (García, 1983; Hakuta, 1986).

Effects on Language Pragmatics

Language
as a Social
Instrument

As previously noted, language is a critical social repertoire, a set of skills that enables children to function in a world of social interactions. The discourse component of any social interaction most often determines the general quality of that interaction. In this, it carries special significance for the culturally and linguistically diverse student. Social tasks that include a language choice are loaded for children who are learning the language as they use it. Most children acquire the ability to use linguistic codes differentially, as determined by the social attributes of the specific speaking context. Children who are culturally and linguistically diverse face the added task of multiple code differentiation. Implicit in this discussion is the general notion that languages must not only be mastered in terms of phonology, vocabulary, and grammar, but also must be used as social instruments.

There are important sociocultural variables that contribute to a child's motivation to communicate in the target language. One of these is the attitude that the learner has toward members of the cultural group whose language he or she is learning. Gardner and Lambert (1972) found that the positive attitude of English-speaking Canadians toward French-speaking Canadians led to high integrative motivation to learn French. A. Ramirez (1985) reported a series of studies that investigated the relationship between Chinese, Japanese, and Chicano students' achievement in English and their attitude toward English speakers as a group. Positive attitudes toward the culture of the target language corresponded to higher language proficiency.

The individual language learner's attitude toward the target culture is not the only important variable. Second-language acquisition is also influenced by the relationship between the two cultures. Schumann (1976) hypothesized that the greater the social distance between the two cultures, the greater the difficulty the second-language learner will have in learning the target language. Conversely, the smaller the social distance, the less difficulty the language learner has. **Social distance** is determined in part by the relative status of cultures. For example, two cultures that are politically, culturally, and technically equal in status have less social distance than two cultures whose relationship is characterized by the dominance of one and the subordination of the other. In addition, there is less social distance if the cultures have attributes that mesh well together.

| Relationship |
| between |
| Cultures |

Once a child is motivated to learn a second language, he or she needs certain social skills in order to establish and maintain contact with speakers of the target language. Wong-Fillmore (1976) and Wong-Fillmore and Valadez (1985) suggest that individual differences in social skills among children influence the rate of second-language acquisition. Second-language learners who seem most successful use three specific social strategies:

| Necessary |
| Social Skills |

1. *Join a group and act as if you understand what is going on even if you do not.* The learner must initiate interactions and pretend to know what is going on. As a result, he or she will be included in the conversations and activities.
2. *Give the impression with a few well-chosen words that you can speak the language.* The child must be willing to use whatever facility with the target language he or she has. As a result, other children will keep trying to communicate.
3. *Count on your friends for help.* The acquisition of language depends on the participation of both the learner and someone who already speaks the language—the friend. The child's friends can help in several ways, for example, by showing faith in the learner's ability to master the language and by including the learner in their activities. They also can provide the learner with natural linguistic input that he or she can understand.

Seliger (1977) has also demonstrated that high-input generators (children who solicit help with the language) are the most successful second language learners. High-input generators place themselves in situations that expose them to the target language and are willing to use it for communication. They therefore receive the necessary input, as well as the opportunity for practice. Following this general rule, most teachers of foreign languages recommend extended visits to a country in which a language learner will be maximally exposed to and required to participate in normal social interactions with native speakers of the language.

Another focus of research into pragmatics has been to investigate ways in which language is used and the rules that govern discourse. Philips's (1972) research at Warm Springs Indian Reservation, now a classic study of discourse rule differentiation between school and nonschool settings, compared the conditions for speech use in the American Indian community and in the government school. She identified basic distinctions in **participant structures,** which are rules that govern who speaks when. American Indian students were reluctant to speak up when called on in class. Philips attributed this reluctance to differences in the ways in which authority is exercised in the Indian community and the minimal role of verbalization in the teaching styles practiced within Indian families. She compared the students' lack of verbal responsiveness in teacher-directed situations with their different participation in peer-learning situations, which are more culturally congruent. Boggs (1972) addressed a similar reluctance among native Hawaiian children to respond to direct questioning by teachers. He documented the low frequency of adult questioning directed at a specific child in native Hawaiian homes. Boggs found that when students were invited to participate in the classroom in ways that were culturally congruent, they did, in fact, produce long narratives.

Heath's (1983) study of ways of talking in middle-class white and working-class African American families in a southern community extended this line of research. Heath suggests that children of working-class African American families were reluctant to answer teachers' questions because of differences in communicative patterns. Working-class African American parents rarely used the "known-answer" question. Heath (1986) later explored "ways with words" within Asian and Latino communities, searching for similar clues to the discontinuities between language use at home and at school. She introduced the concept of the oral genre as a type of organizing unit into which smaller segments of language fit.

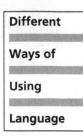

Different

Ways of

Using

Language

Oral genres, such as stories, accounts, and recounts, exist among all linguistic communities. However, their frequency varies among groups, as does the kind of language associated with each. In her research analysis, Heath posited that discrepancies between sociolinguistic conventions are the primary source of misunderstanding between children from language minority families and their mainstream teachers. She argued

Becoming a Responsive Teacher

4.1   Real-Life Practices That Enhance Literacy Development

In October of his first year of school a third-grade Hmong child, Se, carefully copies into his journal a few lines of "The Good Morning Song" from the sentence strips his teacher keeps in a pocket chart. The room is filled with other print sources that he could have chosen to copy. The teacher has allowed the children to draw or write on whatever topic they wish. When Se's teacher asks him to tell her about what he's written, he only smiles, not ready to speak in English except for occasional one-word answers, most often in chorus with other students.

This teacher knows she's doing the right thing by immersing her children in print. She's familiar with the work of researchers, such as Brian Campbourne, who have pointed out that children learning English as second language (ESL) may rely on environmental print as a source of writing for their stories or journal entries for a longer period of time than do native-English speaking children. Sometimes ESL children, like young native-speakers of English, copy print but don't refer to it when they talk to their teachers about their stories; later they may use their copied words to generate a meaningful message or story. But all children, both ESL and native speakers of English, need a print-enriched classroom.

This teacher has also just begun to allow her students to exercise choice about the topics in their journals and stories. Like many other teachers, she thought that her ESL students, with their very limited knowledge of English, needed topics, frames, or sentences to copy. Other teachers did not think that their students could go through all the stages of the writing process. But as teachers at Newcomers School raise their expectations about the language and literacy development their students are capable of, they are finding that their students not only meet those standards but push them upwards.

In a primary grade classroom, the student teacher asks the ESL children about the kinds of birds that they know. She makes a list of their answers and asks them to listen and look for more kinds of birds to add to the list as she reads them the book

Where's the Green Parrot? The book's repetitive structure allows children to predict what will happen next and to "read" the book aloud with their teacher.

This student teacher knows the crucial role of linking ESL children's background knowledge and personal experience to the beginning of any literacy event. She also knows through her reading of ESL research that when she does this, she makes it possible for even those children with little English proficiency to construct meaning with her and with their peers as if they were more proficient in English. Lessons centered on the students' experiences become even more critical when the children are asked to construct meaning in their second language.

This reminds us of how much ESL lessons have changed in terms of materials. We used to think that we needed special vocabulary- and grammar-controlled boxes of materials, with the accompanying dittos. Those are nowhere to be found at this school. Instead, books—whole books, not excerpts—flood the rooms. Rather than buying basal readers and workbooks, the principal allots each teacher money to purchase trade books, the same children's books that are sold in bookstores. The students have access to attractive, whole books and whole poems. These books and poems help ESL students construct meaning by giving them the multiple cues that only authentic children's texts can, such as pictures, complete story grammars, and natural language patterns.

A fourth-grade Russian child's single journal entry at the end of October shows at least four spelling strategies: (1) She has memorized a stock of English words and spells them correctly; (2) She spells an English word using her knowledge of the Russian sound system; (3) She produces a few invented spellings using her fledgling knowledge of the English sound-symbol system; and (4) She writes the last word of her entry in Russian.

Instead of correcting this child's "errors" in the entry, the teacher marvels at the obvious growth in Yelena's writing fluency during the past two months—strategies for communicating her message. The teacher realizes that Yelena is showing successive approximations in her journal entries, approximations that indicate Yelena's use of more and more conventional writing forms.

This attitude toward "errors" represents another recent shift in the ESL field. As ESL teachers, we were first taught to immediately correct children's mistakes, lest they develop bad language habits. Through the work of Stephen Krashen and many other researchers in the field, we came to know, as Yelena's teacher knows, that "errors" are wonderful examples of development—they are the successive approximations our students use as they become English proficient.

Most afternoons children in a combined second- and third-grade classroom choose from an array of centers: dramatic play, art, writing, and math. The talk one hears at these centers—sometimes in Hmong, Vietnamese, Spanish, and Chinese, sometimes in English, as children from different language groups interact—is rich, rapid, and incessant.

The teacher has purposely organized her classroom so that the students are actively engaged in talking and learning. She knows what the recent research trend shows: that limited English proficient children show greater growth in English when they are not in a traditional teacher-directed lesson. This is also a time when the teacher circulates, talking with children and noting their language use in anecdotal records that she will add to their portfolios. She knows that these longitudinal records of observations and interactions give her much more information about her students' language development than can any formal language proficiency test.

The teacher comments: "It is true that setting up these conditions for students calls for a dramatic shift away from the curriculum offered them in the past. It essentially calls for a new view of students, of their learning, and of teachers' roles in facilitating that learning. But it also seems to me that teachers and students at this school start with the understanding that there are no barriers to optimizing instruction for students, except perhaps the ones we construct."

Meeting the Challenge

1. Visit a bookstore that has a large collection of children's literature. Spend some time browsing the shelves. Do these books take into account the diverse backgrounds of children in the United States? Note down the author, title, and publisher of the five most interesting books you discover. Bring your notes to class and compile a master list.

2. Experiment with "story time" with your classmates. Select a children's book written at any grade level that you will bring to class and read aloud. As a reader, remember to speak clearly and distinctly and to consider your audience. As an audience member while others read aloud, remain attentive to your responses to the story and the reader. During class discussion after all the stories, comment on your experience as a reader and as a listener.

3. What do you think of the concept of error as described above—that errors are to be considered as examples of development rather than as mistakes to be corrected? What is your attitude toward your own errors? Toward errors made by others? Using one particular example from a past schooling experience, describe the role error played in your learning process, either positive or negative. Did other people respond to this error in any particular way? If so, explain how.

4. Visit two elementary school classrooms, one which is all English-speaking and one which has a significant number of non-English-speaking students (e.g., an ESL classroom). In these two classrooms, observe the frequency and quality of social communication, both teacher-student and student-student. Note the structure of each classroom and the opportunities for language acquisition, such as environmental print, reading aloud, and writing. Record some interactions that you find significant and explain why they are or are not supportive of literacy development.

that the *discontinuity between home and school languages* (such as Spanish versus English, or Black English versus standard English) is not as disconcerting and detrimental as is the *discontinuity between ways of using language* in the community and at school. This finding addresses Dolson's (1984) report that children from homes in which the first language is used achieve better in school than those whose parents and older siblings try to use English. When limited-English-proficient (LEP) parents and siblings insist on using their weaker language for communication at home, children may be exposed to a far more restricted array of genres.

In a similar mode, Nine Curt (1984) identified areas of pragmatics that can cause particular confusion for Puerto Rican students: personal space, eye contact, touching, and body movements. Nine Curt reported on a study that found a high rate of retention of Puerto Rican gestures among students born and raised on the mainland. This work indicated that students may be retaining more of the nonverbal than the verbal patterns of their parents' native Spanish. Nine Curt's observations about Puerto Rican culture have been further summarized by Iruju (1988). That work details research documenting the cultural variation in eye contact and gaze behavior among African Americans and white North Americans, Arabs, Latin Americans, southern Europeans, East Asians, Greeks, and northern Europeans.

| Nonverbal |
| Contact |

García (1983) reports on an investigation of mother-child interaction. Spanish and English were used by children and adults (the children's mothers) in three different contexts: (a) preschool instruction periods, (b) preschool free-play periods, and (c) the home. Descriptions of these interactions pointed out very consistently that children, in particular, were "choosing" to initiate an interaction in either Spanish or English as a function of the language the mother was using to initiate the interaction. A closer qualitative examination suggested that almost 90 percent of mother-child interactions were initiated by the mother, most often in Spanish (i.e., mothers most often did not allow children to initiate). For those small number of instances in which children did initiate discourse, the topic determined language choice. That is, what the child spoke about was highly correlated with the language he or she chose to use.

| Language |
| Choice |

The richest data on how bilingual children initiate interactions comes from child-child interactions. Genishi (1981), while investigating the use of Spanish and English among first-graders, concluded that the general language initiation rule for these students was "Speak to the listener in his or her best language." Her analysis suggests that when speaking with others, these children first made a language choice based on the history of their previous language use with their fellow students. Zentella (1981) agrees that bilingual students make these decisions. However, she found another discourse rule operating: "You can speak to me in either English or Spanish." Although Genishi's (1981) and Zentella's (1981) discourse rules differ, each observation suggests that bilingual students employ their social and language use history to construct guidelines for discourse initiation. These studies suggest that particular sociolinguistic environments lead bilingual students to be aware of language choice when initiating discourse.

While there is much encouraging research that addresses the awareness of classroom discourse, it is not appropriate to conclude that all is well in those classrooms that serve culturally and linguistically diverse students. The one feature of the learning environments studied in detail by Ramirez and Merino (1990) and J. Ramirez, Yuen, Ramey, and Pasta (1991) was the quality of teacher and student language, whether in English or Spanish, in several language minority education programs. From analyses of tape recordings of classroom interaction, they concluded that teachers in all programs offer a passive language environment, which limits student opportunities to produce language and develop more complex language and thinking skills. This finding parallels similar results for "regular" classrooms in the United States (Cazden, 1988), but it is likely that language use should be a higher priority in classrooms that have many language minority students. Ramirez et al. (1991) concluded:

Passive

Language

Environment

> Direct observations reveal that teachers do most of the talking in classrooms, making about twice as many utterances as do students.
>
> Students produce language only when they are working directly with a teacher, and then only in response to teacher initiations. Of major concern is that in over half of the interactions that teachers have with students, students do not produce any language, as they are only listening or responding with non-verbal gestures or actions. Of equal concern is that when students do respond, typically they provide only simple information recall statements. Rather than being provided with the opportunity to generate original statements, students are asked to provide

simple discrete close-ended or patterned (i.e., expected) responses. This pattern of teacher-student interaction not only limits a student's opportunity to create and manipulate language freely, but also limits the student's ability to engage in more complex learning (i.e., higher order thinking skills). (p. 8)

In order to develop a comprehensive understanding of culturally and linguistically diverse students, we must therefore take into consideration more than the students' linguistic attributes. We must also consider their complex and active communicative environment. Recent data tentatively suggest that social context in and outside of classrooms will determine the specific social language rules for each language and the roles assigned to each language. In turn, these specific rules for social language use can inhibit or enhance communicative development in classrooms. It is the responsibility of any educator to understand these phenomena and organize classroom activities that enhance functional and effective communication both among students and between themselves and their students.

| Social |
| Context for |
| Language |

Use of Dialects

Along with the existence of multiple languages in use in our society, a great many dialects also exist. A **dialect** is a regional variation of language characterized by distinct grammar, vocabulary, and pronunciation. Between speakers of the same language, different dialects are usually mutually intelligible, whereas different languages are mutually unintelligible. However, some languages have dialects so different that speakers of them cannot understand each other. The Chinese language, for example, has two major dialects, Mandarin and Cantonese, which are mutually unintelligible. In contrast, Norwegian and Swedish, which are considered different languages, are mutually intelligible to speakers of each language.

The English language consists of American, British, Australian, and Canadian dialects. Canadian English is more similar to American English than to British English. Each of these dialects has its own further variations. For instance, in American English there are Southern, Midland, Northern, Boston, Appalachian, Cajun, Black, and Hawaiian dialects (Gleason, 1988). Dialects share most linguistic features with the language they are based on, but they differ from each other primarily according to the frequency of certain usages. For example, speakers with a Boston dialect understand and occasionally pronounce the terminal *r* of words but less frequently than do speakers of other American English dialects.

While language is associated with a specific national origin or geographic location, dialects tend to be associated with specific characteristics of the speaker such as race, gender, age, social class, and geographic region of origin. Only when people change their status or role with respect to these important characteristics do they find it necessary to acquire a new dialect (e.g., in the United States, people who move to the South may acquire a southern dialect.) As Harrison (1985) points out, languages are not fixed and isolated entities but are collections of repertoires that have appropriate occasions depending on the setting, topic, and social status of the respective speakers and listeners. In most cultures, not all dialects are considered appropriate for all occasions. Because of this, some speakers never have any need to learn more than one dialect in a single language while others will need to learn many dialects or languages.

U.S. schooling practices presuppose that standard English is a vital tool for success in the United States and recognizes its increasing prominence as an international language. **Standard English** is the version of English that has the grammar, vocabulary, and pronunciation considered appropriate for most occasions of public discourse and for written communication. It is the "standard" in that its rules for grammar, vocabulary, and pronunciation are taken to be authoritative. Most dialects are "nonstandard," meaning that their rules for sentence structure, word usage, and phonology vary from those of standard English. Negative attitudes about speech start with the belief that some dialects are linguistically inferior to the standard version of the language. Until quite recently in the United States, any variation from standard English spoken by children was viewed as limited and debilitating, an educational drawback. However, linguistic research (Labov, 1972) indicates that language variation is a natural reflection of cultural and community differences. People's attitudes toward languages, and particularly dialects, stem from the social class structure. If some dialects of English are more highly regarded than others, this reflects a socially constructed hierarchy that makes deviations from these dialects seem "unnatural, incorrect and inferior" (Thornton, 1981).

| **Standard and** |
| **Nonstandard** |

Becoming a Responsive Teacher

4.2 Learning by Talking

A crucial aspect of nurturing culturally diverse students is to provide an environment in which students feel safe and comfortable speaking aloud, and differences of outlook and opinion can be aired and appreciated. One way to achieve this end is to reconfigure class discussion time so that most discussion takes place among the students. This is in contrast to the traditional classroom, where discussion is typically in the form of a teacher-child interaction. In this alternative model, the adult intervenes only as necesssary to guide, stimulate, and facilitate student discussions, and to support the development of correct concepts. Students no longer direct most of their comments to the teacher, and the teacher steps in only selectively.

Let's look at how this process can work. The first step in developing discussion that teaches effectively is to get all of the students talking about the topic of, for example, a science lesson in pairs or small groups—expressing opinions or beliefs in an unstructured manner, or simply raising questions. Next, the teacher should help the students to listen to others, using the three r's: *recognize* someone else's desire to speak, *respect* that person's thought or opinion, and *restate* what has been said, to show that you understand. Children should learn that skilled communicators are able to anticipate and address other points of view. Good communicators are also aware that paying careful attention to someone else's view is an important prerequisite to developing a counterargument.

While engaging in speaking and listening, students will also develop thinking skills. They will enhance their ability to:

- evaluate and substantiate opinions by giving reliable sources and using logical arguments and evidence.
- become critical consumers of information, developing the view that not everything that is published or is stated by an "expert" is necessarily the ultimate truth.
- think analytically, finding ways to elaborate their own ideas and explanations and be attuned to the complex considerations and tradeoffs between different points of view.
- recognize that there is no right or wrong side in many debates.

Working in this model, the teacher brings the whole class together from time to time, to introduce and clarify important science concepts and to foster development of the thinking skills listed above. In addition, she has the class participate in monthly or bimonthly "dilemma discussions" on complex scientific and environmental issues, such as whether oil spills should be cleaned up or allowed to disperse naturally. Also, there can be personally relevant discussions, in which students make predictions for their own lives based on what they are learning about the topic.

Meeting the Challenge

1. Select an elementary or high school grade level and develop a series of possible topics on which to base a "learning by talking" curriculum. Keep in mind the diversity of backgrounds that will be represented in your classroom, and the different learning issues depending on your students' grade level. Be sure to build in to your plan the opportunity for students to shift the focus or to develop their own topics for discussion.
2. Create some guidelines for language use in your "learning by talking" classroom. Who will get to talk, and for how long? How will speakers be recognized? Is interruption permitted? What will your role be? Devise a way to allow your students input into this decision making so they will feel comfortable abiding by the guidelines.
3. When you next spend some time with friends, take a step back and observe the language pragmatics operating. What are the rules everyone seems to be following? What can be said or not said, and how are tone of voice and body language used? What happens when someone breaks a rule? How long does it usually take a newcomer to catch on to the rules? What if he or she is unable to master the pragmatics?

Black English, also referred to as Black English Vernacular, is the most studied nonstandard American English dialect. It has its roots in African Creole and English but has distinct syntactic, phonological, semantic, and vocabulary rules. Labov (1972) estimated that 80 percent of the black population in the United States speaks Black English. He notes that some Puerto Ricans in New York City speak Black English as well as Puerto Rican Spanish. A more recent estimate is that 60 percent to 70 percent of the U.S. black population speaks Black English (Lucas, 1987).

In the classroom and out, the dialect speaker will confront social attitudes toward dialects other than standard English. For some, the variation in usage may be based in pronunciation and vocabulary (e.g., Boston dialect). For others, it may also involve syntactic changes (e.g., Black English). A student's use of language may influence his or her chances for success in the classroom and may have important social consequences. Rating children's personality and competence from their dialect alone is both inaccurate and unfair, yet it happens over and over. Williams (1970; cited in Dwyer, 1991) asked teachers to rate the voices of black, white, and Mexican American children. Children with nonstandard speech were rated as less competent rather than socially different from the children with a more standard dialect. Cherry (1981) found that teachers were much more supportive, in terms of allowing requests and supplying information, to students who used the standard dialect.

Dialect in
School

Harrison (1985) concludes that a dialect can affect the initial judgment about how smart a child is likely to be, how well he or she will fare as a learner, how he or she is grouped for instruction, and how his or her contributions to class will be treated. This judgment, in turn, may affect (1) the child's attitude about herself or himself as a student, (2) the child's willingness to participate, and (3) the child's expectations for the results of participation. A child's competence is not easily predicted from dialect, but as Edwards (1981) found, it is more probable that teachers who expect problems with children who speak a dialect may treat those children differently, creating a self-fulfilling prophecy.

Learning to
Adjust
Dialect

Research on code switching in children whose original dialect was Black English indicates that children quickly learn to use a more standard dialect in the classroom as they grow older. Destefano (1972) recorded the classroom and nonschool speech of black children between 8 and 11 years old. Their classroom speech appeared to be more formal or careful and to contain a greater frequency of standard features than their nonschool speech. Furthermore, it was reported that in a repetition task, first-graders who spoke Black English responded in standard English 56 percent of the time. It appears that even the younger children already knew most of the standard forms and were learning to use them in the appropriate contexts. A study conducted by Melmed (1971) revealed that black third-graders used standard English 70 percent of the time in school-related tasks.

Lucas (1987) refers to a study of instructional discourse that describes dialect features in predominantly black classrooms in Washington, D.C. The study reports a developmental progression in the use of dialect from kindergarten through fourth grade to sixth grade. Children in kindergarten are still in the process of learning which situations are appropriate or inappropriate for dialect. By fourth or sixth grade, the learning process

The Study of
Dialect

is practically complete. Group interviews showed dialect awareness mostly in the fourth and sixth grades. With regard to the instructional use and effects of dialect on academic outcomes, little data are presently available. Wolfram (1986; as cited in Dwyer, 1991) proposed that it is possible to introduce students to dialect as a type of language study in its own right. He suggested that the study of dialect would teach an understanding of language variation along with a deeper appreciation of the richness of American dialects. Moreover, he concluded that there is no evidence to suggest that Black English, as a dialect for school-aged children, negatively affects academic achievement.

Conclusion

Humans seek meaning and understanding in every encounter. As educators, we seek to enhance understanding by introducing instructional environments that address our students' desires to make meaning. The environments we create must be structured around the multidimensional aspects of the communicative act and each participant's diverse set of cultural devices for making meaning. Table 4.1 presents a noninclusive set of strategies for educators to use to enhance communication in the classroom. They are offered here as specific practical suggestions that follow directly from the concepts presented in this chapter. Hopefully they will be a start toward the development of more specific guidelines for constructing effective instructional environments.

Table 4.1 **Instructional Strategies for Helping Students Become More Effective Communicators**

	INSTRUCTIONAL STRATEGIES	
ISSUE/GOAL	**Topics for Class Discussion**	**Class Demonstrations**
Oral Communication	Unique functions and appropriate uses of oral communication	Techniques for identifying appropriate uses of oral communication in specific situations
Audience Analysis	The role of audience analysis in speech preparation	Techniques for identifying audience characteristics (i.e, motivations, needs, lifestyle objectives) to maximize communication with a specific audience
Language Choices	Types, functions, and limitations of language use	Methods to analyze and use effective types of nonverbal communication
Nonverbal Communication	The role and limitations of nonverbal communication in face-to-face oral interactions	How to use the most effective language choices for specific audiences
Vocal Characteristics and Articulation	Role and variables of vocal presentation, including social reactions to different types of vocal presentation	Techniques to enhance the articulation process, particularly in terms of social meanings conveyed to and from others (i.e., standard versus subculture pronunciation usage)
Delivery and Style	The range of speaking styles (e.g., formal, conversational) and varied reactions to speaking styles	How to match delivery style to a specific circumstance or social setting
Organization	Audience need for patterned, systematic presentation of information and how organization affects audience perception and comprehension	Techniques to select most effective organizational pattern
Speaker Credibility or Ethos	The factors that affect a speaker's credibility and image with an audience	Selection of linguistic choices and nonverbal behavior that enhance speaker credibility
Logical and Emotional Appeals	How logic and emotional appeals can influence the audience	Methods to anticipate audience reactions to specific logical and emotional appeals

Table 4.1	Instructional Strategies for Helping Students Become More Effective Communicators (cont.)	
	INSTRUCTIONAL STRATEGIES	
ISSUE/GOAL	**Topics for Class Discussion**	**Class Demonstrations**
Speaking Situation	Opportunities and constraints associated with specific types of speaking situations (e.g., interpersonal, intercultural, international)	How to adapt to unique communication requirements of a particular type of speaking situation
Oral Message Construction	Characteristics of effective oral messages (i.e., characteristics that distinguish an oral message from a written message)	How best to construct oral messages
Feedback	The interaction between speaker and audience and how to monitor what is conveyed to and understood by listeners	Methods to monitor how effectively speakers achieve their objectives with an audience

SUMMARY OF MAJOR IDEAS

1. Communication consists of both verbal and nonverbal systems that enable humans to encode meaning and transmit it to others. Language is a complex interaction of many variables, including the verbal signal, the signal sender, the manner and context in which the signal is sent, the signal receiver, and previous experiences the sender and the receiver may have had with similar signals. Children begin to communicate in infancy and in a matter of a few years develop skills in vocabulary and grammar. Communication is at the core of all teaching and learning activities.

2. Metalinguistic awareness is the conscious awareness of how one uses language. Schooling experiences that increase children's metalinguistic awareness can develop a child's understanding of his or her own culture and the cultures of others.

3. Phonology is the study of speech sounds. Infants exposed to environments in which English is spoken begin to produce speech sounds at 5 to 8 months of age. Children in all language groups proceed through similar stages of language development. Spanish-language learners acquire vowel sounds

early, and English-language learners focus on consonant sounds early.

4. Vocabulary is the sum of words understood and used by an individual in any language group. Children typically acquire their first word at about age 1 and then gain vocabulary rapidly between the ages of 2 and 6.

5. Grammar is the system of rules implicit in a language that allows words to be arranged with some regularity of structure. From normal communicative interactions with adults, children typically acquire the rules of grammar in their native language with little difficulty.

6. Language pragmatics refers not only to the rules of a language but also to cultural notions about what is considered appropriate and effective use of the language. Children's knowledge of language pragmatics continues to develop throughout the school years. Among the most important skills in language pragmatics are the ability to be responsive to the needs of listeners and the ability to adjust one's use of language for different audiences.

7. Children must learn the rules of language pragmatics for conversation, for written language, and for different discourse situations. The rules for discourse can vary widely across cultures. School discourse also has its own specific rules.

8. Bilingualism and second-language acquisition are becoming more common among students in U.S. schools. Bilingualism is the ability to speak two languages with equal fluency. Second-language acquisition is a process of language development whereby a child first acquires one language and then is exposed to and required to learn a second language.

9. Research into bilingualism indicates that children between 2 and 4 can acquire skills in both Spanish and English without any evidence of negative linguistic effect. Bilingual children also exhibit code switching as a normal state of language development. Code switching is the production of mixed-language utterances.

10. Research into second-language acquisition indicates that children use cognitive strategies they learned while acquiring their first language to acquire the second. They also rely on rote memorization and exposure to conversation with native speakers of the second language.

11. Language skills enable children to function and grow in a world of social interactions. Sociocultural variables that can affect an individual's motivation to learn a second language are the learner's attitude toward native speakers of the lan-

guage and the degree of social distance between the two cultures the languages represent. Second-language learners need social skills in order to successfully acquire the target language.

12. Second-language learners must acquire the discourse rules of the target language along with the language itself. Research shows that it is not so much the use of different languages as it is a discrepancy in language use between the home and the school that constitutes the primary source of confusion for language minority students. The passive language environment of many classrooms may provide linguistically diverse students with only limited opportunities to produce language and to develop more complex language and thinking skills.

13. Dialect is a regional variation of language characterized by distinct grammar, vocabulary, and pronunciation. The English language consists of American English, British English, Australian English, and Canadian English dialects. American English has a number of regional dialects. Speakers of dialect, such as Black English, may encounter negative attitudes from those who believe that dialect is linguistically inferior to more standard versions of English. Research shows that children who speak in dialect learn to adjust their speech and switch to more standard usage in school-based contexts.

EXTENDING YOUR EXPERIENCE

1. Interview the parent of a child under the age of 3. What has he or she discovered firsthand about language development from interacting daily with this child? Formulate your interview questions around the concepts discussed in the text: phonology, vocabulary, grammar, pragmatics, and metalinguistic awareness.

2. Review the text sections on language pragmatics and sociolinguistic conventions. Make a list of social communication "rules" for language use you have noticed in your general public interactions with others. Have you ever unintentionally violated such a rule for the way language should be used? Describe that experience. Now think about the varied communication settings and types of audiences you encounter in a typical day (home, work, school, and so on.) List some of the rules for language pragmatics that operate in each of those settings. Do the "rules" vary depending on setting and audience? If so, why?

3. For this activity you will need a television and a VCR. With a group of your classmates, select and view a foreign film you have not seen before. Block off the lower portion of the television screen, where the subtitles appear, and try to follow the events in the film. Note your strategies for interpreting meaning and your feelings as you try to understand what is going on. Does your ability to "read" nonverbal communication help at all? Stop the film intermittently and compare notes. What do other group members think and feel? Prepare a report of your group experience for the whole class.

4. Informally survey your classmates in all your current courses and find out how many are bilingual. How many have acquired a second language (English or other)? Ask them to describe their schooling experiences as speakers of more than one language, and record their comments, honoring those who wish to remain anonymous.

5. This chapter describes a good deal of research into language development and use. Why is it important for teachers to attend to the questions asked by educational researchers and to understand their findings? Why is it important for teachers to understand the issues raised by educational theorists?

6. As you learned in this chapter, a child's motivation to learn a second language depends on three things: the child's social skills, the child's attitude toward the second language culture, and the social distance between the two language cultures. Create some teaching strategies for positively addressing these influences on motivations.

RESOURCES FOR FURTHER STUDY

García, E. (1983). *Bilingualism in early childhood*. Albuquerque, N.M.: University of New Mexico Press.

> This research focuses on the language children between 3 and 5 years old use when communicating with their mothers. The findings support the notion that there are differences in language acquisition in early childhood. Using statistical measures, home observations, and recordings of subjects, the author concludes that no significant differences in English were detected in monolingual and bilingual students and that bilingual students used different speech patterns at home.

Gleason, J. B. (1988). *The development of language*. Columbus, Ohio: Merrill.

This book is a collaborative effort targeted primarily at college students. The chapters present various topics and are written by individuals familiar with language theory, research, and practice. Models and theoretical perspectives are also presented. The book provides an insightful perspective on how language development occurs and what forces and issues foster it.

Hakuta, K. (1986). *Mirror of language: The debate on bilingualism.* New York: Basic Books.

This book offers a detailed overview of how bilinguals (including multilingual and non-oral-aural languages) develop their linguistic skills and argues the need to move beyond simplistic research into bilingualism. The overall aim of the book is to dispel myths and misconceptions about bilingualism. It presents pressing issues that will be at the center of bilingual education in the future.

Heath, S. B. (1986). Sociocultural contexts of language development. In Evaluation, Dissemination and Assessment Center, *Beyond language: Social and cultural factors in schooling language minority students.* Los Angeles: California State University.

This chapter places the issue of native tongue and second-language acquisition at the forefront of educational reform. Using California as an example, the author argues that academic success has to do more with how students "use" the language they know than with "what" language they know. Educators can help students by involving them in a range of oral and written exercises. In order for educators to unlock new venues of academic delivery, such encouragement must take into account not only the students' language but also their past and present experiences.

Ramirez, J. D., Yuen, S. D., Ramey, D. R., and Pasta, D. J. (1991). *Final report: Longitudinal study of structured English immersion strategy, early-exit and late-exit transitional bilingual education programs for language-minority children.* San Mateo, Calif.: Aguirre International.

This extensive report was prepared for the Department of Education using three different models to educate language minority students: structured English immersion and early- and late-exit bilingual models. The overall results suggest that there are no significant differences between the three models examined. The factors that influence language acquisition and development have more to do with teacher qualification and parental involvement than the time spent learning the language. Without question, the author concludes, bilingual programs might not be proper for all language minority students, and more effective and structured means should be utilized to educate those students.

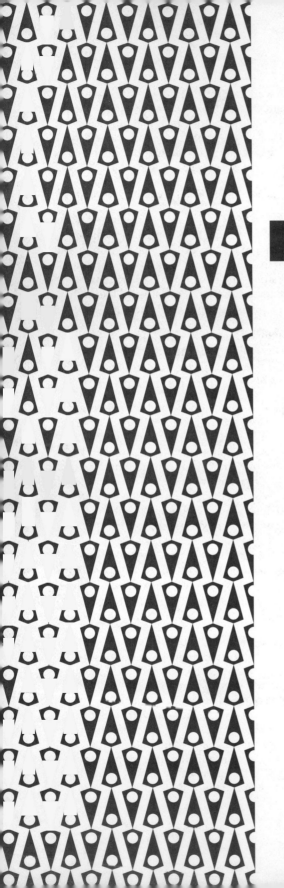

LANGUAGE,

CULTURE, AND

COGNITION

CHAPTER 5

Focus Questions

○   What is sociocultural theory, and how does it provide a framework for approaching the education of culturally diverse students?

○   How does children's language development relate to their development of higher-order thinking skills?

○   What does the general trend in research suggest about the use of intelligence tests?

○   What is instructional discourse, and how can it be used to develop students' ability to think and to communicate?

○   What part does writing play in a child's symbolic repertoire?

"It is not the voice which commands the story, it is the ear."

—CICERO

As the quotation above suggests, and in some contradiction with ideas presented in the previous chapter, it is the listener, the receiver of communication, who is a significant player in the communicative act. Understood in its broadest sense, the "ear" represents the intellectual and social attributes of the receiver of communication. Listeners bring all of their language skills, sociocultural background and experiences, and thinking abilities to bear during the process of communication.

How and what the listener attends to in communication represents all of the processes going on in the listener's mind. We saw in Chapter 3 that for humans the process of making meaning is a constructive act. Human cognition, the mental processes we use to acquire knowledge, is complex and multidimensional. Recent developments in cognitive science have generated a new description of the mind as including both "structural" and "representational" aspects (Donald, 1991). Over the ages humans have evolved new systems of representation: not just new information but new ways of thinking. The mind is our storehouse of symbolic reference. It is a library of symbols that are distinctly assembled by our inherited mental "structures" but are also specifically ordered as "representations" of our own personal set of experiences.

Let's look at how this description of the mind as both structural and representational might apply to an educational situation. A new teacher (or a new student, for that matter) encountering the first day of school has prepared herself or himself for the encounter. He or she has called on previous experiences with formal education, on informal family and nonschool experiences in teaching and learning, and on expectations for social interaction and approaches to problem solving. In short, a variety of experiences recorded and ordered in the "library" of the teacher's or the student's mind are mobilized to prepare for the classroom encounter: How should I behave toward others in the classroom? What language and tone of voice should I use to make my messages understood? What do I want to accomplish? All participants in education call on their own mental libraries in order to gather their present understandings of the classroom and related experiences and apply them to new classroom experiences.

But what, really, do we mean when we say the mind is like a library? Compared to the world, a library is very small. In the form of books, though, a large part of the world can be represented in that library. This is also true of the human mind: it is physically tiny but it can contain representations of anything in the world. The mind is also shaped by what is put in it and how that represented world is organized (should we put nonfiction on the first floor or on the tenth floor?).

The represented world within our minds is determined both by the mental structures we have inherited and by our own personal experiences and how we tend to order these experiences mentally. Our inherited mental structures are the intellectual faculties that allow us to think, and to think in many different ways—by means of formal argument, systematic categorization, induction, deduction, verification, differentiation, quantification, idealization, theoretical synthesis, and so on. But we do not think in a vacuum. We think in a context of our experience, and the world represented in our minds is shaped by that experience. There is an interaction between thinking processes and cultural experiences. We may all possess the thinking skills listed above, but if our experiences and mental representations of those experiences differ, the results of our thinking will differ. Herein is the basis for recognizing that diversity in experience leads to diversity in mind. In day-to-day living, and in the classroom, the workings of the human mind and the representations of culture are inseparable.

This chapter begins by discussing a theoretical framework for understanding the interaction of language, culture, and cognition as it relates to education. We then examine the problematical notion of "intelligence" and intelligence testing and consider research indicating that multilingualism may be an advantage in cognitive development. The second half of the chapter describes two elements of teaching that may be particularly effective with culturally diverse students.

The Role of Culture in Cognition

Early theories of teaching and learning focused on the individual learner and were influenced most directly by findings in the field of psychology. Within the last twenty to thirty years, however, scholars trained in such fields as anthropology, sociology, cognitive science, and sociolinguistics have begun to look into the question of how thinking processes and cultural experiences interact in schooling situations. The extent of fit or mismatch between home and school cultures provide a dynamic understanding of a wide variety of variables that affect student learning. Researchers in developmental and educational psychology are now devoting increased attention to the social context of learning and to the role of family, peer group, and community in children's school achievement.

During the last decade, many educational theorists have become interested in **sociocultural theory,** an international intellectual movement that brings together the disciplines of psychology, semiotics, education, sociology, and anthropology. This movement draws on work done earlier in this century by the Russian theorists L. S. Vygotsky and Mikhail Bakhtin and relates it to the thought of such theoreticians and philosophers of education as William James, John Dewey, C. S. Peirce, and Jean Piaget. The aim is to find a unified way of understanding issues of language, cognition, culture, human development, and teaching and learning.

The importance of sociocultural theory for education is its proposal that individual learning and social interaction are inextricably connected. Sociocultural theorists argue that the psychology of the individual learner is deeply shaped by social interaction—in essence, that both student and teacher are engaged in the process of constructing their minds through social activity. In this view, knowledge is not a given set of fixed ideas that are passed from teacher to student. Rather, knowledge is *created* in the interaction between teacher and student. Higher-order mental processes, the tendency to look at things in certain ways, and values themselves are produced by shared activity and dialogue (Rogoff, 1990).

Our social lives, often considered to be the major products of culture, are instead for sociocultural theorists the major ingredients of culture. Social experience is inseparable from thought. Moment by moment we construct reality. That process of construction, and the understanding it generates, depend on our previous understandings and our previous social experiences.

The focus of sociocultural theory holds particular import for education, partly because education has been a major interest of many of its founding writers, but mostly because educational practice and theory is particularly needful of a unifying theory of teaching and learning. Educators of culturally diverse stu-

Variables Affecting Learning

Learning and Social Interaction

dents will find this theoretical framework helpful because it conceives of learning as an interaction between individual learners and an embedding context. That embedding context may be as immediate as the social environment of the classroom or as indirect as the traditions and institutions that constitute the history of education. Both contexts and many more come into play whenever teachers and students interact. Important contexts for teaching and learning range from (1) close, detailed instruction of individual learners and (2) concern for the social organization of classrooms to (3) a consideration of the cultural attributes of teachers, students, and peers. These contexts interweave, and we can follow their strands to gain a new understanding of the relationship between language, culture, and cognition.

Language and Culture as Tools of Thought

How do language and culture relate to cognitive development? Recall that human cognition—how and what we know—is a process of mental representation shaped by experience and the structural aspects of our minds. According to Vygotsky, language acquisition is the momentous occasion when internal mental representation and external reality converge. For him, "external reality" is first and foremost cultural: through the development of language in interpersonal experiences, children begin to construct meaning. In this view, language functions significantly as a tool of thought. As stated by Hamers and Blanc:

> The shared representations and scripts which are basic to language proficiency arise in the interaction between the child and the significant others around him. The representations the child will construct are highly dependent on the shared social representations in his environment. The child will internalize those language functions that are valorized and used with him; it is through the socialization process that he becomes cognizant of functions and representations. (Hamers and Blanc, 1989)

Mental Frameworks

Thus, as children develop their ability to use language, they absorb more and more understanding of social situations and improve their thinking skills. This in turn allows them to learn how to control their own actions and thoughts. It is through a culturally bound and socially mediated process of language development that children construct mental frameworks (or

schema) for perceiving the world around them. If language is a tool of thought, it follows that as children develop more complex thinking skills, the mental representations through which language and culture embody the child's world play a significant role.

If as Vygotsky proposed, a child's cognitive schema for operating in the world are culturally bound, what are the effects of trying to learn in an environment where the culture of the classroom differs from the culture of the home? Culturally diverse students face the challenge of either accommodating their existing schema or constructing new schema. When the educational focus is on transitioning culturally diverse students to a mainstream culture rather than building on what they already know, the students are forced to change in order to meet the needs of the classroom. As Georges Duquette concludes:

> Children need to be understood and to express themselves (in the same positive light experienced by other children) in their own first language, home context and culture. Their minority background brings out the limitations not of the children but of the professionals who are asked to respond to those needs. (Duquette, 1991)

| Negation of |
| Cognitive |
| Tools |

Language minority students face a far greater challenge. It is through a child's first language that he or she creates mechanisms for functioning in and perceiving the world. If the culture of the classroom negates a child's first language and accompanying representations of the child's world, it is thus negating the tools the child has used to construct a basic cognitive framework.

In a discussion of Vygotsky's theory, Diaz and Klinger (1991) outline how language as a tool of thought has major consequences for a child's cognitive development. As language skills develop, a child's cognitive processes become more independent from the directly perceived environment. Through the use of language, children can organize and reconstruct their perceptions in terms of their own goals and intentions. Language development allows the child to act reflectively according to a plan rather than merely on impulse. As their language abilities mature, children can ultimately gain control over their own cognitive processes.

From the perspective of sociocultural theory, cognitive development is reflected by the increasing ability to use language in abstract ways. If the relationship between language and cognitive development operates as Vygotsky and later theorists claim, educational practices that ignore or regard negatively a student's native language and culture could quite possibly have negative effects on the student's cognitive development. If a student's first language and culture are used only as a means to learn English and mainstream school culture and not to build on previous experiences and representations, then the student's cognitive development could be hindered or interrupted.

A Foundation for Language Proficiency

To further understand the link between language and cognition, various investigators have made the distinction between contextualized and decontextualized language. **Contextualized language** conveys meaning using physical cues such as gestures, intonation, and other concrete representations characteristic of face-to-face communication. **Decontextualized language** relies on more abstract linguistic and cognitive cues that are independent of the communicative context (Duquette, 1991). An example of decontextualized language is a reading assignment in science class. Such an assignment requires the student to construct meaning from a written context only. There is no opportunity to observe a physical demonstration of new concepts or to ask questions of others.

Abstract Linguistic Cues

As students progress in school, they are increasingly required to use language in an abstract, decontextualized way (reading and writing as opposed to only listening and speaking). Proficiency in decontextualized language is considered to be most indicative of future academic success. In an extensive review of different research, Cummins shows that a high level of literacy (a decontextualized skill) in the first language is more closely related to development of literacy in the second language than is social communicative competence (a contextualized skill) in the second language (Cummins, 1991). Cummins argues that it takes students much longer to develop decontextualized language and cognitive skills than it takes to develop face-to-face, contextualized language skills. He further argues that removing students too soon from educational programs which utilize their native language will lead to their future academic failure (Cummins, 1989). In essence, children utilize native language abilities as a tool to construct higher-order thinking processes. Limiting their opportunities to learn in their first language will limit their cognitive growth and related academic achievement.

Learning in the First Language

Because it focuses primarily on oral acquisition of English, current policy and practice regarding the education of culturally and linguistically diverse students is overly simplistic. Such an approach does not take into consideration the complex interweaving of students' cultural, linguistic, and cognitive development. In their study of the possible effects of language on cognitive development, Hakuta, Diaz, and Ferdman (1986) recognize the importance of acknowledging these three important strands in children's development and addressing them in our schools. They concluded that most of the variance in cognitive growth directly relates to the way in which society affects and manipulates cognitive capacities. Therefore, cultural and contextual sensitivity theories that examine the social and cultural aspects of cognitive development will best serve diverse students.

An Assessment of Intelligence Testing

Over the last five to seven decades, the educational establishment has been guided by theories that consider the concept of "intelligence" to be the central factor in learning. **Intelligence** is generally defined as the ability of an individual's mind to perceive, organize, remember, and utilize symbolic information. To its credit, this idea of intelligence attempted to explain (albeit somewhat ambiguously) the relationship between the physical aspects of the brain and the human ability to reason and to symbolize. To its discredit, this concept depended extensively on the notion of biological determination (we "inherit" our intelligence) and on the assumption that an individual's intelligence could be validly and reliably assessed through a simple set of test items. Historically, culturally diverse children have been negatively affected by this enduring definition of intelligence (García, 1983).

Concept of
Intelligence

Careful examination of the testing literature has revealed several problems in using the results of intelligence tests to understand the cognitive development of culturally diverse students. Personal, social, and cultural differences among students typically are not accounted for in **psychometrics,** which is the measurement of psychological attributes. Intelligence tests in particular have failed to assess adequately the "intelligence" of culturally diverse populations because of language discrepancies, inappropriate test content, and failure to consider diversity in

Problems
with
Intelligence
Tests

the development of test-scoring strategies. Because of its devastating effects on culturally diverse student populations, it is appropriate to discuss the problematical topic of intelligence testing. Inherent in this discussion is the message that explanations of the human mind that rely on the concept of intelligence and on intelligence testing have been educationally misinformed.

The use of intelligence tests with culturally diverse students and adults has generated much interest because of differences in scores found between this population and normative groups. As early as 1924, Sheldon compared the intelligence of 100 "white" and 100 "Mexican" children of the same age and same school environment. The Cole-Vicent group intelligence test was administered and was followed by the Stanford-Binet individual intelligence test. Sheldon's results were as follows:

1. The average Mexican child was below the normal development of the average white child by fourteen months.
2. On a group comparison, Mexican children had approximately 85 percent of the scored intelligence of their white counterparts.
3. By combining several studies, Sheldon found that Mexican children scored lower than American, English, Hebrew, and Chinese children but scored higher than American Indian, Slavic, Italian, and Negro children.
4. As chronological age increased, differences in mental age became greater. A conclusion reached by Sheldon was that the average mental age of the Mexican group seemed to have reached its maximum at 9 years.

These indicators of lower mental ability were supported by further research. In 1932, Manuel and Hughes administered the Goodenough Intelligence Test to 440 Mexican and 396 non-Mexican children from the San Antonio public schools. Based on an age and grade comparison, the Mexican children scored in the retarded stage. The educational hypothesis that "Mexicans" were mentally inferior began to crumble, however, with such research as by Garth, Elson, and Morton (1936). These researchers tested 445 Mexican children between the ages of 8 and 16 on the Pintner Non-Language Intelligence Test and the Otis Classification Test. Their aim was to obtain a reliable nonverbal test to ascertain the influence of language and education when subjects' ability on a nonverbal intelligence test was known, and to determine how these subjects would perform when administered a verbal achievement test. Results showed

Becoming a Responsive Teacher

5.1 How Two Students Developed through Collaborative Learning

The Weaker Student: Valuing Not Knowing Amiri entered school situations expecting failure. He could be heard saying over and over again, "Boy, am I stupid," as he struggled through academic tasks. He assumed he was unable to do whatever was asked of him on his own and therefore sought a great deal of help from both teachers and peers. He did not appear to believe that he had anything of importance to contribute to others, nor that his participation in activities or discussions was valued. He often engaged in disruptive, attention-seeking activities or just "spaced out." His behavior was consistent with a belief that intelligence is something you are born with, that he hadn't been given much, and that no amount of effort would change that fact.

Some teachers who had worked with Amiri held a different view of his abilities; they thought he was more able than he himself believed, yet they found themselves at a loss to change his outward behaviors, his low social status in the class, or his apparent poor self-image. All this began to change when computers were introduced to the classroom. In Amiri's words:

> See, really, when I first started off on computer—it was O.K.
> because we got to play games. And then I got a little bit serious
> about it...serious about it around April. At first I didn't really...I was
> like the dull one...really. I didn't know what was going on.

By the end of the school year, Amiri's school experience was very different from the one he was used to. He had become an "expert," and the information he had acquired during the previous several months of research was valued by teachers and peers alike. The very expressions of uncertainty that previously marked him as unsuccessful in school were valued in this new environment. Repeated participation in reciprocal teaching groups and large group discussions provided Amiri with ample opportunities for guided practice in new social behaviors, in ways to enter and participate in group discussion, and in more successful learning strategies.

Amiri's developing confidence and increasing skills are evidenced by his growing eagerness to participate in large group discussions, as well as in the quality of the questions he posed. This extract from a class discussion demonstrates his new thoughtfulness.

> PAULETTE: The bamboo grove is real shady and the pandas is black
> and white so they sort of blend in.
>
> AMIRI: Why is it that the pandas eat all of the bamboo if they need to
> be protected?...Why would they eat all their, their camouflage?

This previously unsuccessful student came to be appreciated—by others and by himself—for qualities of mind that his learning environment enhanced and made visible. Amiri, and other students like him, found that their willingness to say, "I don't know," born of much real world experience of not knowing, was valued here. And, as he reflected at the end of the year, learning was both possible and enjoyable to him: "I'm not going to drop this...I have a lot to learn."

The Stronger Student: Learning to Reflect Wilson scored in the 98th percentile on standardized tests of achievement in both reading and mathematics. He read voraciously, learned facts quickly, and performed school-related tasks with ease. He was articulate and confident. But Wilson rarely listened to others, did not work well in groups, and preferred finding things out on his own. He most often was heard making declarative statements or directing the activities of his peers. He was sure his way was best, and resisted suggestions by others to the contrary. Despite Wilson's high test scores, his inability to reflect interfered with his capacity to be a flexible and responsive learner.

As might be expected, it was difficult for Wilson to participate in a project emphasizing collaborative activity. Would a successful student like Wilson find such a project sufficiently challenging,or would the slower rate of Wilson's peers hold him back and frustrate him?

Becoming a Responsive Teacher *(continued)*

As it turned out, while working with a group, Wilson continued to develop skills and expertise in numerous areas. He learned to listen and to share his knowledge with others, and he began to engage in more flexible and reflective thinking behaviors. He also became more open to learning from his peers. As the following segment illustrates, Wilson reflects on changes in his own thinking and the classroom experiences that stimulated those changes. Later, for the first time, he seeks clarification of new data rather than holding rigidly to his original point of view.

At first I thought I agreed with Stuart [that pandas are fat because they are indolent] except it really takes a lot of exertion to climb trees. It does. They must burn their energy climbing, because remember, we saw them in that laser disc...how the panda was climbing trees to get to the bamboo.

I'm sort of getting two pictures. First you're saying there's plenty of bamboo, and they sit around and munch it all day, and then you say that their bamboos is dying off. Can you sort of set me straight?

Meeting the Challenge

1. Describe your reactions as you read the above stories of Amiri and Wilson. Were you surprised by either of these outcomes? Does the underlying teaching approach alluded to here seem to be "transmitting" or "facilitating"?
2. Do you feel you are like Amiri or more like Wilson as a learner? Devise some strategies for broadening the role of social interaction in your own learning process.
3. Observe a class and record two phenomena: (a) the number of times the teacher responds to the way a child learns, and (b) the number of times the teacher responds to what a child learns. Describe a teacher response that seemed to be particularly effective for some student.

these Mexican children to be "inferior" to white American children in verbal tests across age and grade. However, on the nonverbal test, their scores were about equal to white American children's scores. The authors suggested that the verbal test could be unfair to the Mexican children.

Despite evidence to the contrary, the hypothesis that some populations were "mentally inferior" to others continued to prevail. In the 1940s, Altus reported research findings related to racial and bilingual group differences within U.S. Army populations. An initial study (Altus, 1945) examined racial and bilingual group differences in predicting trainees' classification (discharged as inept or kept in the army) and in mean aptitude test scores by using the Wechsler Mental Ability Scale (WMAS) to test American Indians, Mexicans, Filipinos, Chinese bilinguals, whites, and Negros. The study results showed that the four different bilingual groups scored lower than the two monolingual groups on all WMAS subtests. A subsequent study (Altus, 1948) addressed the topic of group differences in intelligence and the type of test administered. The subject populations used in the study were "Anglos, Negros, Mexicans, and Indians, who had been classified as illiterate when entering the army." Results from these comparisons showed that in the verbal subtest, the "Anglo" and "Negro" had higher scores than the "Mexican" and "Indian." However, there were no differences on the nonverbal subtests. Importantly, these data suggested that group inferiority or superiority was in part a consequence of the test used.

In another significant study, Christiansen and Livermore (1970) compared the effects of social class and ethnic origin on intelligence test scores. They divided the group of subjects into two categories: those with middle-class status and those with lower-class status. The results indicated that social class was a more important factor than ethnic origin in "intelligence" differences among children. With this information, important cautions about test bias began to emerge.

More recent review of the use of intelligence tests with culturally and linguistically diverse populations has pinpointed several serious concerns. First, the language of the test can bias the test results, promoting lower scores for non-English-speaking populations. Second, social class is highly correlated with test performance, which calls into question any conclusions about intelligence and ethnic background. Third, the content of the tests is biased toward mainstream U.S. culture. It seems appropriate to conclude that differences in test performance may be an artifact of the tests themselves or of other linguistic,

| Hypothesis of Mental Inferiority |

| Social Class and Intelligence |

| Test Bias |

psychological, or social factors as yet imperfectly defined. Intelligence tests and the concept of intelligence that underlies them have done and continue to do an educational disservice to culturally diverse students. The limitations of these educational "tools" should be recognized and educators should be extremely cautious when using them to generalize about students.

Multilingualism and Cognitive Development

In the previous chapter, we looked into some of the research that has explored bilingualism and second-language acquisition from the perspective of language development. A separate but significant research approach to the understanding of multilingualism and its effects has focused on the cognitive (intellectual) attributes of the student. Past correlational studies indicating a negative relationship between childhood bilingualism and performance on standardized tests of intelligence made it tempting to link bilingualism to "depressed" intelligence, and this negative conclusion characterized much early work (Darcy, 1953). Due to the many methodological problems in studies investigating this type of relationship, any conclusions about multilingualism and intellectual functioning (as measured by standardized individual or group intelligence tests) are extremely tentative in nature (Darcy, 1963; Diaz, 1983).

In one of the first investigations of German-English bilingual acquisition, Leopold (1939) reported a general cognitive plasticity for his young bilingual daughter. He suggested that linguistic flexibility (in the form of bilingualism) was related to a number of nonlinguistic cognitive tasks such as categorization, verbal signal discrimination, and creativity. Peal and Lambert (1962) summarized their work with French-English bilinguals and English monolinguals by suggesting that the intellectual experience of acquiring two languages contributed to advantageous mental flexibility, superior concept formation, and a generally diversified set of mental abilities.

More recent research (Feldman and Shen, 1971) reports differential responding between Chicano Spanish-English bilinguals and English monolinguals across three separate tasks reflecting Piagetian-like problem solving and metalinguistic awareness. Results indicated significantly increased cognitive flexibility for Chicano bilinguals. Other studies have compared matched bilin-

| Mental |
| Flexibility |

guals (Afrikaans-English) and monolinguals (either Afrikaans or English) on metalinguistic tasks requiring separation of word sounds and word meanings. Comparison of scores on these tasks indicated that bilingual speakers concentrated more on attaching meaning to words rather than to sounds. Ben-Zeev's (1977) work with Hebrew-English bilingual children also comments on the metalinguistic abilities of these children. Subjects in these studies showed superiority in symbol substitution and verbal transformational tasks. Ben-Zeev summarizes:

> Two strategies characterized by thinking patterns of the bilingual in relation to verbal material: readiness to impute structure and readiness to reorganize. (p. 1017)

Even more recent research, specifically with Chicano bilingual students (Kessler and Quinn, 1987), supplies additional empirical support for the emerging understanding that, all things being equal, bilingual children outperform monolingual children on specific measures of cognitive and metalinguistic awareness. Kessler and Quinn (1987) engaged bilingual and monolingual children in a variety of symbolic categorization tasks that required their attention to abstract features of concrete objects (for example, the relative size of toy blocks). Chicano Spanish-English bilinguals from low socioeconomic backgrounds outperformed English monolinguals from both high and low socioeconomic backgrounds on these tasks. Such findings are particularly significant given the criticism by McNab (1979) that many bilingual "cognitive advantage" studies utilized only subjects from high socioeconomic backgrounds and from non-U.S. minority populations. It is important to note that findings of metalinguistic advantage have also been reported for Puerto Rican students from low socioeconomic backgrounds as well (Galambos and Hakuta, 1988).

| **Greater** |
| **Metalinguistic** |
| **Awareness** |

Theoretical attempts to link multilingualism with cognitive attributes have begun to emerge. To identify more specifically the relationship between cognition and bilingualism, Cummins (1979, 1981, 1984) has proposed that children who do achieve balanced proficiency in two languages may be cognitively "advantaged," whereas those who do not achieve balanced proficiency in two languages may be cognitively "disadvantaged." Interestingly, Diaz (1985) has proposed an alternative hypothesis and supportive data that suggest that the cognitive "flexibility" of the multilingual is at its maximum during the early stages of multilingual development, before balanced proficiency is attained.

As yet, it is not quite clear how bilingualism or multilingualism directly influences cognitive development. Is it always an advantage? Can it be a disadvantage? Is early (and balanced) proficiency advantageous, and is late (and unbalanced) proficiency disadvantageous? These questions are not yet answerable (García, 1991; Hakuta, 1986). What we do know is that multilingual children have been found to score higher on specific Piagetian, metalinguistic, concept formation, and creative cognitive tasks. Gone are the old myths that multilingualism is an intellectual and psychological liability.

Two Aspects of Effective Teaching in Culturally Diverse Classrooms

Since the time of Socrates, educators and philosophers have argued for a kind of teaching that does more than impart knowledge and teach skills. Knowledge and skills are important enough, the argument goes, but true education and real teaching involve far more. They involve, fundamentally, helping students understand, appreciate, and grapple with important ideas while developing a depth of understanding in a wide range of issues.

> **Goals of Education**

Teaching aimed at these important goals is presently most notable for its absence from U.S. classrooms. Goodlad (1984), for example, reports that:

> A great deal of what goes on in the classroom is like painting-by-numbers—filling in the colors called for by numbers on the page . . . [teachers] ask for specific questions calling essentially for students to fill in the blanks: "What is the capital city of Canada?" "What are the principal exports of Japan?" Students rarely turn things around by asking questions. Nor do teachers often give students a chance to romp with an open-ended question such as "What are your views on the quality of television?"(p. 108)

If this portrait is accurate for mainstream American classrooms, it is even more accurate for classrooms in which the students are linguistically and culturally diverse and of low-income backgrounds. Because of the perception that these students fundamentally require drill, review, and redundancy in order to progress academically (Brophy and Good, 1986), their learning opportunities are likely to be excessively weighted toward low-level skills and fact-oriented rather than concept-oriented instruction. As important as skills and knowledge undoubtedly are, no less important are more cognitively demanding learning opportunities that promote, as the philosopher and educator Mortimer Adler (1982) has written, the "enlarged understanding of ideas and values" (p. 23).

With Adler's notion of such an "enlarged understanding" in mind as a goal of education, the rest of this chapter will attempt to consolidate the more theoretical issues of language, culture, and cognition addressed earlier. It is impossible to delineate all the interlocking pieces of this puzzle in this small space. We can make some headway, though. We will examine two recently researched areas that have attended to instructional delivery (the language and discourse of instruction) and the development of literacy. The selection of these two particular areas is not a random one. The basis of enhanced academic productivity for culturally diverse students lies in the manner in which their communicative and cognitive development is organized instructionally in oral and literacy activities. In essence, the way these endeavors are handled in the classroom is highly significant for the student of interest in this book.

Basis for

Enhanced

Achievement

Instructional Discourse

In classrooms throughout the world, but particularly in the United States, teaching events are structured daily around teacher-student dialogues. In a study recently completed (García, 1992), we recorded the following kindergarten classroom with the teacher leading a lesson for six children:

TEACHER: "Okay, Maria, let's see what we can figure out about the shapes of these blocks."

MARÍA: "This one's yellow."

TEACHER: "Sí, yellow is a color, but can you tell me what shape this block is?"

MARÍA: "Todos son amarillos." [They are all yellow.]

TEACHER: "Sí, but we want to talk about *shape*. Tú sabes cómo? [You know how?]

> MARÍA: [Holding up a triangle.] "This one, this one, this one, es
> amarillo" [is yellow].

These sorts of instructional interactions occur repeatedly every day in classrooms. Typically, the teacher asks a question or, as in the preceding example, otherwise requests a student response. The student then replies (as for María, not always the way the teacher would prefer.) Finally, the teacher evaluates the child's response and may request further elaboration.

Effective **instructional discourse** (García, 1992) or **instructional conversation** (Tharp and Gallimore, 1988, 1989) has been demonstrated as highly relevant to the broader linguistic, cognitive, and academic development of linguistically and culturally diverse children. On the one hand, such conversations are an instructional strategy in that they are designed to promote learning. Yet they are structured to take advantage of natural and spontaneous interactions, free from the didactic characteristics normally associated with formal teaching. Such interactions are interesting and engaging. They center on an idea or a concept. They have a focus that might shift as the discussion evolves but remains discernible throughout. They allow a high level of participation without undue domination by any one individual, particularly the teacher. Students engage in extended discussions—interactions—with the teacher and among themselves.

In instructional discourse, teachers and students are responsive to what others say, so that each statement or contribution builds upon, challenges, or extends a previous one. Topics are picked up, developed, and elaborated. Strategically, the teacher (or discussion leader) presents provocative ideas or experiences, then questions, prods, challenges, coaxes—or keeps quiet. He or she clarifies and instructs when necessary but does so efficiently, without wasting time or words. The teacher assures that the discussion proceeds at an appropriate pace, neither too fast to prohibit the development of ideas nor too slow to lose momentum and interest. The teacher knows when to bear down and draw out a student's ideas and when to ease up, allowing thought and reflection to occur. Perhaps most important, the teacher manages to keep everyone engaged in a substantive and extended interaction, weaving each individual participant's comments into a larger tapestry of talking and thinking.

Such discourse is in many ways similar to interactions that take place outside school between children and adults (e.g., Ochs et al., 1989; Rogoff, 1990). These interactions appear to be very important for children's learning and cognitive development

Spontaneous

Interaction

Teacher's

Role in

Discourse

in general. For example, Rogoff (1990) notes that middle-class adults tailor their responses to children, "focusing their attention, and expanding and improving the children's contributions." Although not designed to teach in a formal sense, these tailored responses, Rogoff concludes, "appear to support children's advancing linguistic, thinking, and communicative skills" (p. 157).

Elements of Good Classroom Discourse. Moving beyond such general descriptions, what characterizes good classroom discourse? What are its constituent elements? What must teachers know and do in order to implement successfully these types of learning interactions with their students? Working in a low-income, language minority school in California (García, 1989) and building upon earlier work in Hawaii (e.g., Au, 1979; Tharp and Gallimore, 1988), recent research teams comprised of teachers and researchers have attempted to address these questions (see Goldenberg and Gallimore, 1990, 1991; Goldenberg and Patthey-Chavez, 1991). What has gradually emerged is a more precise description of instructional discourse. As developed by Goldenberg (1992), Table 5.1 compares direct instruction with instructional conversation.

Table 5.1 Characteristics of Direct Instruction and Instructional Conversation

DIRECT INSTRUCTION	INSTRUCTIONAL CONVERSATION
Teacher models	Teacher facilitates
Exact, specific answers Skill directed	Draw from prior or background knowledge
Easier to evaluate	Many different ideas encouraged
Step-by-step systematic instruction	Build on information provided by students
Teacher centered	More student involvement
Guided and independent practice following instruction	Establish common foundation of understanding
No extensive discussion	Extensive discussion
Goal is mastery after each step	Fewer black and white responses
Check for understanding	Guided understanding

Source: C. Goldenberg, *Instructional conversations and their classroom application: Education practice report #2.* National Center for Research on Cultural Diversity and Second Language Learning, University of California, Santa Cruz, 1992. Used with permission.

Although these comparisons in no way represent definitive or comprehensive descriptions of direct instruction and instructional discourse, they suggest important distinctions between these two teaching approaches. They are based on very different assumptions about teaching and learning. Direct instruction assumes that the teacher acts as a "transmitter," imparting knowledge to the student through modeling and step-by-step instructions. Instructional conversation, on the other hand, views the teacher as more of a "facilitator," building upon the student's existing knowledge. The two approaches imply different roles for the teacher. Instructional conversation emphasizes the teacher's role in facilitating and guiding student learning through extended verbal interactions, rather than emphasizing the direct delivery of instruction (Goldenberg, 1992, pp. 5–6).

As the preceding discussion suggests, a primary issue in determining the educational needs of linguistically and culturally diverse children is understanding instructional interaction. Children from different linguistic cultures will use language in ways that reflect their different social environments. As we saw in Chapter 4, an investigation of mother-child interaction in preschool instruction periods, preschool free-play periods, and the home showed that the mothers of bilingual children, and not the children themselves, generally initiated interactions, and this was generally done in Spanish. On those few occasions when the children initiated discourse, their decision of what language to use was based on what the topic was (García, 1983).

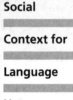

Social Context for Language Use

A comprehensive understanding of instructional interaction must therefore take into consideration the linguistic and cognitive attributes of that interaction. It must consider the child's surrounding environment. Recent data tentatively suggest that social context will determine:

1. The specific linguistic and metalinguistic information important for the development of each language.
2. The specific rules for social use of each language.
3. The roles assigned to each language (García, 1986).

Table 5.2 provides a more fully elaborated vision of instructional discourse in terms of its instructional and conversational elements.

Instructional Discourse for Diverse Students. Tikunoff (1983), in the report of the Significant Bilingual Instructional Features Study (SBIF), also addressed the issue of language use in language minority classrooms. The fifty-eight classrooms observed in the

Table 5.2 Elements of Elaborated Instructional Discourse

INSTRUCTIONAL ELEMENTS

1. **Thematic focus.**

   The teacher selects a theme or idea to serve as a starting point for focusing the discussion and has a general plan for how the theme will unfold, including how to "chuck" the text to permit optimal exploration of the theme.

2. **Activation and use of background and relevant schemata.**

   The teacher either "hooks into" or provides students with pertinent background knowledge and relevant schemata necessary for understanding a text. Background knowledge and schemata are then woven into the discussion that follows.

3. **Direct teaching.**

   When necessary, the teacher provides direct teaching of a skill or concept.

4. **Promoting more complex language and expression.**

   The teacher elicits more extended student contributions by using a variety of elicitation techniques—e.g., questions, restatements, pauses, and invitations to expand.

5. **Promoting bases for statements or positions.**

   The teacher promotes students' use of text, pictures, and reasoning to support an argument or position. Without overwhelming students, the teacher probes for the bases of students' statements—e.g., "how do you know?" "what makes you think that?" "show us where is says ___."

CONVERSATIONAL ELEMENTS

6. **Fewer "known-answer" questions.**

   Much of the discussion centers on questions and answers for which there might be more than one correct answer.

7. **Responsivity to student contributions.**

   While having an initial plan and maintaining the focus and coherence of the discussion, the teacher is also responsive to students' statements and the opportunities they provide.

8. **Connected discourse.**

   The discussion is characterized by multiple, interactive, connected turns; succeeding utterances build upon previous ones.

9. **A challenging, but nonthreatening atmosphere.**

   The teacher creates a "zone of proximal development," where a challenging atmosphere is balanced by a positive affective climate. The teacher is more collaborator than evaluator and creates an atmosphere that challenges students and allows them to negotiate and construct the meaning of text.

10. **General participation, including self-selected turns.**

    The teacher encourages general participation among students. The teacher does not hold exclusive right to determine who talks, and students are encouraged to volunteer or otherwise influence the selection of speaking turns.

Source: C. Goldenberg, *Instructional conversations and their classroom application: Education practice report #2.* National Center for Research on Cultural Diversity and Second Language Learning, University of California, Santa Cruz, 1992. Used with permission.

study were located in six school sites throughout the United States, and they included a variety of non-English languages. All classrooms in the study were considered effective based on two criteria: (1) they were nominated by members of four constituencies (teachers, other school personnel, students, and parents); and (2) classroom teachers were found to produce rates of academic learning time, a measure of student engagement on academic tasks, as high as or higher than those reported in other research on effective teaching.

Significant

▬▬▬▬▬▬

Features

Instructional features found to be unique to the education of language minority students included the use of two languages, special activities for teaching a second language, and teaching practices that took advantage of students' cultural background. According to the SBIF report, English was used approximately 60 percent of the time. Either the student's native language or a combination of the native language and English was used the rest of the time, with the percentage of English increasing with grade level. An additional significant instructional feature was the particular way in which the two languages were combined. Teachers of limited-English-proficient (LEP) students mediated instruction by using the students' native language and English for instruction, alternating between the two languages whenever necessary to ensure clarity of instruction. Moreover,

Integrative

▬▬▬▬▬▬

Approach

Tikunoff (1983) reports that students learned the language of instruction when engaged in instructional tasks expressed in that language. This integrative approach to developing English-language skills during ongoing instruction in the regular classroom contrasts with the more traditional procedure of "pull-out," in which LEP students leave the regular instructional setting to receive ESL instruction.

A study performed by Wong-Fillmore et al. (1985) provides a detailed analysis of the influence of classroom practices on the development of oral English in language minority students of Hispanic and Chinese background. In this study, 17 language minority classrooms (13 third grade and 4 fourth grade) served as sites. In these classrooms either the native language and English were used during instruction or only English was used during instruction. The researchers obtained specific measures of English-language production and comprehension over a period of an academic year. In addition, classroom observations documented the character of teacher-student and student-student interaction as well as the organizational features of instruction. These authors reported a series of potentially significant observations:

Becoming a Responsive Teacher

5.2 A Tapestry of Interaction

The 32 seventh graders sit in a large circle on the floor. The teacher, who is sitting on the floor with them, begins:

Teacher: What I would like you to do is to look around and call on people to add to what you've said—anything that you left out or that people remember that you haven't said yet....

LaWanda: Is this a thinking lesson?

Teacher: Ah, yes! Exactly. What I'd like you to do is think about your own thinking. That's exactly right.

[LaWanda raises her hand.]

Teacher: Go ahead.

LaWanda: [calling on another student] Elayne, what things does elephants has that is common to otters? Elephants and otters are— what does, what do they have in common?

Elayne: They both get hunted.

LaWanda: And?

Juan: Oh, they both need a lot of space.

LaWanda: What about your animal? The panda and the wolfs?

Marcus: They both need a lot of space....

LaWanda: Is there anything [else] they have in common?

Marcus: They're running out of food.

LaWanda: Their habitats are being destroyed?

Marcus: Yeah....

LaWanda: And the bear group. Is, is, why is your bear becoming extinct? Yolanda?

Yolanda: They kill them for their fur.

Becoming a Responsive Teacher *(continued)*

Robert: They're used as a food source in China.

LaWanda: I know, you said they're using them for a food source.

People eat them, right?

Robert: Right.

Teacher: [forgetting to raise her hand] It sounds like we need to—

[LaWanda frowns, doesn't respond. The adult teacher raises her

hand.]

[LaWanda calls on the adult teacher formally.]

Teacher: How do you know something is an animal?

LaWanda: Let's start with Juan. What do you think an animal is?

Juan: A creature that roams the earth.

LaWanda: Valencia?

Valencia: Anything that's alive, and breathing. Like plants aren't

really animals. They're alive and everything, but they're not really

animals. They can't walk around or do anything. They just sit there.

LaWanda: How do you know something is an animal? Marcus?

Marcus: Anything like mammals, reptile, amphibians, fish, even a

virus are animals.

LaWanda: Can you explain what a virus is?

Marcus: Actually, yes. But I'm sorry, a virus is not a living thing. But

animals can be microscopic.

LaWanda: Darius?

Darius: ...People are animals. Bugs, forest animals, every living thing

is an animal. Plants are like animals. Every living thing is an animal...

LaWanda: I have a question. You say almost everything is an animal.

Why do you say that?

Kaylan: Not human beings.

Darius: Every human being is an animal.

LaWanda: Which way do you mean? 'Cause of behavior?

Darius: Because they're living things, and living things are animals.

Teacher: Let's think about this for a minute. It sounds like everybody would agree that all animals are living things. Turning that around, are all living things animals? What living things are not animals?

LaWanda: [to teacher] Did you raise your hand? [To Chakita, who had gone to get a dictionary] Say it.

Chakita. [reading from dictionary] *Animal...any living being that can move about by itself, has sense organs, and does not make its own food as plants do.*

Meeting the Challenge

1. Reflect on your own experience as a student in U.S. elementary and secondary school classrooms. Does it match the version of American education portrayed above? If not, how does it differ, and what is the significance of that difference? What are these students being encouraged to learn that you may not have been?

2. Is this transcript an example of instructional discourse or direct instruction? Point out moments of interaction that suggest one or the other. Use Tables 5.1 and 5.2 for reference.

3. As the teacher of a fourth-grade class, devise a list of open-ended questions for discussion (versus fill-in-the-blank or known-answer questions). You may select any content field, such as language arts, math, science, social studies, and so on.

4. Develop a writing activity to engage the students portrayed in the above transcript. Be sure to take into consideration the emphasis put on social interaction in this classroom.

1. Instructional practices that were related to English-language development depended on the student's initial level of English proficiency. Therefore, instructional practices such as high levels of teacher and peer interaction were more related to enhanced English development for nonproficient speakers of English.
2. The instructional variables that were significant for the students differed. Students of Chinese background seemed to do best under classroom conditions in which they received independent help on English-language learning and in classrooms in which the instructional style was characterized by teacher-directed instruction. Students of Hispanic background demonstrated enhanced oral English-language development under classroom conditions in which there were more opportunities to interact with English-speaking peers.

In addition, these researchers reported that growth in English-language production and comprehension was related to several attributes of student-teacher interaction. Classrooms in which teachers adjusted the language level of their interaction based on student feedback were more likely to produce overall gains in English-language proficiency. Allowing and encouraging student participation and calling attention to the structure of language while using it were also characterized as instructional features that enhanced language development.

García (1989) examined instructional interaction for linguistically and culturally diverse students under conditions identified as academically successful. Previous research has suggested a potential mismatch between the culture of the home and the culture of the school (Ramirez and Castaneda, 1974). Similarly, research has suggested potential discrepancies in interactional styles (Ramirez and Castaneda, 1974; Zentella, 1981). Specifically, García (1990) examined instructional discourse in "effective" Hispanic classrooms. The study observed and analyzed the instructional styles of "effective" kindergarten, third-grade, and fifth-grade teachers of academically successful Hispanic (bilingual and nonbilingual) students. The results indicated that:

1. Teachers tended to provide an instructional initiation often reported in the literature. They elicited student responses but did so at cognitive and linguistic levels of relatively lower order.
2. However, once a teacher initiated a lesson, students were allowed to take control of the specific lesson topic and were able to invite interaction from fellow students.

Figure 5.1 diagrams the type of instructional discourse identified in this study, or student-dominated discourse, as compared to teacher-dominated discourse.

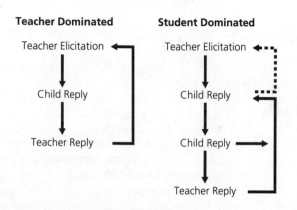

Figure 5.1 **Lesson Discourse Styles**

The finding that teachers were clearly allowing student-student interaction in the child-reply component of instructional discourse was considered significant. That is, the teacher was much more inviting of a student's "call" for peer response once the instructional interaction was set in motion. This finding is particularly important considering what we know about linguistic and cognitive processes. García (1983) has suggested that discourse strategies that emphasize student-student interaction are important to enhanced linguistic development. Moreover, McClintock, Bayard, and McClintock (1983) and Kagan (1983) have suggested that schooling practices which focus on cooperative child-child instructional strategies are in line with social motives in some Mexican American families. Such a style of instructional discourse would be of linguistic and cultural benefit to Mexican American students.

Student-

Student

Interaction

Student Writing Development

Like oral language, writing is crucial in schooling endeavors. As in all other areas of meaning making, children first attempt to manipulate written symbols during familiar, manageable activities. Children may continue to "just write" letters or to use "cursive" (wavy line) writing (e.g., when writing stories or extended texts in dramatic play) but attempt more precise encoding when

Naming

writing smaller units, especially names (Ferreiro, 1988). While such labeling can occur as part of dramatic play, naming is itself an activity of great interest to many young children and one in which they will invest considerable intellectual energy, especially if they are in the company of interested adults and peers.

Initially children's written names do not represent spoken words. Instead, they are letters that belong to certain people or things. That is, rather than trying to encode speech into graphics, children typically make meaningful graphics about what they say (e.g., "This is my Mama's name") (Dyson, 1983). Just as speech helps to organize and elaborate on the meaning of early drawn objects, so too it aids the early writing of names. For children, in fact, names are types of objects; they belong to people and things (Ferreiro and Teberosky, 1982).

Many publications describe for teachers the "developmental stages of writing," which progress from child scribbles to invented spelling. It is important to remind ourselves that these sorts of observations about children's writing are based on attention to superficial manifestations of development, not to the complicated process of representation. There is no linear progression in cognitive development, or in the development of oral and written language. Development is linked in complex ways to the whole of children's symbolic repertoires. Its evolution involves shifts of function and symbolic form and social give-and-take as children explore and gradually control new ways to organize and represent their world and to interact with other people about that world.

Putting writing in its symbolic place—seeing its emergence within the student's total symbolic repertoire—suggests, first, that in the early years children need many opportunities to

Symbolic

Repertoires

freely use the arts: to draw, play, dance, and sing. For young children, the most accessible media are those that most directly capture the movements of their own bodies, the sounds of their own voices, and the images made by their own hands, as lines, curves, and colors take form on paper. This teaching strategy requires a knowledge base of the child's language and culture.

First-grade teacher Karen Gallas (1991) describes an instructional unit on insects and their life cycles, beautifully detailing how drawing, painting, music, movement, drama, poetry, and storytelling, "each domain, separately and together, became part of [the children's] total repertoire as learners." In a classroom in which cultural, social, and language barriers might have kept children apart, use of the arts allowed individuals many avenues for learning, expression, and communication. Some children sketched insects, focusing on visual details, while others dramatized the life cycle of an insect, using their bodies to capture the changing shapes of life. Still others drew grass as seen from the perspective of an insect. New intelligences, in Gardner's (1985) sense, were visible as children forged new understandings through colorful images and felt movements, understandings that will surely enrich each child's later experience with print as a reader and a writer.

The curious world and the students themselves should be the center of the curriculum, not the "steps" in writing or reading. Indeed, making literacy the center of the curriculum may prevent reading and writing from becoming the dynamic, colorful intellectual and social tools they should be. Teachers must help connect print with the liveliness of students' use of other symbolic forms. In a series of books on her own classroom life with children, Paley (e.g., 1981, 1986) has illustrated how elementary students can collaboratively transform themes in their own lives into dictated texts, elaborated texts, and dramas. For many students, dictated words did not sufficiently represent the action, and they needed to share the action through media of their own voices and movements. Transforming their own texts into dramas allows students and teachers opportunities to find words for unarticulated ideas and previously unknown cultural representation of those ideas.

| Literacy as |
| a Tool |

Children's interweaving of language, culture, and thinking does pose developmental challenges, as eventually children must differentiate and gain control over the unique interactive powers of these domains. Therefore, it is important to talk to students about their expressive efforts and in this way to help them reflect upon their development. Indeed, many educators consider such reflective moments with a student about his or her ways of talking, playing, and writing to be an important means of supporting the student's development. What aspects of a student's imagined world are in the pictures? The print? In dramatized action? Which are still unarticulated, waiting for an interested other to help give them shape? At the same time, students must be allowed to remain in charge of their own intentions (Genishi and Dyson, 1984). Children feel no compulsion to put into written words the meanings they express through acting and talking. Their differentiation and control of these varied media is a gradual developmental process, one we nurture but cannot force.

| Importance |
| of Reflection |

In summary, the complexity of development is linked to the whole of children's symbolic repertoire. Unlike oral language, written language involves the use of a deliberately controlled system of symbols to mediate activity. An adult or an older student writing a letter is substituting written communication for the opportunity to speak in person to another individual. A student, however, who says she is pretending to write a letter may not be using written language to mediate her activity. To use Halliday's (1973) terms, the student is showing an awareness of the interactional function of literacy, perhaps, but the letter is fulfilling an imaginary as much as an interactional function. For some students whose native language is not written, such an act is quite revolutionary. It is more prop than mediator. To understand truly how development occurs, it would be necessary to understand how the child attempts to write the letter, the role of letter writing in the child's social activity, the role of other media in the accomplishment of the letter writing, and how the child's interaction with other people and with other media changes over time, as writing is transformed from primarily a prop to a mediator.

To both understand and foster written language development, we must view that development within the particularities of children's social lives. Indeed, we as adult writers may turn to media that seem to fit most comfortably the initial contours of our ideas before struggling to craft those ideas within the linear confines of print: we may draw, map, make gestures in the air, or even scrawl conversational language across a page. Written language emerges most strongly when it is firmly embedded within the supportive symbolic sea of gestures, pictures, and talk—that is, put simply, when it is embedded in our cultures.

> **Control of**
>
> **Written**
>
> **Symbols**

Conclusion

This chapter has attempted to highlight theory and related educational practices that provide a broad understanding of issues of importance to the schooling of diverse student populations: language, culture, and cognition. As indicated, the knowledge base in this area continues to expand, and it is in no way to be considered comprehensive as yet. Also, it would be an error to conclude that the data and theory which have emerged have been used as a primary basis in determining the educational treatment of these students. Too often, the education of these students has been determined instead by "political" variables (Hakuta and García, 1989). However, we can identify possible program and policy implications derived from research and theory highlighted by the foregoing discussion and by other previous reviews, such as August and García (1988); Cazden (1988); Goldenberg and Gallimore (1991); Hakuta (1986); Hakuta and García (1989); Hakuta and Snow (1986); Tharp (1989); Tharp and Gallimore (1988); Wong-Fillmore and Valadez (1985). This research suggests that:

1. One major goal regarding the education of culturally diverse students should be the development of the full repertoire of language, literacy, and cognitive skills.
2. For non-English speakers, time spent learning the native language is not time lost in developing cognitive and academic skills. Children can become cognitively competent best by building on previous language and cultural experiences and representations.
3. There is no cognitive cost to the development of multilingualism in children. Very possibly, bilingualism enhances children's thinking skills.
4. Education programs should be flexible enough to adjust to individual and cultural differences among children, particularly in the development of expected cognitive literacy domains.

We have seen that the linguistic, cognitive, and social character of the child develop simultaneously and that linguistic, cognitive, and social development are interrelated. Cognitive factors may act to influence linguistic and social development. Linguistic development (the ability to operate within the structural and pragmatic aspects of languages) may in turn act to influence social and potential cognitive functioning. The development of social competence directly influences the acquisition of linguistic and cognitive repertoires.

Figure 5.2 presents a model of the interactions among language, cognition, and culture as children develop. This interactive model is not meant to provide a definitive description of human development but simply to reflect the integrated nature of linguistic, social, and cognitive factors in learning. Changes in each of these domains may be attributed to changes in other domains, and in turn may further alter the character of the individual child. This and other similar conceptualizations of integrated development should guide our instructional efforts for all children, but they are particularly important as a foundation for enhancing the cognitive development of our diverse student populations.

Figure 5.2 **A General Integrative Model of Language, Cognition, and Culture**

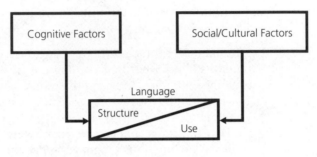

SUMMARY OF MAJOR IDEAS

1. The human mind is a library of symbols shaped by inherited mental structures and by representations of the world that come from our own individual experiences. The cognitive processes by means of which we acquire knowledge develop in conjunction with language background and sociocultural factors. To be effective, teaching and learning practices must consider the interactions of language, culture, and cognition.

2. Sociocultural theory is an international intellectual movement that draws on ideas from psychology, semiotics, education, sociology, and anthropology. Recent work in this area seeks a unified way of understanding language, cognition, culture, human development, and teaching and learning. Proponents of this theoretical perspective claim that the psychology of the individual learner is deeply shaped by social activity and that knowledge is always constructed in a social context. In this view, learning occurs in an interaction between individuals and an embedding context.

3. Because children use language in a sociocultural context to construct meaning, language and culture function as significant tools for cognitive development. Children whose language and culture do not match those of the schools are

usually forced to adjust their schema (their mental frameworks for understanding the world) or to construct new schema. Such negation of a child's language and culture also negates the child's cognitive tools and can seriously hinder cognitive development.

4. Contextualized language relies on more abstract linguistic and cognitive cues. Proficiency in the use of decontextualized language takes longer to achieve and is usually considered indicative of academic success. Limiting opportunities for children to learn in their first language may prevent them from developing the proficiency in decontextualized language required for academic achievement and for literacy.

5. Intelligence is generally defined as the ability of an individual's mind to acquire and apply knowledge. The traditional notion of intelligence presumes that it is an inherited intellectual capacity that can be measured by a test. Research into test bias over the past few decades has identified serious concerns about using intelligence tests to determine the intellectual capacity of culturally diverse students.

6. Research indicates that bilingual language ability may correlate with increased cognitive flexibility and metalinguistic awareness in children. Multilingualism should no longer be considered a cognitive and psychological liability in educational settings.

7. Effective teaching in culturally diverse classrooms involves organizing oral and literacy activities that develop students' communicative and cognitive abilities. Instructional discourse, or instructional conversation, is a teaching strategy that emphasizes discussion in the classroom. Compared to the didactic character of most formal teaching, it is structured to take advantage of natural and spontaneous interactions between teacher and students and among students.

8. In direct instruction as an approach to teaching and learning, the teacher transmits knowledge to students through modeling and step-by-step instructions. In instructional conversation, the teacher acts as a facilitator, building on students' existing knowledge and guiding learning.

9. Children from different language cultures will use language in ways that reflect their different social environments. Research indicates that effective instruction of language minority students includes the use of two languages in the classroom, special activities for teaching a second language, and teaching practices that take advantage of students' cultural backgrounds. Discourse strategies that emphasize stu-

dent-student interactions, rather than solely teacher-student interactions, may also enhance linguistic development.

10. As for oral language, student development in the use of written language is likewise tied to language and sociocultural factors. Unlike oral language, however, using written language requires children to control a highly abstract system of symbols. To help children develop literacy as a social and intellectual tool, teachers must connect the student's use of print with other, more concrete symbolic forms such as physical movement and oral language.

EXTENDING YOUR EXPERIENCE

1. Describe the approaches used by a teacher who is a "transmitter" and a teacher who is a "facilitator," and explain how these approaches differ. Have you had both types of teachers in your student career? Select two teachers who adopted contrasting approaches and describe your experience as a learner with each one. Remember to consider "teachers" you may have had outside the formal school environment, such music or art instructors and sports coaches.

2. As this chapter points out, sociocultural theorists argue that knowledge is not a fixed set of ideas passed from teacher to student but is created in the social interaction between teacher and student. What do you make of this claim? Do you agree or disagree? Note down the reasons for your position and discuss them in class.

3. Interview a psychology professor on your campus or a few friends who are majoring in psychology. Ask them to define the term *cognition* for you and to explain what they have learned about this concept. Then ask them to do the same with the term *intelligence*. Only after you have recorded all their comments, refer to a dictionary or encyclopedia and note the definitions given there. Report the results of your investigation to your classmates.

4. This chapter quotes research showing that children use their ability in their first language as a tool in order to learn how to think. What are the implications of this research for the education of language minority students, whose first language is not English?

5. What do you consider to be the goals of education? List at least three and be prepared to discuss them in class.

6. What patterns of social interaction do you expect to encounter in your own educational experiences? Think back over your past and present classroom experiences as a learner. Would you characterize your interactions as mainly teacher-student or student-student? Has this pattern of interaction shaped how and what you learn? In what way?

RESOURCES FOR FURTHER STUDY

Diaz, R. M., and Klinger, C. (1991). Towards an explanatory model of the interaction between bilingualism and cognitive development. In E. Bialystock (Ed.), *Language processing in bilingual children.* New York: Cambridge University Press.

This article is part of a volume that reports research into basic processes in language acquisition and use for bilingual students. The aim of the book is to describe the acquisition and development of a second language and to explain how such processes affect language awareness. In particular, the authors revisit the old issue of the impact bilingualism has on intelligence. Ultimately they conclude that in order to substantiate the relationship, more detailed research needs to be done. The theoretical foundation for this essay is directly associated with Vygotsky's work, with a minor twist.

Duquette, G. (1991). Cultural processing and minority language children with needs and special needs. In G. Duquette and L. Malave (Eds.), *Language, culture and cognition.* Philadelphia: Multilingual Matters.

This publication is a collection of recent research findings on topics that have generated more discussion of bilingualism and multiculturalism. Presenting an array of perspectives, the work lacks in-depth discussion of any single topic but does provide up-and-coming concepts and instructional approaches in the education of language minority students. Seventeen chapters are divided into three areas that deal with the cognitive process, the nature and role of language in culture, and aspects of teaching and learning. Taken together, all of these essays critically analyze and interpret how bilinguals acquire knowledge and develop academically.

Goldenberg, C., and Gallimore, R. (1990, September). *Meeting the language arts challenge for language-minority children: Teaching and learning in a new key.* Progress Report for 1989–90 to

Presidential Grants for School Improvement Committee, University of California Office of the President.

The authors argue that regardless of the techniques they use, teachers must be adequately prepared and have a solid grasp of the type of education they are delivering to students. The authors present an analysis of direct instruction (DI) and "instructional conversations" (ICs). The two methods differ: ICs are designated so that teachers can produce a natural flow of discussion while maintaining a productive and open learning environment; and DI is considered to be a closed learning environment because what the students are expected to learn has been determined by the teacher. These conclusions are drawn from a research site where extensive and collaborative effort to implement ICs was conducted.

Kagan, S. (1983). Social orientation among Mexican-American children: A challenge to traditional classroom structures. In E. García (Ed.), *The Mexican American Child* (pp. 163–182). Tempe: Arizona State University.

The competitive atmosphere that Mexican American students face in American schools runs contradictory to these students' cooperative nature. Such opposition has detrimental effects on most children who cannot understand the differences between the comfortable home and the competitive institution. Kagen offers some disheartening figures to argue the fact that the educational system is set up to fail Mexican American students. To counter such a record, Kagan discusses how Mexican American students can succeed when their classroom experiences fall within their cultural boundaries.

Tharp, R., and Gallimore, R. (1988). *Rousing minds to life: Teaching, learning and schooling in social context.* Cambridge, England: Cambridge University Press.

This book is considered a new and important contribution to the arena of multicultural education. It offers an improved model to advance the teaching and learning process. Using Vygotsky's theory, the authors present a series of educational concepts and discuss their impact and development in everyday interaction. One chapter examines the theory of teaching and the development of skills to improve teaching. The book centers mainly on the Kamehameha Elementary Education Program (KEEP) and explains how theory and practice developed this project into an exemplary model. It emphasizes the importance of education to society and stresses that the connection between theory and practice must be strengthened to ensure that future generations of students receive the best education possible.

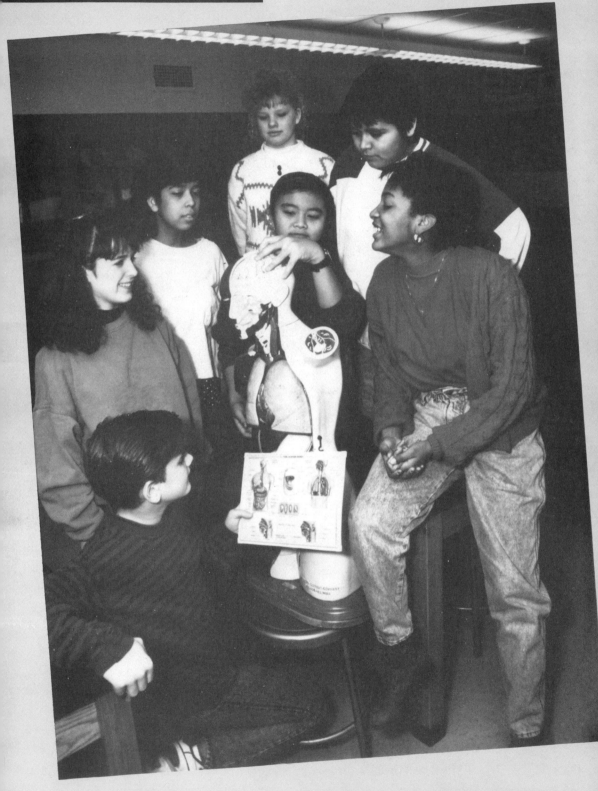

PART THREE

In order to address educational underachievement, U.S. schools must find ways to respond to the needs of culturally diverse students, and educators must understand the multiple cultures these **THE** students are learning to negotiate. Chapter 6 describes the relationships between students' family, school, and peer cultures and suggests how they combine to affect a child's engagement with learning. Which aspects of **EDUCATIONAL** the school environment help students bridge the gap between home and school? Which aspects impede such bridge building?

Chapter 7 turns our attention specifically to the role of the teacher, and Chapter 8 **RESPONSE** focuses on the attributes of the school itself. What are the characteristics of a teacher who effectively serves culturally diverse students? Can current methods of teacher preparation meet the requirements of the changing classroom? What insights can we glean from the study of effective schools? What can schools do to become more effective?

AN ECOLOGY

OF FAMILY,

HOME, AND

SCHOOL

CHAPTER 6

Focus Questions

○ What might prevent children from making successful transitions between their multiple cultures?

○ What is the role of the family in the socialization of culturally diverse children?

○ What are ethnic images, and how might they influence a child's concept of self?

○ How does the cultural systems approach account for persistent educational under-achievement among culturally diverse populations in the United States?

○ What is the difference between a voluntary and an involuntary minority population?

○ What are the advantages of scaffolding and the disadvantages of tracking and ability grouping?

> **"In the seed lies critical ingredients for future growth, but the initial nurturance of that seed also determines the same growth."**
>
> —CONRAD LORENZ

In any culture, important socialization practices formed within the context of family and home circumstances set the stage for a child's development for years to come. This chapter focuses on understanding students' multiple cultures and the transitions between them. In the process, I hope to provide information which will assist educators and others who work with students to build bridges between these cultures. We will look at family, school, and peer cultures, at the interrelationships among them, and in particular at how these cultures combine to affect children's engagement with learning. Of particular interest to us are the features in school environments which either aid or impede students' transitions between home and school.

The Meeting of Cultures

Before we can discuss the bridges we want to build across students' multiple cultures, we must identify the nature of the lines between these cultures, settings, and contexts. Some such boundaries are neutral in that sociocultural components experienced by the people on each side of the boundary are perceived as equal. When boundary lines are neutral, movement between cultures occurs with relative ease because the social and psychological costs to the individual are minimal. Alternately, when cultural borders are *not* neutral and separate cultures are *not* perceived as equal, then individual movement and adaptation across borders is frequently difficult because the knowledge and skills in one culture are more highly valued and esteemed than those in the other. Although it is possible for students to navigate nonneutral borders with apparent success, these transitions can incur psychological costs that are invisible to teachers and others. Moreover, when the psychosocial consequences of adaptation across borders become too great for individuals to face, cultural boundaries become impenetrable barriers.

Cultural

Boundary

Lines

Prior research generally has focused on families, peers, and schools as distinct cultural entities. We know that any one of these components can powerfully affect the direction in which students are pulled. For example, dynamic teachers, vigorous schools, and educational programs targeted to override the negative effects associated with low socioeconomic status, limited motivation, and language and cultural barriers can produce committed, interested, and academically engaged individuals (Abi-Nader, 1990; Edmonds, 1979; Heath, 1982; Johnson, 1981; Joyce, Murphy, Showers, and Murphy, 1989; Rutter, 1979; Sharan, 1980; Slavin, 1988, 1989; Vogt, Jordan, and Tharp, 1987; Walberg, 1986). Likewise, research on peer groups has described the potency and force with which members pull

Influence on
Students

young people toward the norms of groups (Clasen, 1985; Clement, 1978; Coleman, 1963; Eckert, 1989; Larkin, 1979; Ueda, 1987; Varenne, 1982). We know too that family indices, such as socioeconomic status and parents' educational levels are important predictors of students' engagement within educational settings (Jencks et al., 1972), as are cultural expectations and beliefs (Clark, 1983; Erickson, 1987; Fordham, 1988; Gibson, 1987; Hoffman, 1988; McDermott, 1987; Ogbu, 1983, 1987; Spindler, 1987, 1989; Suarez-Orozco, 1985, 1987; Trueba, 1982, 1988). In other words, we know a great deal about how aspects of families, schools, teachers, and peer groups independently affect educational outcomes. But we need to know how these worlds combine in the day-to-day lives of students to influence their engagement within school and classroom contexts.

As we attempt to create optimal school environments for increasingly diverse populations, educators need to know how students negotiate borders successfully—or, alternatively, how they are impeded by barriers which prevent their connection not only within an institutional context but with peers who are different from themselves. Figure 6.1 attempts to graphically portray the interaction of cultures which students must learn to negotiate.

Difference
Seen as
Negative

Although we still have much to learn about the complex interactions of culture, socialization, and education, at least now we are asking the right questions. That is, recent research focuses on understanding and facilitating successful interaction among cultures rather than discounting the attributes of minority cultures to accommodate majority cultures. Sadly, this has not always been the case. In Chapter 3 we saw that it has long been characteristic of U.S. schools to consider the unique

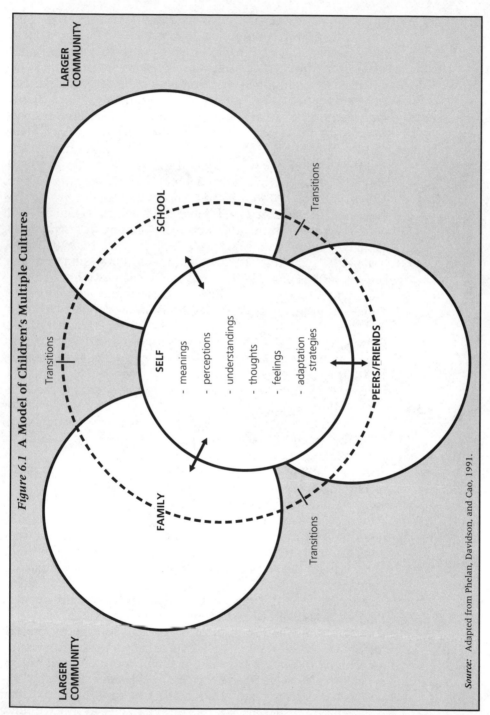

Figure 6.1 A Model of Children's Multiple Cultures

LARGER COMMUNITY

LARGER COMMUNITY

SCHOOL

FAMILY

PEERS/FRIENDS

Transitions

Transitions

Transitions

SELF

- meanings
- perceptions
- understandings
- thoughts
- feelings
- adaptation strategies

Source: Adapted from Phelan, Davidson, and Cao, 1991.

language development of culturally diverse children as a limitation. The social attributes of these children's family and home environments likewise have been viewed as detrimental to social, economic, and educational success.

The desired effect of "Americanizing" students and adults was to socialize the culturally different community. The early response was an attempt not only to change but also to segregate culturally diverse student populations to better serve the "diverse" children while not contaminating the other children. Segregated schools arose for "Negroes," "Mexicans," "Chinese," "Jews," "Germans," "Poles," and so on. Chapter 3 describes how American Indian students were segregated into government schools many thousands of miles away from their families and communities. The belief was that if schools could serve as the social institution which taught students English and succeeded in instilling "American" values, then the negative social and economic conditions of these populations could be eradicated.

Socializing
Difference

Americanization continues to be the goal of many programs aimed at culturally diverse populations in the United States. For students, Americanization means the elimination not only of linguistic and cultural differences but of an undesirable culture. This schooling approach does not recognize the significant boundaries that exist between a student's family, community, and school and the necessity of providing students with transitions and bridges across these borders. Instead, it considers only the most negative perceptions of these differences while ignoring the interaction which always has and always will take place when cultures meet.

The Role of the Family in Socialization of Children

Although the concept of Americanization has predominated, educational research during the last two decades has begun to regard ethnic culture as more than a target for elimination. Building on a foundation established by the noted anthropologist Margaret Mead (1937), more recent researchers have begun to explore socialization as a means by which cultural differences can be understood as opposed to eliminated (notably Gallimore and Tharp, 1989; Kagan, 1983; Lave, 1988; McClintock, 1974; Nieto, 1979; Valsiner, 1989; Wagner and Stevenson, 1982).

One of the most significant functions of **socialization** is the transmission of values. By socialization, Mead (1937) and

Becoming a Responsive Teacher

6.1   How Home Life Shapes Classroom Behavior

Maria was identified by her first grade teacher as very quiet. She hardly ever participated in classroom discussions. Even when the teacher specifically invited her to participate, she was very reticent. She did very well on individual activities, but the teacher worried about her shyness.

A videotaping project was scheduled for this room as part of a larger research project exploring the language development of the children in the classroom. The teacher made a request to make a special effort to video tape Maria's interactions during specific whole-group lessons. These videotapes indicated that Maria was paying close attention to the teacher, but never volunteered to participate and at times avoided eye contact with the teacher as the teacher attempted to make eye contact with her.

Another aspect of the videotaping captured students working together in small groups at "learning stations" that the teacher had throughout the room. During one of those tapings, Maria was observed leading a group of five students through the exercises at the station. She was quite verbal, asking other students questions and directing their activity. In addition, the students in the group looked to her for guidance, overtly requesting her assistance. Subsequent video recordings of similar small-group interactions in which Maria participated always included Maria playing an active or even a leading role. Yet, on the very same days, Maria continued to be non-participatory within any lesson activity led by the teacher.

The teacher was very interested in these contrasting behavior patterns. She watched the videotapes herself and was deeply puzzled by the distinct ways in which she saw Maria behave. Here was her shy Maria acting not shy at all—in many cases looked upon as a leader by her peers.

The teacher decided to ask Maria about her family circumstances and was not surprised by the results. Maria was one of a family of eight children—five older than she and two younger. Her parents and older brothers worked in the local fields, and Maria took major responsibilities for caring for her younger brother and sister whenever her mother was unavailable. Her family lived in a two-bedroom house that required sharing of space and related resources. Mom and Dad made the rules and enforced them, Maria said—you respected their wishes; you knew they knew best. Asked if Maria was ever consulted regarding her opinions, impressions, or suggestions, she politely indicated that Mom and Dad knew best: it would be disrespectful to offer any opinions.

The teacher understood Maria's hesitancy in responding to her during group lessons. The teacher as adult was a person to be respected—she knew best. Maria would likely never volunteer opinions or in any way challenge the authority of the teacher. However, in small-peer-group circumstances, she seemed to be making use of her caretaking skills—those practiced and appropriately regarded in her family. Without the appropriate attention of the teacher, this culture clash could have had negative educational consequences. The teacher's perceptions of Maria's choice not to respond during formal instruction could have led to an impression that Maria could not participate—that she was uninterested, unmotivated, or lacked the ability to handle the academic content in the lessons.

Needless to say, the teacher was appreciative of the newfound information. She understood that Maria worked best in small groups and that she needed to develop the ability to participate in larger groups led by adults.

Meeting the Challenge

1. Share the story narrated above about Maria with a few of your friends outside of this class. Relate to them the teacher's observations about Maria's two different behaviors, and ask your friends why they think she would act so differently in a small group. After they offer some ideas, explain to them the concept of home-school culture clash and how it may influence children's learning experience. Report the results of your discussion to your classmates.
2. If the above-described small "learning stations" had not been an established part of Maria's classroom, what impression would her teacher continue to have about her?
3. What is shyness? Compare your definition with those of your classmates. Describe learning environments that have made you feel reticent to participate and why.

McClintock (1972) refer to the process through which prescriptions (ideas about what one should do) and prohibitions (ideas about what one should not do) are transmitted to members of the social group. The traditional view of socialization generally presented in the literature has emphasized the family, including siblings and members of the extended family, as important agents of socialization. More recent conceptualizations (e.g., Hetherington and Parks, 1988) have considered socialization agents outside the family, such as teachers, peers, the media (especially television), and other persons with whom the child regularly comes into contact.

> **Agents of**
>
> **Socialization**

Several authors have discussed the variables associated with family background, family structure, and the broader social ecology that influence the socialization experiences of culturally diverse children (Keefe and Padilla, 1987; Knight et al., 1988; McClintock et al., 1983; Whiting and Edwards, 1988). The variables of family structure shown to be related to the parents' socialization goals include: (1) the strength of familial interdependence; (2) the pattern of status in relationships within the family; and (3) family size (see McClintock et al., 1983, for more details). Strength of familial interdependence consists of feelings of family solidarity as well as attachment and commitment to the family.

> **Family**
>
> **Variables**

There is some empirical evidence of particularly close family ties among Mexican American families (Keefe, 1979; Keefe, Padilla, and Carlos, 1979). For example, research comparing Hispanic families with Anglo-American families suggests that Hispanic families demonstrate closer relations and greater loyalty among members, more frequent visits among relatives, parental encouragement of family-centered interactions, fewer opportunities for children to invite friends over, less freedom for children to play away from home, greater disapproval of children who contradict authority, and fewer decision-making opportunities for children. Similarly, Johnson, Teigen, and Davila (1983) found parents of Mexican backgrounds to be relatively demanding and restrictive of children compared to Anglo-American parents. While we must be cautious of stereotyping all Hispanic families as showing strong interdependence among family members, McClintock et al. (1983) have speculated about the implications of this characteristic for a child's exposure to nonfamilial peers. Because of the greater emphasis on family-oriented interactions and within-family competition, it may be less relevant for a Hispanic child to compete with Anglo-American peers for recognition and rewards.

Cooper, Baker, Polichar, and Welsh (1991) report a related study of individual and cooperative socialization values. Their study explored the links between individuality and family connectedness in European American, Chinese American, Filipino American, Vietnamese American, and Hispanic American adolescents. Members of the three Asian American groups and the Hispanic American group reported much more concern for familial values than for the individual. In addition, members of these groups were much more likely to consider their siblings and peers, rather than their parents, as major sources of assistance and advice. Anglo-American adolescents were much more individualistic in their perception of themselves in the family and more likely to seek out parents and adults for critical advice or support. Similarly, Seginer's (1989) study of Arab adolescents found that older sisters play a key socialization role. These adolescents see their sisters as important consultants regarding the outside world, future plans, social relations, and education. Mothers are consulted only about pubertal changes, and fathers are consulted about permission, money, and political issues.

Still further evidence of cultural diversity in socialization practices comes from research on Native Alaskan families (Henze, Regan, Vannet, and Power, 1990). Interviews with Yup'ik families yielded a pattern of socialization that was not centered on the family. Socialization in this cultural group is organized around those activities which are required for survival: the "men's house" provides instruction for boys in all aspects of community life, and the home functions as the place where women transmit information to girls. This gender-separate social structure evolved over many years as the functions of each gender were organized to meet harsh survival challenges. The concept or structure of a core nuclear or extended family is nonexistent in this culture. Moreover, as in other findings regarding American Indian cultures (Tharp, 1989), Yup'ik children are expected to learn by carefully observing adults or older peers and siblings, without asking questions or interrupting activities. These diverse socialization practices have too often been interpreted as deviant instead of different. We review such examples here to reinforce the overall thesis that the environment of children outside of school sets the stage for lifelong patterns of

Diversity in

Socialization

social relations, including those which are important in the schooling process.

In this chapter, we will use the concept of "ecology" to gain an understanding of the family, community, and school environments of children. **Ecology** is the study of the relationships between an organism and its environment. Besides the ecology of the family and the community, the broader social ecology has also been suggested as an important determinant in the socialization of children (Kagan, 1984; Keefe and Padilla, 1987). The social ecology includes such factors as the urbanization level of the community in which the child lives, the socioeconomic status of the family and the community, the nature of the minority status of other cultural groups in the community, and prevailing views about these cultural groups in the larger society.

Factors in
Social
Ecology

In many ways, a more rural environment and/or an environment of relatively low socioeconomic status may lead to socialization experiences that foster interdependency, respect for others, and more sharing of resources. In contrast, a more urban environment may lead to socialization experiences that foster independence, competitiveness, and more reliance upon social supports that are external to the family. There has been some empirical demonstration of a relationship between the social behaviors of children and urbanization level (e.g., Kagan, Knight, Martinez, and Espinosa-Santana, 1981) and socioeconomic status (Knight and Kagan, 1977a). Minority status may lead to considerable variability in socialization experiences simply because children from minority populations generally have direct contacts with members of the minority group as well as with members of the Anglo-American majority (Ogbu, 1982, 1987).

An Ecological
System

The model of socialization briefly presented here suggests that characteristics of family background and structure and the broader social ecology are important determinants of the socialization practices to which children are exposed. We have barely scratched the surface of the many cultural differences that exist in socialization practices. Nonetheless, such conceptual rethinking of the child, the family, and the broader society as constituting an ecological system is a far cry from the traditional tendency to regard cultural difference as a negative social attribute to be eliminated. Enlightened understanding of diverse student cultures cannot be founded on the Americanization strategy: take all who are not "American" and make them "American." We will gain a clearer picture of the future for culturally diverse students in this country if we set aside issues of Americanization and instead concentrate on examining the nature of social variables and their relationship both to "cultural differences" and to educational practices and outcomes.

Ethnic Image and Its Effects

In recent decades, American society has made considerable progress in the area of race relations. White Americans have become more supportive of integration and racial equity (Jaynes and Williams, 1989; Schuman, Steeh, and Bobo, 1985; Smith, 1990; Smith and Sheatsley, 1984). Federal and state governments have instituted numerous programs to promote integration and to assist members of minority groups in their efforts to attain educational and economic equality of opportunity (e.g., through busing, affirmative action, minority contracting). In the next section we discuss the findings of research studies that explore the ethnic images that continue to prevail in our society despite this progress toward equity.

Ethnic Images in Society

Recent research has explored shifts in racial tolerance and changes in the images that people have of different ethnic groups. This research has addressed two questions: (1) What are the images that people have toward several major ethnic groups along various dimensions? (2) Do the images people have about ethnic groups influence their attitudes and behaviors toward those groups?

Two

Questions

In this research, the term **ethnic** is used as a general term to refer to six groups of people (whites, Jews, African Americans, Asian Americans, Hispanic Americans, Native Americans, and white Southerners) who are differentiated partly by race, religion, nationality, and region of origin. We use the term **images** rather than words such as *stereotypes* or *prejudices* in order to avoid some of the baggage that is frequently associated with these words. For example, stereotypes and prejudice are often considered to contain a component of irrationality and to involve such fallacious thinking as improper generalization, excessive categorization, and rejection of counterevidence (Allport, 1953; Jackman, 1973; Schuman and Harding, 1964). We use the term **ethnic images** to designate general beliefs that people have about cultural groups, in particular beliefs about group characteristics and attributes.

Contemporary relations between cultural groups in the United States cannot be understood without examining the images that members of these groups have about themselves and one another. The notion that Americans are approaching a color-and-creed-blind society is easily disabused by the data on ethnic images collected in the 1990 General Social Survey (Smith, 1990). First, these data indicate that people are willing and able to rate others on the basis of their ethnicity. Second, with one exception, minority groups were evaluated more negatively than whites in general. The one exception among minority groups was Jews, who were rated more favorably than whites on each characteristic except patriotism. No other group scored above whites on any characteristic. In this study, Jews were rated most positively overall (first on wealth, industry, nonviolence, intelligence, and self-support, and third on patriotism). Asian Americans and white Southerners were ranked next (second or third) on almost every dimension. Finally, African Americans and Hispanic Americans were ranked last or next to last on almost every characteristic.

Ethnic images also are associated with the social distance that people wish to maintain between themselves and the members of other groups. As the rating scale for each group moves from positive to negative, this research shows, people are less favorable toward living in a neighborhood where half of the neighbors are from particular groups and are less favorable toward having a close relative marry a group member. While all of the groups showed a significant relationship between ethnic images and desired social distance, the relationship between these factors for Jews and white Southerners was modest, whereas the relationship for African Americans, Asian Americans, and Hispanic Americans was strong.

This research shows that images about ethnic groups are significant predictors of support for racial integration and desired social distance. Despite the demonstrable progress in tolerance of cultural difference over the last several decades, ethnic images are still commonplace in contemporary U.S. society. On the whole these images are neither benign nor trivial. Most members of the majority population in the United States see most minority groups in a decidedly negative light on a number of important characteristics. African Americans and Hispanic Americans in particular receive very low ratings. These negative ethnic images in turn help shape people's attitudes toward civil rights and

Rating of

Ethnicities

Desired

Social

Distance

policies of racial integration. Ethnic images remain important determinants of public opinion on affirmative action, school desegregation, and many other group-related issues.

Effects on Children

How do ethnic images shape a child's personality? Following from the work of Smith (1991), **personality** may be understood as a structure that reconciles children's interpreted experiences and emotional states. Those experiences and emotions, in turn, are shaped by the social attributes ascribed to an individual by others. A sense of ethnic identity is part of that synthesis. In a world populated by people of many different ethnic backgrounds who often interact and conflict with each other, a child's developing sense of ethnic group identity is an important social issue. Several studies of the development of ethnic identity have focused both on children's ability to identify their own ethnic group and on their attitudes toward their own and other groups (McAdoo and McAdoo, 1985).

Research performed by Kenneth and Mamie Clark (1939, 1958) was perhaps the most famous inquiry into the development of ethnic identity, because the results became evidence that led the U.S. Supreme Court to declare racially segregated education illegal. African American and Anglo-American children aged 3 years and older were presented with pairs of dolls representing each ethnic group. On successive trials the children were asked to choose "which boy [doll] you would like to play with" or "which girl you don't like." They reported that most of the youngest children distinguished between the gender categories of the dolls and that both the African American children displayed a preference for the Anglo-American dolls. These results were interpreted by the justices of the Supreme Court as evidence that segregation resulted in the development of a negative sense of self among African American children. Studies conducted since the 1950s both confirm the Clarks' original findings (McAdoo, 1985; Spencer, 1989) and extend them to other minority ethnic groups including Native Americans (Beuf, 1977), and Bantu children in South Africa (Gregor and McPherson, 1966). In all of these cases, children of minority groups were more likely to prefer Anglo-American dolls.

Negative

Self-Concept

Importantly, these same studies have cast doubt on the notion that children from minority ethnic groups acquire a generalized negative self-concept. Beuf (1977), for example, reports incident after incident in which Native American children who

<table>
<tr><td>

Recognition

of

Inequalities
</td><td>

display a preference for Anglo-American dolls also demonstrate with devastating accuracy an understanding of the economic and social circumstances that make their lives difficult in contrast with the lives of Anglo-Americans. Five-year-old Dom was given several dolls representing Anglo-Americans and Native Americans (whose skins were represented as brown) to put into a toy classroom.
</td></tr>
</table>

> Dom: (holding up a white doll) The children's all here and now the
>
> teacher's coming in.
>
> Interviewer: Is that the teacher?
>
> Dom: Yeah.
>
> Interviewer: (holding up a brown doll) Can she be the teacher?
>
> Dom: No way! Her's just an aide.
>
> (Beuf, 1977).

In Beuf's view, children's choices when presented with pairs of dolls are less an expression of their self-concept than of a desire for the power and wealth of the Anglo-Americans with whom they have come into contact.

Other recent research has shown that when psychologists attempt to test their social concepts and self-concepts, young children's expressed ethnic preferences change according to the circumstances. Harriet McAdoo (1985) reports that the degree to which African American preschoolers show a preference for

<table>
<tr><td>

Environment

and Self-

Concept
</td><td>

Anglo-American dolls has decreased relative to the results obtained in studies performed prior to the 1960s. She does not speculate on the reasons for these trends, but the end of racial segregation and several decades of political and cultural activism in the African American community are likely candidates. This
</td></tr>
</table>

conclusion is reinforced by Beuf's (1977) finding that young children whose parents were active in promoting Native American cultural awareness and social rights chose dolls representing Native Americans more often than children whose parents took little interest in Native American affairs.

Additional evidence of the power of the environment to shape children's ethnic preferences comes from an experimental study that rewarded children 3 to 5 years old for choosing black versus white pictures of animals and people (Spencer and Horowitz, 1973). Initially all of the children showed a preference for white stimuli (both animals and people), but after training sessions in which they received symbolic rewards for either choice (receiving marbles that could be traded for cookies) they displayed a marked preference for black stimuli that remained intact over a period of several weeks.

In sum, the results of studies on ethnic identity indicate that children are aware of differences by the time they are 4 years old. At the same time, or not long after, they also become aware of and form judgments about their own ethnicity. Their attitudes toward their own and other people's ethnicity seem to depend both on the attitudes of their adult caregivers and the perceived power and wealth of their own ethnic group.

A Cultural Systems Account of Underachievement

So far, this chapter has discussed the relationship between culture and education by concentrating on issues of family, home, and socialization practices experienced by individual students. By its very nature, such a closely focused, "micro" approach concentrates on an individual student's social contact with parents, siblings, peers, and other representatives of social institutions. These interactions are seen as guiding and constituting the communicative, cognitive, social, and educational development of the student. In short, these interactions prepare the way for either educational success or educational failure.

An alternative to this close focus on the individual students is the "macro" approach proposed by a number of anthropologists and sociologists. This approach broadens the focus to one on cultural systems. A system is a network of interrelating elements that form a complex whole. A cultural system, then, is an interacting group of cultural elements. The **cultural systems approach** to education considers the organization of a society, specifically the roles and status assigned to cultural groups within a society,

Broader

Approach

to be a major determinant of educational underachievement (Gibson and Ogbu, 1991; Matute-Bianchi and Ogbu, 1987; Ogbu, 1982, 1987, 1991; Suarez-Orozco 1991). Known by such various names as the **structural inequality theory** (Gonick and Chinn, 1990), **institutional racism** (Ovando and Collier, 1985), the **perceived labor market explanation** (Erickson, 1987), and most notably the **secondary cultural systems theory** (Ogbu, 1991), this approach suggests that the specific social placement of a cultural group within the broader social fabric will directly affect the values, perceptions, and social behavior of members of that group.

As it pertains to the education of culturally diverse groups in the United States, the cultural systems approach suggests that members of minority groups become convinced by the overall social order that their "place" in society is distinctively disadvantaged. In essence, students from minority backgrounds recognize that they are generally perceived as less intelligent, as lazy, as dependent, and begin to take on these attributes themselves, particularly in response to perceptions held by social groups that wield political and economic power. As we saw in the previous section, the ethnic images that label some cultural groups as "lesser" have long persevered in our society despite outward signs of progress.

| Response to |
| Overall Social |
| Order |

Ogbu (1991) has been an important spokesperson for the cultural systems approach to understanding the disproportionate school failure of some minority populations in the United States and throughout the world. His analysis carefully distinguishes between immigrant or voluntary minorities and nonimmigrant or involuntary minorities (also called castelike, outcast, pariah). The term *minority* suggests a group that is smaller in the numerical sense. When considered in a social context, however, the term **minority** usually refers to a group that is subordinate to another dominant group and that is subject to a negative power relationship. Numerical majority does not guarantee a group dominant status. In Latin America, India, and Africa, for example, millions of native peoples historically were in a subordinate position to a minority of "ruling" colonial powers (Golnick and Chinn, 1990).

| Types of |
| Minority |
| Groups |

Ogbu's (1991) analysis suggests that members of voluntary and involuntary minority groups may live in the same society and experience the same circumstances: prejudice, discrimination, residential segregation, inferior education for their children, and exclusion from desirable jobs. However, voluntary minorities often do well in school and sometimes are more successful academically than students in the dominant group. In the United States, for example, East Asian students often test higher on standardized testing than Anglo-American students. By contrast, involuntary minorities such as African Americans, Hispanics, and American Indians consistently have problems in school, perform below grade level, and have higher dropout rates.

Ogbu and Matute-Bianchi (1986) begin to elaborate on a conceptual framework regarding the distinction between voluntary and involuntary minority groups. Table 6.1 presents these differing terms of minority status. Ogbu (1991) proposes that the cultural models for voluntary and involuntary minorities differ in five key elements:

1. A frame of reference for comparing present status and future possibilities (see Table 6.2).
2. A folk theory of getting ahead, especially through education (see Table 6.3).
3. A sense of collective identity (see Table 6.4).
4. A cultural frame of reference for judging appropriate behavior and affirming group membership and solidarity (see Table 6.5).
5. An assessment of the extent to which one may trust members of the dominant group and the institutions they control.

According to Ogbu, "the different cultural models resulting from these differing theories and frameworks are learned by the children and shape the attitudes, knowledge and competencies they bring to the school" (Ogbu, 1991, p. 141). Tables 6.2 through 6.5 describe the two types of minorities Ogbu identifies and chart their responses to and interpretations of prejudice and discrimination. The comparison presented in these tables is a synthesis of two articles by Ogbu and Matute-Bianchi (1986) and Ogbu (1991).

As a theoretical framework, this conceptualization of educational underachievement is worth considering. It allows us to begin to understand the reasons for different educational outcomes for different populations of students. For example, Suarez-Orozco (1987) proposes that the different Hispanic American groups—Mexican Americans, Puerto Rican Americans, and Americans of Cuban, Central American, and South American descent, as well as recent refugees from Central America—are distinct populations and should be understood as such. They face different issues and have different patterns of educational adaptation. Suarez-Orozco (1991) reports that whereas one-fourth of Mexican Americans nationwide aged 25 years or older had less than five years of schooling, the same was true for only 6 percent of other Hispanics. In the southwestern states, only 60 percent of Mexican Americans were reported to have graduated from high school compared to 86 percent of Anglo-Americans. Many Central American refugees, however, are experiencing school success.

An ethnographic study of two hundred Central American refugees at two school sites in San Francisco found that the ideas these new immigrants had developed about the nature of opportunity in this country allowed them to succeed academically.

Different

Educational

Outcomes

Table 6.1 Terms of Minority Status

VOLUNTARY MINORITY	INVOLUNTARY MINORITY
1. Moved voluntarily to host society.	1. Involuntarily incorporated through slavery, conquest, colonization, birth, and relegated to menial status.

2. Chose to emigrate for
  a. greater political freedom (including escaping death, imprisonment, torture, in homeland.)
  b. economic well-being.
  c. better overall opportunities.
	2. Did not choose to emigrate.

3. Experience in host society may include prejudice, exploitation, and discrimination in the form of
  a. residential segregation.
  b. inferior education for their children.
  c. job ceiling: exclusion from jobs when qualified, particularly desirable jobs.
  d. low wages.
  e. cultural and intellectual derogation.
	3. Experience in "host" society is one of prejudice, discrimination, and exploitation in the form of
	  a. residential segregation.
	  b. inferior education for their children.
	  c. job ceiling: exclusion from jobs when qualified, particularly desirable jobs.
	  d. low wages.
	  e. cultural and intellectual derogation.

4. Primary cultural discontinuities (cultural and language barriers):
  a. existed before minority group came into contact with dominant group.
  b. perceived as barriers to be overcome to achieve goals of immigration.
  c. specific; have to do with "content."
  d. cause initial problems for teachers, peers, and in learning but diminish over time; attributed to deficiencies in cultural assumptions.
	4. Secondary cultural discontinuities (cultural and language barriers):
	  a. arose as coping mechanisms after minority group was subjected to the power of dominant group.
	  b. perceived as markers of social identity to be maintained.
	  c. general; have to do with "style" (interactional, communication, cognitive, learning)
	  d. cause problems that do not tend to diminish over time; attributed to social opposition and negative personal characteristics.

Table 6.2 Frame of Reference for Comparing Present Status and Future Possibilities

VOLUNTARY	INVOLUNTARY

1. Positive dual frame of reference:
 	
  a. compare life in host society to homeland of "there."
 	
  b. perceive position "here" to be much better.
 	
  c. perceive themselves as foreigners, outsiders, guests.
	1. Negative dual frame of reference.
	
	  a. compare life to that of members of dominant group.
	
	  b. perceive position to be much worse.
	
	  c. perceive themselves as denigrated and subordinated members of dominant society.

2. Believe that "foreigners" must tolerate prejudice and discrimination of dominant group to achieve emigration goals; not highly influenced by it.	2. See no justification for dominant group belief that minorities are biologically, religiously, socially, and culturally inferior; highly influenced by it.

3. View situation as temporary because
 	
  a. they can return home.
 	
  b. they can emigrate elsewhere with wealth and credentials.
 	
  c. it will improve through education and hard work.
	3. View situation as permanent and institutionalized because
	
	  a. they have no other home.
	
	  b. they cannot leave present circumstances.
	
	  c. it will not improve through education and hard work.

4. Perception of job ceiling:
 	
  a. menial position "here" compared with worse position at home.
 	
  b. interprets exclusion from better jobs to "foreign" status, inability to speak the language, educated elsewhere.
	4. Perception of job ceiling:
	
	  a. menial position compared with jobs held by dominant group members who are better off.
	
	  b. interprets exclusion from better jobs to the fact that they are a disparaged group relegated to menial position.

Table 6.3 Folk Theory of Getting Ahead

VOLUNTARY	INVOLUNTARY
Value education, hard work, individual effort as a means of "making it" and diminishing discrimination. As a result, a. accept parts of the mainstream dominant culture. b. adopt the challenge of assimilating into the dominant culture.	Do not perceive education as a way to "make it"; believe it will require more than hard work and individual effort; believe discrimination is permanent. As a result, a. reject the value system of the mainstream dominant culture. b. develop a folk theory in opposition to the dominant group.

Table 6.4   Sense of Collective Identity

VOLUNTARY	INVOLUNTARY
Maintain sense of old social identity they had before emigration at least through the first generation. Thus, a. may not approve of certain aspects of dominant culture or want to be like dominant group members, but do not develop oppositional identity.	Form a new sense of peoplehood or social identity in opposition to the "oppressor." Thus, a. identity is forged from group's ancestral heritage and present interpretations of discrimination and denial of equal treatment.

Table 6.5   Cultural Frame of Reference for Judging Appropriate Behavior and Affirming Group Membership and Solidarity

VOLUNTARY	INVOLUNTARY

1. Alternation model: group members
  a. believe it is possible and acceptable to participate in two different cultures or two different languages for different purposes, alternating one's behavior to the situation.
  b. become acculturated without assimilating; dominant culture is not seen as threatening; necessary to cross cultural boundaries to achieve emigration goal.
2. Stress cultural values of "homeland" in family and community, but members
  a. must accept the rules of the host society
	1. Cultural inversion model: group members
	  a. assume it is not possible or appropriate for the same individual to participate in culture of the dominant group and in culture of the minority group.
	  b. experience linear acculturation; crossing cultural boundaries is seen as threat to minority identity, culture, and language.
	  c. communicate disapproval for "acting white."
	2. Stress collective efforts and collective struggle, so members
	  a. legitimate civil rights activities, as well as rioting to change rules because the rules don't work for them.

The school success of the Central American refugees was surprising. They "were routinely routed to overcrowded, understaffed, poor inner city schools, into a poisonous atmosphere of drugs and violence," where teachers were afraid of their students (Suarez-Orozco, 1991). They learned English quickly but were tracked into other low-level classes they had already completed in their own country. Yet many were highly motivated to persevere and to succeed in school. The Central American immigrants were perceived as desirable students by their teachers—eager to learn, appreciative, polite, respectful, and hard working.

According to Suarez-Orozco (1991), these recent Central American immigrants developed a dual frame of reference in which they compared their situation in the United States with that in their "homeland." Most perceived that they had more and better opportunities here. The students believed it was self-evident that the future was open to them. Their parents overlooked difficulties and emphasized the positive: the United States was fairer, they didn't have to pay for schools, hot lunch and libraries were free, and teachers seemed sincerely interested in their students. These immigrants developed a folk theory of "making it" in which *education* became the single most significant factor in getting ahead. This was in contrast to the method of getting ahead at home, which was "who you know." In the United States, they felt, it was "what you know." The students felt their parents were doing everything for them and felt a duty to succeed and to remove other loved ones from dangerous situations in the homeland. No matter how bad things were "here" and now, they were not as bad as at "home."

How to

Get Ahead

With a similar interest in distinctions between populations, Matute-Bianchi (1991) focused on diversity within a population of students of Mexican descent. In her ethnographic research at Field High School on the central coast of California between 1983 and 1985, she distinguished among five major categories of students of Mexican descent: recent Mexican immigrants, Mexican oriented, Mexican Americans, Chicanos, and Cholos. These categories emerged from interviews with teachers, counselors, aides, administrators, students of Mexican descent, and her own observations. She emphasized the different forms and functions of ethnic labels and self-identity in immigrant and nonimmigrant Mexican groups in the United States. She traced the relationships among these factors to variations in school performance. Matute-Bianchi (1991) observed a pattern of school

Patterns in

School

success among immigrant Mexican-oriented students and a pattern of school failure among nonimmigrant Chicanos. The two groups were perceived differently by teachers and students, and members of the groups themselves had different perceptions of what their futures held in terms of employment.

Specifically, Matute-Bianchi found five distinctive "cultural" groups within her student population:

1. *Recent Mexican immigrants.* Self-identify as "Mexicanos"; arrived in the last three to five years; refer to Mexico as home; came to the United States for economic opportunity; considered "unstylish" by other students; proficiency in Spanish (oral and written) tends to be an indicator of school success.
2. *Mexican oriented.* Maintain a strong identity as Mexicano; frequently Mexican-born, but have lived in the United States most of their lives; parents are immigrants; tend to be bilingual; adept at academic work in English, having received most schooling here; speak English with school personnel, Spanish and English with peers, Spanish at home; active in Sociedad Bilingüe; proud of Mexican heritage; many students with Spanish surnames who are in college prep from this group.
3. *Mexican Americans.* U.S.-born English speakers, much more American oriented than previous groups; may not speak Spanish unless necessary at home; participate in mainstream activities; tend not to call attention to their ethnicity; some of the most esteemed Mexican descent students in the school; described by staff as "totally acculturated."
4. *Chicanos.* At least second generation of their family in the United States; loyal to their own group and avoid school activities; call themselves "homeboys" and "homegirls," call academically successful students "schoolboys" or "wannabes" ("want to be white"); among the most alienated students in the school.
5. *Cholos.* Smallest group in the school; noted for culturally distinct style of dressing that represents an identity that is not Mexican or American; "gang-oriented" or "gang sympathizers"; "low riders" perceived to be gang members; feared and held in contempt by both other students of Mexican descent and mainstream Anglo-American students.

According to Matute-Bianchi, the successful students of Mexican descent were achievement and goal oriented. They saw a connection between high school success and adult success.

Characteristics

of Student

Groups

They defined success as having a nice car, a nice house, a good job, and no money worries. They wanted to go to college, although they were not sure of a career choice. They had Anglo-American and Mexican role models in school. Most stated that interest and support from their parents were essential to their school success. School success was defined as the result of regular attendance, doing homework, asking for help, getting along with teachers, and working "as hard as you can." Some had received support from teachers and counselors.

The Chicanos and Cholos expressed the desire to get good jobs but did not have an idea of how it was accomplished. They did not feel a connection to the future in a positive way and lived for the moment or the weekend. They doubted that they would graduate, even though they wanted to. They had little exposure to occupations other than the menial and physically difficult jobs of low status at which their parents worked. They could not think of one successful adult of Mexican descent whom they knew well. Although they expressed desire to do well, they exhibited behaviors that resulted in school failure: truancy, poor attendance, disruptive behavior, failure to bring books and homework, poor performance in class, failure to pass enough classes to maintain academic standing. They were apathetic and defiant of school culture.

Gibson (1991) describes similar findings in fieldwork carried out in St. Croix during the 1970s to study the relationship between ethnic identity, immigrant status, and school performance. Her results were similar to those found by Matute-Bianchi (1991). In the St. Croix public schools, immigrants were more successful than natives, even though they are similar in class status, color, and cultural background. This pattern shows up in other settings. In the United States, for example, "Asian Americans (Koreans, Japanese, and Chinese) are the only minority group whose academic achievement surpasses that of whites" (Lee, 1991). They exhibit higher college attendance rates and higher achievement scores than the majority. But Korean students, who in the United States achieve as well as Japanese students do, in Japan have much lower achievement rates than Japanese students. In Japan the college attendance rate of Korean high school graduates was less than 60 percent that of Japanese high school grads. Lee (1991) suggests that the historical experience of Koreans in their two host societies provides valuable insight into the effect of cultural systems on academic achievement.

Success for

Immigrants

Specifically, Lee argues, Koreans have had an increasingly positive image in the United States for two reasons: (1) Korea has become of strategic and economic importance to the United States, and (2) most Koreans in the United States are educated people with middle-class backgrounds. With the exception of physicians, however, Koreans have found it difficult to enter the U.S. middle-class mainstream because of the language barrier, their inability to transfer skills acquired in Korea, and discrimination against them in large businesses.

In Japan, Koreans have been legally entitled to public education since 1965. By 1981, 80 percent of Koreans were attending Japanese rather than Korean schools, hoping a Japanese education would contribute to upward mobility and integration. Korean schools do not have the status of Japanese schools, and their graduates are turned away from qualifying exams for universities and are not eligible to attend barber, beauty, and chef schools. Within Japanese schools, Korean students are discriminated against by staff, by other students, and even by textbooks, which portray Korea in a negative way and distort its history. Japanese children are brought up to consider Korean culture a "lower" culture. More than half of Koreans use Japanese names to avoid harassment by Japanese students. Teachers often treat Korean students with contempt and feel very negatively towards them. Korean parents must pledge that their children will not disturb order, and if tuition is required, Koreans must pay more than Japanese. According to Lee (1991), Koreans are perceived to have and actually assume a disadvantaged role in Japanese society.

Korean Students in Japan

However, American teachers and American students and their parents perceive Koreans in a completely different light. American teachers welcome Korean students. They are praised for qualities that many teachers feel are lacking in Anglo-American students. They have proven themselves to be highly successful academically. Educators attribute this to the high standards held by East Asian parents and to strict discipline and close management of their children's time. They believe that once East Asians overcome the language barrier, they will get jobs. American parents perceive East Asian children as setting good examples for their own children and welcome them as friends (Ogbu, 1991).

Korean Students in the United States

In the United States, as we saw above, Koreans have higher college attendance rates and higher achievement scores than Anglo-American students. Korean parents value education and have high expectations for their children, often teaching them at home before they are of school age. In Japan, Koreans are a castelike minority with little power in their host society. In the United States, Koreans are one of the most successful immigrant minorities.

Although some claim (Erickson, 1987) that Ogbu (1986) sees "a social revolution" as the only way out of the situation involuntary minorities find themselves in, Ogbu (1991) does not in fact reach that conclusion. What he does stress is that educational practices and programs must be based on appropriate research. He points out that many intervention programs are based on the idea that ethnic minorities are "culturally deprived," "culturally deficient," or "socially disadvantaged" and that the school's role is to "redeem" them. He differentiates between "improvement research" and "explanatory research." He is interested in providing explanatory research, in particular comparative ethnographic research, "the long range goal of which is to provide knowledge for better and more effective educational policy as well as for preventative and remedial efforts" (Ogbu, 1987). He cautions against instigating educational change without first understanding both the "micro" and the "macro"—the individual and the societal—aspects of underachievement in ethnic minority populations.

Research
That Explains

Educational Implications

Mehan (1988) makes a distinction between ethnic studies (the study of ethnic groups) on the one hand, and a sociocultural approach to language, culture, and education on the other. This distinction does not diminish the significance of ethnic studies. From the point of view of schooling practices, however, approaching contexts of learning for culturally diverse youth with a focus on ethnic studies poses difficulties. It can be dangerous. Because it is impossible for educators to acquire complete ethnological knowledge of the student groups they will encounter, the knowledge they do acquire tends to be laden with stereotypes. It is also dangerous because these stereotypic notions often lead to the assumption of cultural deprivation—that because a culture is characterized as different, it is characterized as deficient. Educators should focus on understanding the intersection of the school context with the student's family, home, and community contexts, not only on understanding the differences among ethnic cultures.

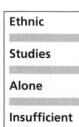

Ethnic
Studies
Alone
Insufficient

Building Bridges Between Diverse Cultures

In Chapter 2 we saw how school, and certainly the classroom arrangements within it, can be seen as analogous to a culture. The classroom has many explicit cultural elements, but there are also hidden cultural dimensions that Sue Philips (1984) and others have described. Children themselves often feel deeply the numerous cultural demands of the school.

Some classic work has been done in this area by William Labov (1972). He looked at the same children across different social domains of the school culture. Specifically, he observed educational testing encounters arranged in a number of ways. The theme of school culture is clear in his work: depending on the context in which one observes a child, one obtains a different view of that child. For example, in one intelligence testing situation (using a test such as the Weschler) the IQ tester places an object (e.g., a toy airplane) in front of the child (in this case a third- or fourth-grade African American student). The tester says, "Tell me everything you can about this." There is a twelve-second silence. Twelve seconds is not a very long time in everyday life, but during an IQ test or in a classroom environment twelve seconds is a very long time. So the tester changes the question: "What would you say it looks like?" The child says nothing for eight seconds. When one reviews such a transcript, and examines the testing results from such an event, one is likely to conclude that the child lacks critical cognitive and linguistic abilities.

But Labov did not stop there. He looked at the same child in a number of different domains. Labov thought that this outcome might have something to do with the relationship between the African American child and the white tester, so he brought in an African American tester from the neighborhood to remove the racial boundary. When he repeated the test, with the tester on one side of the table and the child on the other side, the results were not much different. Then Labov did something that is now famous: he removed the trappings of power from the situation. He took the children away from table, removed the adult, and observed the children interacting among themselves on the floor. Their verbal production increased incredibly. Much like Philips (1982), who found communicative differences between American Indian students and school, Labov found significant communicative differences between the domains of the school itself. In short, if you look at a child in only one situation, you get only one kind of picture.

> Effect of
>
> School
>
> Culture

Moll and Diaz (1986) contributed to this understanding of context specificity. They observed children, not at home and at school, but under different constraints of instruction. The children were enrolled in a bilingual program, the goal of which was to allow Spanish-speaking children to acquire English as quickly as possible. At this school, children had two different teachers. They were taught by one teacher in English and by another in Spanish. Moll and Diaz (1986) videotaped lessons in both settings and asked each teacher to watch the videotapes of the other. The Spanish-speaking teacher was appalled when she saw the children in the English-speaking teacher's classroom: they were not reading. They were engaged in drill and practice activities, and very little cognitive activity was taking place. In the Spanish-speaking classroom, where the children were being given comprehension activities, they were reading in Spanish. Moll and Diaz discussed this situation with the Spanish-speaking teacher and hypothesized that reading is specific to the domain of language. So they performed some experiments. They had the children apply the reading comprehension skills they had acquired in Spanish to read in English. In doing this, by the way, they violated one of the basic tenets of bilingual education: keep the two languages separate. But when they let the children call upon all the intellectual resources they had available, their progress was remarkable. The students began to comprehend written English very nicely, even though they did not have complete mastery of the language. A bridge between the two cultures was developed in support of the goals of the school.

| Effect of |
| Instructional |
| Constraints |

Ron Gallimore's study of the Kamehameha Early Education Program, or KEEP (1984), is another example of how bridge building can be accomplished. One recommendation is to allow cultural elements that are relevant to the children to enter the classroom. This is the practice of scaffolding, which was introduced in Chapter 2. Scaffolding enables children to move through relevant experiences from the home towards the demands of the school. For example, in the KEEP project, teachers incorporated cultural elements into the classroom at the beginning of reading lessons, which were divided into three parts. The first part centered on the children's experiences. The children talked about their home experiences and things they knew about in the world, prior to reading a book. Then the teacher made transitions from those experiences to the book and directed the children to read the text that was in front of them. For example, the teacher would say something like: "We're going to read article x. As you read this, can you think of

| Scaffolding |

three things that he says are important about culture?" The students then read the text silently, not aloud, in order to avoid pronunciation difficulties. Now the children have been oriented toward the text. In the end, the children's home experiences are linked with the text reading.

Close discourse analyses of lessons that utilize scaffolding are very interesting: the questioning structures change. In the early part of the lessons, questioning structures are open-ended. Joint responses and joint progressions of narrative are allowed. By the end, they look like traditional lessons. The children have been slowly guided through the lessons in a very microgenetic way, so they can decide what is important. The teaching is done in such a way that the children's culture, interest, and experiences are preserved.

Tracking and Ability Grouping

Ability grouping is managed by elementary school teachers within classrooms, and tracking distributes students among classrooms, usually in secondary schools. Both of these practices bring together groups of children with similar perceived academic abilities—for example, slow readers versus fast readers, and high achievers versus low achievers. Many studies (Oakes, 1984; Rueda and Mehan, 1987) indicate that there is a pattern in the distribution of children between different tracks: children from low-income and minority backgrounds invariably end up in lower tracks, and children from middle- and upper-income backgrounds are in upper tracks. Educational practices are also differentially distributed between these tracks. Students in higher tracks receive challenging educational opportunities; students in lower tracks receive much more practice and drill.

> **Patterns in**
>
> **Student**
>
> **Distribution**

If children were also given equal opportunity to change tracks, this finding would not be quite so troublesome. But children get locked in: if a child is placed in a low-ability group in first grade, he or she will remain there throughout elementary school. If a student is in a vocational track in the seventh grade, that student is unlikely to change to a college-preparatory track. The school, instead of supporting the democratic ideal of a classless society, tends to reproduce the divisions within society.

The question is, why do the practices of tracking and ability grouping practices continue? Most of these activities are organized as practical solutions to a very difficult problem: too many children in class, not enough resources, and the existence of distinct levels of student ability. But the recent research supports heterogeneity, as opposed to homogeneity, in grouping. There is extensive evidence that mixed groupings have a particularly beneficial result for those who need it the most: students from low-income backgrounds who have trouble with school. In Spencer Kagan's review (1986) of the literature, study after study shows that children who do not perform well academically succeed best in heterogeneous groups. That idea resonates very well with parents of culturally diverse students but not with middle- and upper-income parents (Oakes, 1989). These parents think their children will suffer academically under those arrangements. However, recent research results demonstrate that middle- and upper-income children from majority populations are also more likely to succeed in heterogeneous groupings rather than in homogeneous groupings (Slavin, 1989). That wonderful adage—that the best way to learn something is to teach it—truly does work in practice. When children are involved in the teaching process, they learn as well.

The extent to which tracking and ability grouping have become institutionalized practices is demonstrated by a poignant account related by Trujillo (1988), who was a high school principal. He tells of two counselors, advising two almost identical youngsters in preparation for the tenth grade. They were both Filipino, both sets of parents had limited English-language skills, and the students had almost identical records and test scores. As he watched, the first counselor talked the first student and his parents out of the program they had signed up for. He took the youngster out of algebra and talked him into another year of remedial math. He talked the parents out of college prep science class and put their child in a basic English class. In the other conversation, however, the second counselor began describing the courses that the second youngster would need when he enrolled in college. The student was trying to get out of taking the harder classes, but the counselor insisted that she would meet with the student once a week to see how he was doing. The father protested, saying, "We are very poor people. College is not one of the goals we have for our child. We could not afford that, and we don't want to deceive him." And the counselor said, "Don't worry about that, we'll get him a scholarship."

Both counselors were probably trained in the same program with the same methodology. The techniques and rationale the first counselor used to talk the student out of a college prep curriculum were classic; they would make a beautiful chapter in the counseling textbook. In technique, there was nothing the counselor did wrong, and he could use the test scores to prove

Benefits of Mixing Ability Levels

Beliefs That Limit Students

Becoming a Responsive Teacher

6.2   A Community of Learners

Every day, during a one-and-a-half-hour science segment in a self-contained sixth grade class, and in two seventh grade and one eighth grade science classrooms, students engage in collaborative research in which they participate in designing their own curriculum. The class is organized into small research groups. Each group is responsible for investigating and writing about one subtopic from a larger content area. For example, different groups chose to study condors, whales, otters, and wolves during a sixth grade class unit on endangered species.

The students conduct their research with the aid of an extended community that includes all members of their own classroom, students and teachers in other project classrooms, research staff and scientists at the University of California at Berkeley, and various experts, such as forest rangers, furriers, and zoo personnel, whose work is related to the students' research. The project provides a core set of resources on environmental science (including books, articles, newspaper and magazine clippings, videotapes, and videodiscs), which the students and teachers supplement with other materials.

As the students gather information, adults guide them in note-taking, outlining, and writing, as well as in learning how to read technical material. Adults also intervene when students appear to need help working together on group tasks.

To aid students in their research, the project provides a state-of-the-art computer environment based almost entirely on commercially available software. Each classroom contains six or seven Macintosh computers and a laser printer. Students are provided word processing, spreadsheet, database, and graphics applications; access to a scanner; and a computer-based index to the core set of resources (known as a "browser") to help students locate research materials.

An electronic mail package allows students to send messages and requests for help or information to their peers, their teachers, students and teachers in other classrooms, and even to project staff at the university. When appropriate, these questions are forwarded to university scientists who have agreed to be available for occasional consultation.

Once the students have recorded the results of their research, they reassemble into "jigsaw learning groups" composed of one "expert" from each of the previous research groups. Students then take turns leading discussions on their areas of expertise, using the materials prepared by their respective research groups.

This collaborative research approach differs from more traditional approaches to teaching in several ways. The approach intentionally favors depth over breadth, and the process of learning over the learning of content only. Given the rate at which knowledge is changing, particularly in the sciences, we believe that a student who merely acquires current knowledge will be inadequately prepared for future demands in school, at work, and as a responsible citizen.

Meeting the Challenge

1. Working with a few of your classmates, draw a diagram of this community of learners from the point of view of one of the students. Draw connecting lines to all the major groups of people the student can call on during the research process. Draw dashed lines to the research materials and technology available, showing the pathways by which the student would gain access to them. Compare your group's diagram with diagrams drawn by other groups.

2. With your whole class, discuss the extent of organizing, planning, and networking that was required by the educators who established the learning community described above. What barriers to education are being crossed here? How, do you think, have some of these interconnections between groups been set up?

3. Develop a list of broad content areas that would be amenable to the process of learning in such a community. For each area, brainstorm with your whole class all the resource groups you can think of that could contribute to the learning network.

4. As a teacher of the students described above, how comfortable would you be with the hardware and software used daily in your classroom? List the items you would need to learn more about. See if one of your classmates can shed light on your questions.

that the youngster belonged in those remedial classes. There seemed to be two belief systems operating: the second counselor had overcome the belief system that she was taught, and the first counselor was still very much a part of that belief system. In short, Trujillo (1988) concludes that the majority of educators in the U.S. schools know their subject matter and are fairly well steeped in the appropriate methodologies. But the biggest problem is that they do not understand the students they will be teaching: "In other words, the people who do well with children are those who understand them—who don't demean them" (Trujillo, 1988).

Conclusion

Educators must understand and digest the fact that children, all children, come to school motivated to enlarge their worlds. Educators start with the many cultures of students. Educators should not look at them, certainly not initially, as organisms to be molded and regulated. Educators should view them to determine what they know, what they seek to know, and what experiences can be used as the fuel to fire the process for enlargement of interest, knowledge, and skills. Educators must not look at students in terms of deficits: what they do not know but need to know. Far from having deficits, they are asset rich.

SUMMARY OF MAJOR IDEAS

1. Students must learn to negotiate the boundaries between the multiple cultures of family, school, and peers. Depending on the nature of the boundary, culturally diverse students may face great psychological and social consequences when making the transition from one culture to another. Sometimes the psychosocial costs are so great that a boundary becomes a barrier students are not able to cross. A complete understanding of underachievement among minority populations requires a full consideration of the interactions among culture, socialization, and education.

2. Socialization is the process through which prescriptions and prohibitions are transmitted to members of a social group. The family is a major agent of socialization, along with teachers, peers, and the media, especially television. Research

shows much diversity in socialization practices across cultures. A child's socialization sets the stage for lifelong patterns of social relations, including those important in schooling.

3. Ecology is the study of the relationships between an organism and its environment. The socialization of children is determined not only by the ecology of the family and the community but also by the broader social ecology. The social ecology includes such factors as the urbanization level of the community, the socioeconomic status of the child's family and community, and prevailing societal views about cultural groups in the child's community.

4. Ethnic images are the general beliefs people have about the characteristics of cultural groups. Research indicates that ethnic images are tenacious in the United States and that people are willing and able to rate others on the basis of their ethnicity. Ethnic images are significant predictors of support for racial integration and desired social distance and for public opinion on affirmative action, school desegregation, and other group-related issues.

5. Personality is a structure that reconciles children's interpreted experiences and emotional states. The social attributes ascribed to the child by others may greatly influence this process of reconciliation and result in a particular sense of ethnic identity. Research shows that children are aware of attitudes toward ethnic differences by the age of 4.

6. The cultural systems approach to education considers the organization of a society, specifically the roles and status assigned to cultural groups within a society, to be a major determinant of educational underachievement. This approach suggests that peoples' values, perceptions, and social behavior are directly influenced by the status the larger society grants to the cultural groups to which people belong.

7. A voluntary minority group is a population whose members moved voluntarily to the host society. An involuntary minority group is a population whose members were involuntarily incorporated through various means that degrade their status.

8. Members of voluntary and involuntary minority groups may live in the same society and experience similar effects from discrimination and prejudice. Their responses may widely differ, however, depending on five aspects of the cultural model under which they operate: (1) a frame of reference for comparing present status and future possibilities; (2) a folk theory of getting ahead, especially through education;

(3) a sense of collective identity; (4) a cultural frame of reference for judging appropriate behavior and affirming group membership and solidarity; and (5) an assessment of the extent to which one may trust members of the dominant group and the institutions they control. Children absorb these cultural models and bring them to bear in their schooling experiences.

9. A focus on ethnic studies is not sufficient for addressing the educational needs of culturally diverse students because it is too often based on stereotypes. Educators must instead adopt a broader sociocultural approach to language, culture, and education. It is necessary to understand the child, the family and community, the school, and the larger society as constituting an ecological system with interacting elements.

10. The cultural arrangements of the school can affect student performance. Instructional strategies such as scaffolding that provide a bridge between home and school can allow culturally diverse children to make a successful transition to school. Tracking and ability grouping, on the other hand, perpetuate cultural barriers and make it more difficult for such students to succeed academically.

EXTENDING YOUR EXPERIENCE

1. Study the diagram in Figure 6.1. How might a culturally diverse child's self-concept change as he or she crosses the border between one culture and another? What, specifically, are the psychological costs of crossing a "nonneutral" border? Describe any such experience you may have had. What or who did you confront while trying to negotiate this border? What, if anything, helped you build a bridge and make the transition?

2. With a small group of your classmates, review the concept of social ecology discussed in this chapter. Why will it be important for you as an educator to understand the environmental context—family, community, and peers—for each student in your classroom? With your group, develop a list of all the possible *environmental* factors that might affect a student's ability to achieve academically. Think of a male or female student at a particular grade level, and be as specific as you can.

3. Examine various media such as newspapers, magazines, films, and television shows for portrayals of ethnic images. Bring

some of this evidence to class and compare it with material gathered by your classmates. With this evidence in mind, discuss the implications of research quoted in the chapter indicating that a child's awareness of and attitude toward his or her own ethnicity is formed by age 4.

4. Observe an ESL classroom. Note the teacher's positive strategies for building bridges across language and cultural boundaries and for providing scaffolding. In writing, describe the students' reactions to these strategies.

5. In your own words, explain the difference between a voluntary and an involuntary minority status. Read closely the descriptions given in Tables 6.1 through 6.5 and select a contrast between voluntary and involuntary minority status that you find particularly striking. How might this contrast in cultural experience influence a child's academic success?

RESOURCES FOR FURTHER STUDY

Mead, M. (1937). *Cooperation and competition among primitive people.* New York: McGraw.

This landmark collection written by different authors and interpreted by Mead provides a framework useful for the collection, analysis, and theorization of distinct cultures. Each article in the volume is strong and can stand on its own merits. The connecting thread of the book is Mead's point of view. She argues that to truly understand individual behavior, one must first recognize and understand the patterns by which members of the group pass on knowledge and culture to the individual. The subjects in the book are from distinct parts of the world yet share similarities. Overall, this publication opened a new window on how research into different cultures should be analyzed and presented.

Ogbu, J. (1987b). Variability in minority school performance: A problem in search of an explanation. *Anthropology and Education Quarterly, 18(4),* 312–334.

Based on a comparative analysis, this article suggests that the school adjustment and academic performance of minority students are directly influenced by differences encountered outside the school. Minority students, it is argued, perceive economic and social opportunities for the future to be dismal. This view interferes with school work and consequently affects academic performance. Ogbu provides a historical account through educational anthropology. Such background strengthens the author's case that minority students perceive society differently and that such views affect their schooling.

Ogbu, J., and Matute-Bianchi, M. E. (1986). Understanding sociocultural factors: Knowledge, identity and school adjustment. In Bilingual Education Office, California State Department of Education (Ed.), *Beyond language: Social and cultural factors in schooling language minority students*. Los Angeles: Evaluation, Dissemination, and Assessment Center, California State University.

The central theme of this work deals with the issue of why minority students experience a continual disproportionate school failure. Why do some minority groups do better than others? What historical and social forces affect the perspective some minority groups have of education? Why do such failures keep on persisting? The authors present two cases to illustrate the perceptions such students have of the U.S. educational system and the consequent response of these students to their educational opportunities and job outlook.

Weis, L. (1988). *Class, race and gender in American education*. Albany, N.Y.: State University of New York Press.

School experiences set the tone for how future citizens function in society. The expectations students have about school are influenced by the students' gender, race, and class background. This book discusses some of the most heated issues, with in-depth ethnographic and statistical data, that are at the core of the educational system. It describes the traditional debate between the "culturalists" and the "structuralists" and elaborates on both to enrich and promote discussion between the two camps. Such different frameworks constitute a book full of tension with a broad range of perspectives and goals.

THE EFFECTIVE TEACHER:

PREPARATION,

ASSESSMENT, AND

CHARACTERISTICS

CHAPTER 7

Focus Questions

○ How are teachers of culturally and linguistically diverse students currently prepared in the United States, and what institutions are responsible for assessing their competence?

○ What are the patterns in state credentialing available for teachers of bilingual education and English as a Second Language?

○ What are some of the competencies, roles, and responsibilities that have been identified for teachers of language minority students?

○ How has the connoisseur model been implemented in at least one local school district to further the professional development of inservice teachers?

○ What attributes in the domains of knowledge, skill, disposition, and affect characterize effective teachers?

"You are the giver of a lifelong gift. An impulse; an enduring tool; a prolific engine called learning. The infectious transfer of enthusiasm."

—F. X. TRUJILLO

Today's educational professionals have a common concern regarding the education of culturally and linguistically diverse students in the United States: how to identify, implement, and evaluate effective instruction that takes into consideration language and cultural difference. Research into this question has brought scholars in many different fields—psychology, linguistics, sociology, politics, and education—together in a cross-disciplinary dialogue.

This chapter discusses effective teachers. We assume that *who* does the teaching is of major importance regardless of the educational model being implemented. We will extend our understanding of this basic idea by cautiously but directly addressing the development, assessment, and specific attributes of "effective" teachers who serve diverse student populations. We will look closely at credentialing policies and analyze their political and empirical underpinnings. The overall purpose of this discussion is to suggest ways of enhancing the education of culturally diverse students by focusing on the educational professionals who serve them every day.

The Current System of Professional Preparation and Assessment

Professional preparation and assessment of teachers who serve culturally diverse students are problematic, complex, and cumbersome processes. It is an area ripe for criticism. A variety of programmatic efforts have been developed in response to the growing number of culturally diverse students in the U.S. schools, but it has become evident that professional preparation, particularly for teachers, has not kept pace with the demand for educational personnel who are specifically trained to implement these new programs. The following discussion provides an overview of the preparation and credentialing of educators and builds a foundation for understanding the relevant issues.

In our society, teaching is considered a profession. A **profession** is characterized by two general features (Friedson, 1986): (a) acquisition of knowledge obtained through formal education endeavors and (b) an orientation toward serving the needs of the public, with particular emphasis on an ethical altruistic concern for the client. Practices for preparing and judging the competence of professionals have always been embedded in a local time and place, in line with generally accepted concepts and purposes—the profession's Zeitgeist. Thus, educational endeavors and assessment of professional educators usually called teaching credentials, develop in concert with the general intellectual and ethical climate and needs of the time (McGahie, 1991).

Our present concerns about teaching credentials are derived from the ethical considerations of our time and the pressing need to prepare competent teachers to serve diverse student populations. As it stands, the training and assessment of educators is a function performed by the states or by professional societies, or by some combination of these institutions. Typically, the focus is on either (1) assessing the individual as a preprofessional (usually through an examination such as the National Teaching Exam) before allowing him or her to enter the profession or (2) assessing the professional institutions and programs that produce teaching professionals (the NCATE Reviews are an example of such a review by an association, and the California Commission on Teaching Credentialing Program Reviews are an example of state-authorized reviews). In some cases, both individual and program review is required.

Teachers Are
Professionals

Types of
Assessment

Professional Credentialing of Teachers

It is important to note that professional preparation for teachers of linguistically and culturally diverse students is a relatively new enterprise. Not until the mid-1960s did substantial educational initiatives exist in this specialized arena, and not until 1974 did the U.S. Congress authorize resources for institutions of higher education to use in teacher education (August and García, 1988). The recent nature of this innovation, much like similar developments in the field of special education, has spawned many new programs in teacher preparation that are still struggling to establish themselves alongside longstanding programs in elementary and secondary education. These new programs tend to have a more complicated content with a more multidisciplinary perspective. Such teacher-preparation programs must be concerned not only with subject matter and pedagogy but also much more directly with language, culture, and instructional practices.

The 1980–1982 Teachers Language Skills Survey identified the need for 100,000 bilingual teachers in the U.S. schools. This figure was based on the number of schools in which limited-English-proficient students from one language background were sufficiently concentrated to make bilingual programs feasible. Compare this finding with reality: in 1982, there were an estimated 27,000 to 32,000 bilingual teachers, which means there were 68,000 to 73,000 teachers yet to be prepared. A total of 168 institutions of higher education graduate approximately 2,000 to 2,600 trained bilingual teachers each year (Blatchford, 1982), which means the shortage will continue. Furthermore, the Teachers Language Skills Survey reported that of 103,000 teachers assigned to teach English as a Second Language, only 40 percent had received any preparation in the methods of doing so. It is estimated that at least 350,000 teachers currently need such specialized preparation (O'Malley, 1981; Waggoner, 1984). Most unfortunate, the preparation of credentialed teachers of language minority students proceeds at a snail's pace. In California, for example, which is experiencing record increases in language minority students, the number of teachers credentialed per year in areas related to language minority education increased by only 5 percent between 1982 and 1989, whereas overall yearly teacher credentialing increased by 48 percent (California Commission on Teacher Credentialing, 1990). During this same period, there was a 13 percent increase in the general student population, but a 45 percent increase in the population of language minority students (Olsen, 1988).

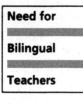

Need for Bilingual Teachers

Over 3 million children in the United States attend their first day of school from home environments in which English is not the primary language. As is the case for preparation and credentialing of "regular" teachers, the credentialing of teachers whose main function is the education of linguistically and culturally diverse students is quite variable. Table 7.1 provides a summary of teacher certification requirements and specific professional teaching services directed at language minority students in 1991. The table identifies the type of teaching credentials which are available in all fifty states and U.S. territories and shows each state's or territory's legislative stance toward such credentialing.

Table 7.1 Credentialing for Teachers of Language Minority Students: 1991 State Profiles

State or Territory	Mandates	Permits	Prohibits BE	No Statutes	BIL Education	ESL or Other	State or Territory	Mandates	Permits	Prohibits BE	No Statutes	BIL Education	ESL or Other
Alabama				•			New Hampshire		•			•	•
Alaska	•						New Jersey	•				•	•
Arizona	•				•	•	New Mexico		•			•	•
Arkansas				•			New York		•			•	•
California		•			•	•	North Carolina				•		
Colorado		•			•		North Dakota				•		
Connecticut	•						Ohio				•	•	•
Delaware				•	•		Oklahoma				•		
District of Columbia				•	•	•	Oregon		•				
Florida				•	•	•	Pennsylvania				•		
Georgia				•			Rhode Island		•			•	•
Hawaii				•		•	South Carolina				•		
Idaho				•			South Dakota				•		
Illinois	•				•	•	Tennessee				•		•
Indiana		•					Texas	•				•	•
Iowa	•						Utah		•				
Kansas		•					Vermont				•	•	
Kentucky				•		•	Virginia				•		•
Louisiana				•		•	Washington	•				•	•
Maine		•					West Virginia			•			
Maryland				•			Wisconsin	•				•	•
Massachusetts	•				•	•	Wyoming					•	
Michigan	•				•		American Samoa		•			•	
Minnesota		•			•	•	Guam	•				•	
Mississippi				•		•	Northern Marianas				•		
Missouri				•			Puerto Rico				•		•
Montana				•			Trust Territory of the Pacific				•		
Nebraska				•	•	•	Virgin Islands		•				
Nevada	•				•	•							

*Indicates whether state legislation mandates, permits, or prohibits special educational services for limited-English-proficiency (LEP) students, e.g., transitional bilingual education (TBE), English as a second language (ESL), immersion, and maintenance programs.

†Indicates whether state offers teaching certification in bilingual education, ESL, or other related areas.

Source: U.S. Department of Education, National Clearinghouse for Bilingual Education, (1986). Forum, IX, 3; Updated by each SEA listed (1991).

| Availability |
| of |
| Credentials |

As this table indicates, twenty-five states and territories presently offer no professional credentialing for teachers of culturally diverse students. Half of the country does not attend to this category of educators even though 20 percent of U.S. students might require specially prepared teachers. It is not coincidental that those states least affected as yet by increases in the population of language minority students are in this group. Keep in mind that all states require some type of certification of teaching professionals in the public schools.

California, Florida, Illinois, New York, New Jersey, and Texas are home to almost two-thirds of this nation's language minority students. In these states, teacher credentialing in bilingual education and ESL or in some other related credentialing area is available. However, only three of these six states mandate professional credentialing (Illinois, New Jersey, and Texas). Therefore, even in states that are greatly affected by growing numbers of language minority students, concern for professional teaching standards is uneven. Valencia (1991) has suggested that because of the segregation of language minority students, particularly Chicano students in the Southwest, state school systems do not feel the full affect of these students. Chicano students, for example, tend to be concentrated in a few school districts within the state, and even though their academic presence is felt strongly by these individual districts, this same pressure is not exerted statewide. I will return to this important observation, since it identifies a possible alternative forum for professional assessment.

| Uneven |
| Concern |

Limitations of Current Assessment Methods

Looking again to Table 7.1, even for those states (a total of 27) which either mandate or permit credentialing for teachers of culturally and linguistically diverse students, the present modes of assessment are highly problematic. As we saw in Chapter 1, present methods of professional assessment can be criticized in several ways (McGahie, 1991; Shinberg, 1983; Sternberg and Wagner, 1986):

1. Professional competence evaluations usually address only a narrow range of practice situations.
2. Professional competence evaluations are biased toward assessing formally acquired knowledge, rather than what the teacher can do in a classroom.

3. Almost no attention is given to the "disposition," "affective," and "commitment" domains of teacher behavior, which have been identified as being significant as content knowledge and practice skills (Pease-Alvarez, García, and Espinosa, 1991).

We also saw that professional assessment instruments are subject to severe violations of reliability and validity (Berk, 1986; Feldt and Brennan, 1989).

Chapter 1 also introduced the concept of assessment by "connoisseur." According to McGahie (1991), teacher assessment operates within the connoisseur model of professional assessment, which presumes that (1) not all professional practices can be quantified, (2) a professional problem or question may have more than one answer, and (3) practicing teachers are the most effective evaluators of teachers in training. As the need for more teachers who can effectively serve diverse student populations grows, the need to develop and assess the competence of these professionals will be of critical importance. The connoisseur model of assessment is not fully developed enough to implement on any large scale, but later in this chapter we will discuss the potential for using it at the school district level.

Connoisseur Model

Recommended Competencies for Teachers of Linguistically Diverse Students

Methods of assessment aside, what are the skills we want teachers of language minority students to have? All teacher-preparation programs must identify the desired end product of their efforts as some set of performance competencies imparted to teachers. The literature abounds with numerous listings of such competencies (Collier, 1985). The most recent and most detailed is presented by Chu and Levy (1988). This list of competencies is derived from a review of federally and nonfederally supported teacher-preparation programs presently operating within U.S. universities. It focuses on some thirty-four intercultural competencies, no small number, that serve as a foundation for success for a well-prepared teacher of linguistically diverse students. These competencies cover the instructor's knowledge in three areas: educational theory, social trends, and classroom strategies.

Areas of Expertise

The most widely distributed list of teacher competencies to be used for credentialing was developed and published in 1984 by the National Association of State Directors of Teacher Education and Certification (NASDTEC). That list, presented in an abbreviated format in Table 7.2, was a result of combining previous competency lists developed by the Center for Applied Linguistics in 1974 and the Teachers of English to Speakers of Other Languages Association in 1975. Although not as comprehensive as the Chu and Levy (1988) list, it has served as a cornerstone of teacher-preparation programs and credentialing analysis in the United States.

Recently, states and school districts have begun to articulate the expected roles and responsibilities of teachers of language minority students. New Jersey details these roles and responsibilities in the *New Jersey State Board of Education Handbook* (1991). The handbook is excerpted below.

| State |
| Handbook |

Role of Bilingual Teachers. The following responsibilities should be considered by the district when defining the role of bilingual teachers (New Jersey State Department of Education, 1991). The bilingual teacher should:

- help identify limited English proficient students;

- communicate with other teachers in planning for the teaching of bilingual programs that meet the needs of eligible students;

- communicate with ESL and other teachers in planning for the bilingual program students in ESL and special subject areas;

- provide input in areas covered by pupil personnel services;

- apply current research findings regarding the education of children from diverse cultural and linguistic backgrounds;

- develop language proficiency in the native language of the students enrolled in the program and in English;

- have knowledge of techniques, strategies, and materials that aid teaching in two languages;

- structure the use of two languages to systematically make the transition from the native language to English;

- select activities and materials for classroom use which indicate an understanding of the developmental level of the students;

- help students to identify similarities and differences for successful interaction in a cross-cultural setting;

- provide experiences that encourage positive student self-concept; and

Table 7.2   NASDTEC Certification Standards: Competencies Required for Teachers of Language Minority Students*

IN BILINGUAL/MULTICULTURAL EDUCATION (B/M ED)	POSSIBLE UNIVERSITY OFFERINGS
1. Proficiency in L1 and L2 for effective teaching	Foreign language and English department courses
2. Knowledge of history and cultures of L1 and L2 speakers	Cross-cultural studies, multicultural education (ME), history and civilization, literature, ethnic studies
3. Historical, philosophical, and legal bases for B/M ED and related research	Foundations of BE (or introduction to BE)
4. Organizational models for programs and classrooms in B/M ED	Foundations of BE
5. L2 methods of teaching (including ESL methodology)	Methods of teaching a second language
6. Communication with students, parents, and others in culturally and linguistically different communities	Cross-cultural studies, ME, school/community relations
7. Differences between L1 and L2; language and dialect differences across geographic regions, ethnic groups, social levels	Sociolinguistics, bilingualism

IN ENGLISH FOR SPEAKERS OF OTHER LANGUAGES	POSSIBLE UNIVERSITY OFFERINGS
1. Nature of language, language varieties, structure of English language	General linguistics; English phonology, morphology, and syntax
2. Demonstrated proficiency in spoken and written English	English department courses
3. Demonstrated proficiency in a second language	Foreign language courses
4. L1 and L2 acquisition process	Language acquisition
5. Effects of sociocultural variables on language learning	Language acquisition, ME, cross-cultural studies, sociolinguistics
6. Language assessment, program development, implementation, and evaluation	Language assessment, program development, and evaluation

*Supplemental to the standards required for *all* teachers.
Source: National Association of State Directors of Teacher Education and Certification, 1984.

- promote and understand the supportive role and responsibilities of parents/guardians and explain the bilingual program to them.

Role of ESL Teachers. The following responsibilities should be considered by the district when defining the role of ESL teachers. The ESL teacher should:

- help identify limited English proficient students;

- participate with administrators in designing an ESL program that meets the needs of eligible students;

- communicate with other teachers in planning for the teaching of the ESL program student in the bilingual or English-only classroom;

- demonstrate awareness of current trends in ESL and bilingual education;

- demonstrate proficiency in English commensurate with the role of a language model;

- use English as the principal medium of instruction in the areas of pronunciation, listening, comprehension, speaking, structure, reading and writing;

- select activities and materials for ESL use which indicate an understanding of the language proficiency level of the students;

- express interest in, and have an understanding for the native culture of the students;

- provide experiences that encourage positive student self-concept; and

- promote and understand the supportive role and responsibilities of parents/guardians and explain the ESL program to them.

Preparing teachers of culturally and linguistically diverse students remains an innovative process. Assessment and credentialing of these teachers are new areas of research inquiry. We have no time-tested methods and specific educational results to direct us. The connoisseur model, however, holds great promise.

District-Level Implementation of the Connoisseur Model

If the connoisseur model of teacher assessment and preparation is not possible on a grand scale, it may be possible to implement the model on a smaller scale. Recognizing that university-based teacher-preparation programs were not able to meet the growing demand in the short term for development of a new cadre of teachers, educators have turned to extensive inservice initiatives for meeting these growing professional needs. **Inservice preparation** is professional training for teachers who are already working in a classroom. In 1974 federal resources were dedicated to the inservice enterprise, and those resources have continued. From 1975 through 1982, federally funded Bilingual Education Service Centers conducted regional needs assessments and implemented regular inservice preparation activities. In the late 1980s, a smaller federal effort continued this activity with regional Multifunctional Resource Centers. State offices of education in states highly affected by culturally and linguistically diverse students have also developed their own resources for inservice preparation programs.

Inservice

Initiatives

Significantly, local school districts have implemented extensive inservice programs to increase the linguistic expertise of their teaching personnel. One such program, in Denver, Colorado, exemplifies this inservice development activity. This urban district, which serves a diverse population of Hispanic, African American, and Southeast Asian students, determined that its needs could be partially met by the professional development of its existing teaching staff. Several training presuppositions guided the development and implementation of their inservice preparation:

Denver

Program

1. Teachers needed theoretical grounding and opportunities to apply theory practically in instructional settings.
2. External consultants with expertise would work collaboratively with a cadre of local teachers over an extended period of time (4 to 6 years).
3. A local group of teachers demonstrating enhanced expertise would provide mentor support to their district colleagues.
4. Development of new mentor groups at individual school sites would ensure the systematic augmentation of expertise throughout the district.

The school district also developed its own "credentialing" requirements, since state requirements were not responsive to the local needs of professional teaching development. A recent analysis of this inservice strategy in Denver indicates that over 500 district teachers participated in this preparation from the mid-1980s to the late 1980s. Significant gains in service delivery to Denver's growing population of diverse students have been documented. A corps of one hundred mentor teachers specifically available to train their colleagues has formed to meet local needs. This mentor corps continues to provide formal preparation experiences, classroom demonstrations, local site networking, and curricular leadership. These experts, or connoisseurs, also serve to evaluate new teaching professionals.

| Results |

What was born out of great necessity in Denver may give us insight into the appropriate development and evaluation of teaching professionals. First, professional development takes on a localized flavor. Such a local emphasis reflects the diversity of students and programs present in the specific school district. Second, over time a corps of connoisseurs develops and can serve in an evaluative capacity. Highly relevant local knowledge of educational needs is developed in experts who in turn evaluate the professional expertise of their colleagues. This is the connoisseur model at its best in response to the complex nature of the diversity challenge in education.

| Local |
| Expertise |

Significantly, professional development also relates to teacher "burnout." **Burnout** is physical or emotional exhaustion, most often caused by a great deal of stress experienced over a long period of time. Burnout is particularly apparent in teachers whose major responsibility is serving highly diverse student populations (Calderon, 1991). Recent studies have made it very clear that ongoing support, particularly through the first few years of teaching, is particularly important to instructors. Calderon (1991) has displayed this data in graphical form. Figures 7.1 and 7.2 portray the cycles of teacher engagement with the profession, with and without the presence of ongoing support in the form of professional development. As the figures show, all teachers experience anticipation, disillusionment, reenergizing, and periods of reflection. But only those with ongoing professional development support experience substantive growth without withdrawal/termination from the profession.

| Benefits of |
| Teacher |
| Support |

The alternative form of teacher preparation and district-level professional development, credentialing, and support that took shape in Denver was born of immediate needs that could not be

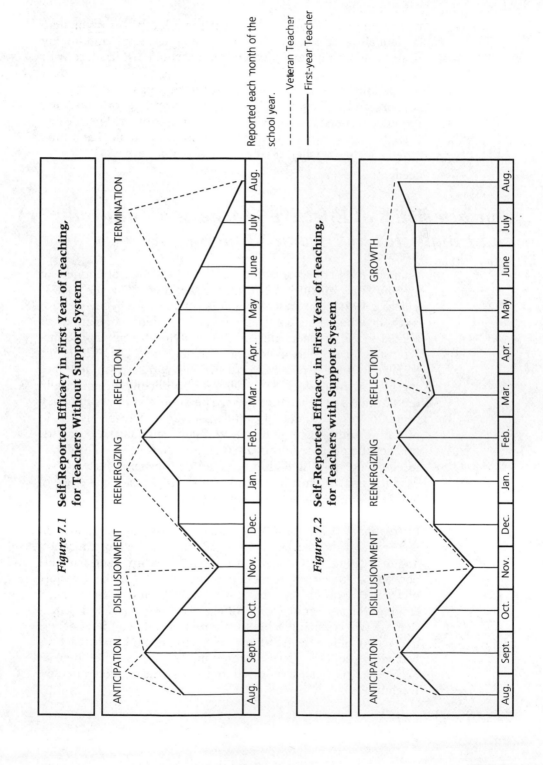

Figure 7.1 **Self-Reported Efficacy in First Year of Teaching, for Teachers Without Support System**

Figure 7.2 **Self-Reported Efficacy in First Year of Teaching, for Teachers with Support System**

Reported each month of the school year.

-------- Veteran Teacher

———— First-year Teacher

met through more typical teacher-preparation pathways or state credentialing standards. It demonstrates a useful and highly responsive solution to a problem many school districts face with respect to serving culturally and linguistically diverse student populations. This alternative form of local preparation, ongoing support, and "credentialing" could be appropriate for enhancing the effectiveness of most educational professionals. Specifically, though, it is worthy of particular attention to the field at a time when effective teachers are needed more than ever.

Characteristics of Effective Teachers of Culturally and Linguistically Diverse Students

Chapter 1 described research reports that have attempted to identify the qualities of effective teachers (Dwyer, 1991; Villegas, 1991). This research emphasis on the effectiveness of teachers who serve culturally diverse student populations is related to the broader interest in identifying "exemplary" characteristics for teachers in general (Reynolds and Elias, 1991). To go beyond these generalizations, the following section describes specific research which has attempted to document empirically the attributes of "good" teachers. The studies are few, but they begin to provide a set of standards which may be useful in preparing and evaluating teachers of culturally diverse students. It is not the purpose of this discussion to suggest that all "good" teachers must be like the ones described here. Instead, we examine this information in order to see if we may make use of it to better understand the needs of students.

Tikunoff (1983), in his analysis of the Significant Bilingual Instructional Features (SBIF) study, reports commonalities in the "exemplary" teacher's response to classroom organization and instruction. As we saw in Chapter 5, the fifty-eight teachers observed in this study represented six sites and spoke a variety of non-English languages (Spanish, Chinese, Vietnamese, Hmong, Navaho, and Hopi). All classes were considered "effective" on two criteria: teachers were nominated by other teachers and school personnel, students, and parents, and their teaching behaviors produced rates of academic learning time as high as or higher than rates reported in other research on effective teaching.

| Attributes of |
| Effective |
| Teachers |

An initial set of instructional features identified as characteristic of effective teachers pertains to the organization and delivery of instruction:

1. Successful teachers specify both task outcomes and what students must do to accomplish tasks. In addition, teachers communicate high expectations for students in terms of learning and a sense of efficacy in terms of their own ability to teach.

2. Successful teachers, not unlike effective teachers in general, exhibit use of "active teaching" behaviors found to be related to increased student performance on academic tests of achievement in reading and mathematics. These teaching behaviors include (a) communicating clearly when giving directions, specifying tasks, and presenting new information; (b) obtaining and maintaining students' engagement in instructional tasks by pacing instruction appropriately, promoting involvement, and communicating their expectations for students' success in completing tasks; (c) monitoring students' progress; and (d) providing immediate feedback whenever required regarding students' success.

3. Successful teachers of limited-English-proficient (LEP) students mediated instruction for students by using the students' native language and English for instruction, alternating between the two languages whenever necessary to ensure clarity of instruction. Although they used this type of language switching, teachers did not translate directly from one language to another.

Recent research (García, 1992; Villegas, 1991) has focused on teachers who were consistently identified at the level of the school site and the district as "effective." In these classrooms, approximately 50 percent to 70 percent of the students were non-English speakers, and the remaining English-speaking students represented several ethnic groups. For the purpose of discussion, I will divide the findings of these studies of teacher attributes into four distinct but interlocking domains: (a) knowledge, (b) skills, (c) disposition, and (d) affect.

Knowledge

Teachers held the prerequisite state teacher credentials and had graduated from programs with specific emphasis on multicultural and/or bilingual education. They had an average of 7.1 years of experience as teachers of culturally diverse students. These were not novice teachers. They reported that they routinely participated in staff development efforts, either taking courses or attending workshops on teaching techniques they wanted to implement in their classrooms. Some of the workshops were sponsored by the school or district and were mandatory. These teachers also participated in courses that they sought out and financed on their own, some related to language development and others related to pedagogy and curriculum.

These teachers were knowledgeable and articulate with regard to the instructional philosophies which guided them. They communicated these philosophies coherently in their interviews. They never hesitated to explain "why" they were using a specific instructional technique and usually couched these explanations in terms of how they saw their role with regard to teaching and "how" students learn. Principals and parents also commented on the ability of these teachers to communicate the rationales for their instructional techniques. One principal commented, "She's always able to defend her work with her students. When I first came here, I didn't agree with all that she was doing, and sometimes I still do not agree. But she always helps me understand why she is doing what she is doing. I respect her for that. She is not a 'recipe teacher'" (García, 1992).

One parent commented about her child's journal writing: "I didn't understand why she was letting ____ make all these spelling mistakes. It annoyed me. During the teacher-parent conference, she showed me the progress ____ was making. His spelling was getting better without taking a spelling test every week. I was surprised. She knows what she's doing" (Pease-Alvarez et al., 1991). A parent concerned about his daughter's lack of English competency indicated, "Me explicó que aprendiendo en español le va a ayudar a mi hija hablar mejor el inglés. Dice bien, porque mi hijo que vino conmigo de México, hablando y escribiendo en español, aprendió el inglés muy facil" [She explained that my daughter's learning of Spanish would help her learn English. She was right, because my son knew more Spanish when he came to the U.S. and he learned English

Experienced Teachers

Coherent Teaching Philosophy

easily] (García, 1992). Moreover, these teachers seemed to be quite competent in the content areas. The upper elementary teachers who were instructing students in fractions had a solid and confident understanding of fractions. They did not seem to be only "one step ahead of the students."

Skills

Despite their differing perspectives, the teachers demonstrated specific instructional skills. Bilingual teachers used English and Spanish in highly communicative ways, speaking to students with varying degrees of Spanish and English proficiency in a communicative style requiring significant language switching. Direct translation from one language to another was a rarity, but utilization of language switching in contexts which required it was common.

Variations of course existed among these exemplary teachers, but each had developed a particular set of instructional skills which, they indicated, led to their own effectiveness:

Teachers had adopted an experimental stance toward instruction. Along with many of their colleagues, these exemplary teachers had abandoned a strictly skills-oriented approach to instruction. To varying degrees they organized instruction in their classes so that children focused first on what was meaningful to them. Teachers in the early grades used an approach to reading instruction that treated specific skills in the context of extended pieces of text (e.g., an entire book, passage, or paragraph). They initiated shared reading experiences by reading to and with children from an enlarged book, pointing to each word as they read. Because most of these books relied on a recurring pattern (e.g., a repeating syntactical construction, rhyming words, repetitions), children who could not read words in isolation were able to predict words and entire constructions when participating in choral reading activities. With time, teachers encouraged students to focus on individual words, sound-letter correspondences, and syntactic constructions. The teacher also encouraged children to rely on other cueing systems as they predicted and confirmed what they had read as a group or individually.

These teachers utilized a thematic curriculum. Science and social studies themes were often integrated across a variety of subject areas. Once a theme was determined, usually in consultation with students, the teachers planned instruction around a

| Shared |
| Reading |

Becoming a Responsive Teacher

7.1 A Successful Practitioner in Math

Kay Tolliver's math program has been celebrated—and for good reason. She teaches at Harlem Tech Middle School— 15% Afro-American, 85% Hispanic, and located in a poor New York City neighborhood. Yet her teaching strategies exemplify those recently recommended by the National Council of Teachers of Mathematics.

Tolliver, who is not a textbook fan, makes math interdisciplinary. Her students constantly hypothesize and engage in hands-on activities. In one activity, they constructed two paper bridges, one made of quadrilaterals and the other of triangles, and found that the triangle was better suited as a building block. Tolliver's students also create and illustrate math problems based on their own lives. For example; "There are two fire escapes on the outside of the building. If one is rusted and opens twice as slowly as the other, which opens in 7.4 seconds, how long will it take the rusted one to open?"

Tolliver prefers authentic assessment methods to conventional testing. Her students have been asked to form a pentagon from any combination of six pattern-block pieces which included a square, an equilateral triangle, a rectangle, as trapezoid, a parallelogram, and a rhombus. They then had to determine the sum of the interior angles of the pentagon and explain how they arrived at their answer.

Not surprisingly, many of Tolliver's students have gone on to prestigious schools, such as the Bronx High School of Science, and to college and vocational schools.

Source: Based on an article in *Teacher* magazine, March 1993. Used with permission.

Meeting the Challenge

1. Develop two interdisciplinary math activities, one for an elementary-level classroom and one for a secondary-level classroom. Assume that your students are culturally and linguistically diverse. Include a collaborative aspect.
2. Contact the National Council of Teachers of Mathematics by letter or telephone. Ask a representative of the organization how you might view the material referred to above regarding the strategies the council recommends for teaching math. Share any information with your classmates.

series of activities that focused on that theme. For example, a unit on dinosaurs included reading books about dinosaurs, categorizing and graphing different kinds of dinosaurs, visiting a museum that featured dinosaur exhibits, writing stories or poems about a favorite dinosaur, and speculating on the events that led to the dinosaurs' disappearance. In one third-grade classroom, a student suggested that the theme address "the stuff in the field that makes my little brother sick" (García, 1992). The teacher developed a four-week theme which engaged students in understanding pesticide use, which is a relevant topic for the children of migrant farm workers.

Despite the use of instructional strategies that depart from traditional skills-based approaches to curriculum and instruction, these teachers did sometimes structure learning around individual skills or discrete components. It was not uncommon for a teacher to form an ad hoc group of students needing special help with particular academic skills. Interestingly, the teachers reported that they devoted a week or two toward preparing students for standardized tests. During this time they taught skills that would be tested, and administered practice tests: "I don't like testing. But we have to do it. I teach my kids how to mark the bubbles and I make sure that they take their time. We practice test-taking" (García, 1992).

Teachers provided opportunities for active learning. A good portion of class time was organized around a series of learning activities that children pursued either independently or with others. During science and math, children worked in small groups doing a variety of hands-on activities designed to support their understanding of a particular concept (e.g., classification, estimation, place value) or subject area (e.g., oceanography, dinosaurs).

Each teacher's commitment to active learning was revealed by the consistent use of a studio or workshop format for literacy instruction. Instead of teaching students *about* reading and writing, teachers organized their program so that students actively *did* reading and writing. Real reading and writing took place in the context of a literature-based reading program and during regularly scheduled times when students wrote in their journals on topics of their own choosing with teachers reliably responding to their entries. There was also time for students to engage in writer's workshops. During this time students generated their own topics and wrote, revised, edited, and published their finished writings for a larger audience. Like published authors, they shared their writing with others and often received input

Thematic Curriculum

Learning by Doing

that helped them revise and improve upon what they had written. For example, one teacher commented, "These kids produce their own reading material and they take it home to share it with their parents. It's real good stuff. I help a little, but it's the kids that help each other the most" (Pease-Alvarez et al., 1991).

Teachers encouraged collaborative and cooperative interactions among students. These teachers organized instruction so that students spent time working together on a wide range of instructional activities. Primary-grade teachers structured their day so that students worked on group and individual activities (e.g., graphing, journal writing, science projects) in small heterogeneous groups. Students who worked in small groups on their own art project, journal, or experiment did not necessarily interact with other members of their group. Teachers explained that students, particularly those who did not share the same dominant language, often ignored one another during these kinds of group activities. They felt that cross-cultural interactions were much more likely to take place when students were obliged to work together to complete a single task. Middle-grade teachers followed this same collaborative approach.

Disposition

A person's **disposition** is his or her usual temperament and frame of mind. We describe the following attributes of "effective" teachers as constituting disposition because no other category seems relevant. The individual characteristics that these teachers possessed explain their success as professionals. For instance, they were highly dedicated. They reported working very hard, getting to school first and being the last to leave, working weekends, and sometimes feeling completely overworked. They reported spending close to $2,000 of their own resources to modify the classroom and obtain the materials their students needed. They indicated that they saw themselves as "creative," "resourceful," "committed," "energetic," "persistent," and "collaborative." They sought out assistance from their colleagues and were ready to provide as much assistance as they received.

| Personal |
| Commitment |

Although these teachers felt that they were effective, they were not complacent. They reported that they continued to change their instructional practices and in some cases their instructional philosophies over the years. These teachers reported undergoing great change in their approach to learning and instruction—of having "shifted paradigms." For example, teachers who once advocated skills-based and authoritarian modes of instruction such as DISTAR were now considering and experimenting with child-centered approaches. Teachers felt

Change

that they enjoyed a certain degree of autonomy in their school. They felt free to implement change. In recent years, when they have wanted to implement a new classroom approach, they have presented a carefully thought-out rationale and eventually enlisted the principal's support.

The changes these teachers were involved in affected other classrooms as well as their own. With other teachers, they have worked to eliminate ability grouping across subject areas. They were involved in individual and group efforts to improve the quality of education at the school and district level. In short, these teachers were highly committed to improving themselves and the services to students in general.

Above all, they were highly confident, and even a bit "cocky" regarding their instructional abilities:

"I have changed my own view on how students learn—we need to understand learning does not occur in bits and pieces. Why do teachers still insist on teaching that way?"

"I know what I am doing is good for kids. Some of my colleagues say I work too hard—I say they do not work hard enough. Not that they are lazy, they just don't seem to understand how important it is to do this job right."

"I know my kids are doing well, all of them. I would rather keep them with me all day than send them to someone who is supposed to help them in their 'special' needs but doesn't help them at all" (García, 1992; Pease-Alvarez et al., 1991).

Affect

The term **affect** is used in psychology to refer to people's feelings and emotions as distinguished from their thoughts and actions. The emotional energy these teachers bring to their work contributes to their effectiveness. These teachers felt strongly that classroom practices that reflect the cultural and linguistic background of minority students are important ways of enhancing student self-esteem. They recognized that part of their job was to provide the kind of cultural and linguistic validation that is missing in the larger society, which more often deprecates minority cultures and language. According to teachers working with Latino students, learning Spanish and learning about Latino culture benefits Anglo-American students as well as Latino students. In their eyes, people who learn a second language tend to be more sensitive to other cultures. Like other teachers, these teachers felt that multicultural awareness enriched their students' lives.

These teachers had high expectations for all their students: "No 'pobrecito' [poor child] syndrome here—I want all my students to learn and I know they can learn even though they may come from very poor families and may live under 'tough' conditions. I can have them do their homework here and I can even get them a tutor—an older student—if they need it. I understand that their parents may not be able to help them at home. That's no excuse for them not learning" (García, 1992). In many respects, these teachers portrayed themselves as being quite demanding, taking no excuses from students for not accomplishing assigned work, and willing to be "tough" on those students who were "messing around."

High

Expectations

Most significant was the teachers' affinity for their students:

"These students are like my very own children"

"I love these children like my own. I know that parents expect me to look after their kids and to let them know if they are in trouble"

"When I walk into that classroom I know we are a family and we're going to be together a whole year . . . . I try to emphasize first that we are a family here . . . . I tell my students, 'you're like brothers and sisters' and some students even call me Mom or Tía [aunt]. It's just like being at home here" (García, 1992).

Each teacher spoke of the importance of strong and caring relationships among class members and particularly between the teacher and the students. They felt that this provided students with a safe environment that was conducive to learning.

Parents also reported a similar feeling. They referred to the teachers in the interviews as extended family members—someone to be trusted, respected, and honored for service to their children. These teachers were often invited to *bautismos* [baptisms], *bodas* [weddings], and *fiestas de cumpleaños* [birthday celebrations], soccer games, and family barbecues. And they attended such occasions, reporting that such participation was inherently rewarding and instructive with regard to their own

Parent Trust

personal and professional lives. Parents commented during interviews:

"La señorita ____ , le tengo mucha confianza, quiero que mi niño la respete como a mí" [Ms. ____ , I trust her, my son respects her as he does me]

"Nunca se larga mi nina de ella, se porta como mi hermana, siempre le puedo hablar y me gusta mucho ayudarle" [My daughter stays close to her, she is like my sister, I can always talk to her and I like to help her]

"I know my son is well cared for in her class, I never worry— she even calls me when he does something good" (García, 1992).

In summary, the teachers who are considered "effective" for culturally and linguistically diverse students are highly experienced, not novices to teaching or to the instruction of these students. They are skilled in communication with students, parents, and their administrative supervisors. They think about and communicate their own instructional philosophies. They work hard to understand the community, families, and students whom they serve, and they incorporate into the curriculum attributes of the local culture. They have adopted instructional methods that are student centered, collaborative, and process oriented—no "worksheet" curriculum was found. They are dedicated and hard workers who collaborate with colleagues and continue to be involved in personal and professional growth activities. Most significantly, these teachers care deeply for and personally connect with their students. They are advocates: having "adopted" their students, they watch out for their students' welfare while at the same time challenging them with high expectations and refusing to accept the "pobrecito" syndrome.

Conclusion

It seems clear that culturally and linguistically diverse students— often referred to en masse as "at risk"—can indeed be served effectively by schools and educational professionals. Schools must develop educational structures and processes that consider both the general attributes of effective schooling practices and the specific attributes of effective teachers (Carter and Chatfield,

1986; García, 1988; García, 1992; Tikunoff, 1983). Although the training of such teachers is in a developmental period and is in need of further clarifying research, it is clearly not in its infancy. A serious body of literature examining instructional practices and organization, and their effects, is emerging.

The preparation of teaching innovators is a challenge for university, federal, state, and local educational agencies. The needs are great, and the production of competent professionals has lagged. Teacher organizations, credentialing bodies, and universities have responded with a new array of competencies, guidelines, and professional evaluation tools. The most often utilized professional evaluation tool is the connoisseur model of professional assessment. Like other assessment methods, the connoisseur model is not yet sufficiently reliable or valid to use at a statewide level. It has been employed with some success, however, at the level of the individual school district, using locally derived credentials. This district-level credentialing process is an alternative worthy of serious consideration. The challenge for all those engaged in the preparation, assessment, and credentialing of linguistically and culturally diverse teachers is to consider the rapidly expanding research literature, to evaluate its implications critically, and to apply it in educational contexts with the help of locally developed connoisseurs.

SUMMARY OF MAJOR IDEAS

1. A profession is characterized by (a) acquisition of knowledge obtained through formal education and (b) an orientation toward serving the needs of the public, with an emphasis on ethical and altruistic concern for the client. The professional preparation of teachers has not kept pace with the educational needs of culturally and linguistically diverse students in the United States.

2. At present, educators are prepared and assessed by state agencies, by professional societies, or by both. Assessment may focus on the individual preservice teacher, through a test such as the National Teaching Exam, or on the programs that prepare teachers, though state or association reviews. The professional credentials that teachers are required to have reflect the general intellectual and ethical climate and needs of the time.

3. Not until 1974 did the U.S. Congress provide institutions of higher education with resources for use in preparing teachers

of culturally and linguistically diverse children. The 1980–1982 Teachers Language Skills Survey estimated that whereas 100,000 trained bilingual teachers were needed in the U.S. schools, barely a third of this number were available. The survey also reported that only 40 percent of teachers assigned to teach English as a Second Language in the U.S. schools had been formally prepared to do so.

4. As of 1991, twenty-five states and U.S. territories offered no professional credentialing for teachers of bilingual education or ESL. Less than one-third of the states required schools to provide services to limited-English-proficient students, even in such states as California, Florida, and New York which are greatly affected by growing numbers of language minority students.

5. Present methods of professionally assessing teachers are limited and are often unreliable and invalid. The connoisseur method of assessment, by which experienced practitioners evaluate the effectiveness of teachers in training, is not sufficiently developed for use on a statewide level.

6. Performance competencies expected for teachers of culturally and linguistically diverse students cover the instructor's knowledge of (a) educational theory, (b) social trends, and (c) classroom strategies. In 1984 the National Association of State Directors of Teacher Education and Certification (NASDTEC) developed a list of competencies to be used for certifying teachers of language minority students. Some states, such as New Jersey, have detailed the roles and responsibilities of these teachers in published handbooks.

7. Inservice preparation is professional training for teachers who are already working in a classroom. The local school district in Denver, Colorado, developed an inservice program for teachers that was based on the connoisseur model. From the mid- to late 1980s, over 500 district teachers participated, and a corps of 100 mentor teachers was formed to meet future training needs and to evaluate new teaching professionals. Such a local emphasis permits schools to respond to the specific diversity present in the district.

8. All teachers experience anticipation, disillusionment, reenergizing, and periods of reflection. Burnout is exhaustion caused by stress experienced over a long period of time and is prevalent among teachers who serve highly diverse student populations. Burnout may cause even good teachers to leave the profession. Research shows that first-year teachers can resist the effects of burnout and experience substantive

growth if they are provided with ongoing support in the form of professional development.

9. Effective teachers organize and deliver instruction in a characteristic way. They specify task outcomes and communicate high expectations for students. They use "active teaching" behaviors. Effective teachers of LEP students switch back and forth between the students' first language and English without directly translating.

10. Effective teachers have also been found to have specific attributes in the domains of knowledge, skill, disposition, and affect. Disposition is a person's usual temperament and frame of mind, and affect is a person's feelings and emotions as distinguished from thoughts and actions. These effective teachers were highly experienced and skilled at communicating with students, parents, and administrators. They used student-centered, collaborative, and process-oriented instructional methods. They were dedicated to their own personal and professional growth. They personally connected with and advocated for their students.

EXTENDING YOUR EXPERIENCE

1. Locate your state in Table 7.1 and determine the credentialing available for teachers of language minority students. Refer elsewhere in the table to determine how your state compares with others in the region. Write or call a representative of your state board of education, or a state legislator, for an explanation of current credentialing practices.

2. Write to the National Clearinghouse for Bilingual Education at the U.S. Department of Education. Find out what information and services they provide that would be of interest to teachers of culturally and linguistically diverse children. In particular, compile a list of inservice training available through state education departments or local school districts.

3. In your local school district, who are the educators who might be called on to serve as mentors, or connoisseurs, in a training and assessment program for teachers of culturally diverse students? How would you go about identifying these experts and learning what they do to provide their students with an effective education?

4. This chapter describes the characteristics of effective teachers of culturally and linguistically diverse students according to four areas: knowledge, skills, disposition, and affect. How

would you rank these areas in terms of importance? Write each one as a heading on a sheet of paper and take an inventory of yourself. Can you identify your own strengths and weaknesses in these four areas?

5. Working with a group of your classmates, design a series of questions to be used to interview candidates for a teaching position in an elementary or secondary school with a large population of linguistically and culturally diverse students. Base your interview questions on the four areas of teacher characteristics discussed in the chapter.

6. Interview one or two elementary or secondary school teachers about their experience with burnout. Ask them to describe their *specific* experiences and to explain how they battled burnout. Share your findings with your classmates, respecting the teachers' anonymity, if necessary.

RESOURCES FOR FURTHER STUDY

Collier, J. P. (1985), University models for ESL and bilingual teacher training. In National Clearinghouse for Bilingual Education (Ed.), *Issues in English language development*. Rosslyn, Va.: Editor.

This publication is a collection of papers presented at a national exchange entitled "Issues in English Language Development for Minority Language Education." This particular paper points to the great challenge faced by programs created to help language minority students. From the point of view of staff, most professionals in the field are new, inexperienced, and young. The task of educating all students sometimes is counterproductive due to the duplication of resources and the inability to effectively direct resources to needed areas. It is clear to the author that many interested and determined individuals are willing to face the challenge to provide a better education to language minority students.

Pease-Alvarez, C., García, E., and Espinoza, P. (1991). Effective instruction for language minority students: An early childhood case study. *Early Childhood Research Quarterly*, in press.

The authors offer a descriptive analysis of two teachers in order to illustrate effective instructional perspectives and practices. Such effective practices are quoted from large-scale studies. The two teachers' experiences demonstrate how to educate language minority students. The teachers' personal, professional, and educational goals provide the reader with insight into how language and culture can become an integral part of the classroom along with innovative perspectives, effective instructional practices, and different philosophies.

Valencia, R. (1991). *Chicano school failure and success.* New York: The Falmer Press.

This book is a collaborative effort focusing on school success and failure for Chicano students. The contributors point out that Chicano students are influenced by social, economic, and historical forces that promote and maintain inequality. The author's goal is to confront the disparities that form barriers for Chicano students and to outline solutions for overcoming such barriers. The obstacles that all students face cut across race and economics. A wide variety of scholars discuss this complexity and suggest ways to improve the schooling of Chicano students.

Villegas, A. M. (1991). *Culturally responsive pedagogy for the 1990's and beyond.* Princeton, N.J.: Educational Testing Service.

The author's main goal is to identify the most current and significant literature dealing with promising instructional practices for minority students. The document reviews the most current thinking on minority students. A number of authorities from different disciplinary perspectives, such as anthropology, sociology, linguistics, sociolinguistics, psychology, psycholinguistics, and curriculum and instruction, were invited to provide input.

EFFECTIVE INSTRUCTION

OF LINGUISTICALLY

AND CULTURALLY

DIVERSE CHILDREN

CHAPTER 8

Focus Questions

○ What are some of the charactcristics of elementary schools and high schools that effectively serve culturally and linguistically diverse students?

○ How radically must schools be transformed in order to educate all of our students?

○ How will acknowledgment of linguistic, sociocultural, and cognitive factors in children's development bring about change in educational practices?

○ What classroom strategies have been identified as effective for enabling language minority students to achieve academically?

"Knowledge is not something separate and self-sufficing, but it is involved in the process by which life is sustained and evolved."

—JOHN DEWEY

It seems only appropriate to begin our discussion of effective instructional practices by addressing the above statement by one of this country's most renowned educators, John Dewey. Too often, the greatest purpose of our schools is perceived to be the "dispensing" of knowledge. Dewey would remind us that knowledge cannot be dispensed. It must be constructed, reconstructed, and located in our own individual ways of living. It is more a process than an entity, something which maintains us while at the same time transforming us.

Today's teachers face numerous challenges. To begin with, he or she must interact with thirty or more children, each with a unique learning biography, interests, strengths, and limitations of experience. Schools exist, at least in part, to provide an opportunity for students to encounter ways of knowing and doing that they would not be likely to encounter routinely out of school. Under these conditions, it seems essential that the teacher give careful thought and preparation—both material and intellectual—to the creation of instructional events. Dewey (1916) recommends instruction that engages the interest of students so that each is enabled to meet the challenges and make meaningful, on his or her own terms, the "educational" material available in that milieu. Only then can the school, the classroom, and the teacher "step back and follow the student's lead" (Dewey, 1916, p. 19).

As the U.S. population continues to diversify racially and ethnically, particularly among the population of young and school-age children, the nature of schooling must reflect this significant demographic transformation. Schools today are being asked not simply to improve their functioning but to adapt to new populations, new societal expectations, and new intellectual and employment demands. Our next generation of young people, and ethnic and racial minority children in particular, will continue to be vulnerable if our schools do not successfully complete the required metamorphosis. The future lies in understanding how a diverse population, with many individuals at risk for underachievement, can achieve *social, educational,* and *employment* competence. As always, in youth reside the new ideas, the energy, and the resources for our society's future.

We have seen that educational vulnerability is a historical reality for culturally and linguistically diverse students in the United States. The phrase "culturally and linguistically diverse" is a relatively new educational term that does not fully portray the stunning diversity among the populations it labels. Recent educational leaders, such as the former U.S. Secretary of Education, have concluded that populations identified as such have been perceived by the majority of society as linguistically, cognitively, socially, and educationally inferior (Cavazos, 1990). This perception gave rise to a variety of social and educational programs that attempted to eliminate these "inferior" characteristics (August and García, 1988). Meanwhile, linguistically and culturally diverse populations continue to struggle to attain educational success.

Recent educational research and related instructional practices have revealed the nature of educational vulnerability as it relates to language, culture, and cognition. In the following section we review some of the theoretical underpinnings of new educational strategies. We then look at some of the research into characteristics of effective schools and effective instructional practices. Particular emphasis is placed on how an instructionally responsive stance can lead to a more productive educational future for culturally diverse student populations.

A Theoretical Framework: Two Divergent Views

Before we examine "effective" schools and instructional practices, let's go back a few chapters and review the theoretical base available to us. Recall from Chapter 3 that at one end of the continuum of educational theory, educators argue that addressing the academic underachievement of linguistically and culturally diverse populations requires a deeper understanding of the interaction between a student's home and school cultures (Tharp, 1989). These theorists claim that educational failure can be explained by the "culture clash" between home and school. Alternatively, other theorists state that the academic failure of any student rests on the failure of instructional personnel to implement the principles of teaching and learning that we know "works."

In any sincere attempt to address the educational circumstances of students, these theoretical positions need not be incompatible. In fact, both positions offer a more informed perspective on the effective and efficient education of *all* students. Making distinctions among theories is a necessary starting point in our discussion of instructional practices which might enhance education for historically unsuccessful student populations. The continued failure of past and present schooling practices to serve these students effectively is highly significant. The rest of this chapter describes the extent to which schools and schooling practices must change in order to reverse this failure.

Both Are
Useful

Characteristics of Effective Schools

Within the last twenty years, researchers have compiled a considerable body of data on effective school practices. A review of the accumulated data identifies the following characteristics of effective schools (Purkey and Smith, 1985):

> *Administrative leadership.* Effective principals are actively engaged in curriculum planning, staff development, and instructional issues.

> *Teacher expectations.* Teachers maintain high achievement expectations for all students.

> *Emphasis on basic skills.* There is a deliberate focus on reading, writing, math, and language arts.

> *School climate.* An orderly, safe environment conducive to teaching and learning is maintained.

> *Regular feedback.* Continual feedback on academic progress is provided to students and parents.

Variables

Edmunds (1979) contributed to the emerging picture of effective schools, particularly with regard to "minority" students. He identified two groups of variables—organizational and structural variables, and process variables—which together define the climate and culture of the school. Organizational and structural variables include:

> *School site management.* School leadership and staff have considerable autonomy in determining the exact means by

which they address the problem of increasing academic performance.

Instructional leadership. The principal initiates and maintains procedures for improving achievement.

Curriculum planning and organization. In elementary schools, the curriculum has a clear focus on the acquisition of basic skills. Instruction takes into consideration students' linguistic and cultural attributes across grade levels and throughout the entire curriculum.

Staff development. This variable is essential to change and consists of a schoolwide program closely related to the instructional program. This activity is crucial in schools serving language minority students.

Parent support and involvement. Support from parents is essential to the success of any educational program for language minority students.

Schoolwide recognition of academic success. Recognition of student achievement is reflected in the school's activities.

District support. Financial and administrative support is fundamental to change and to the maintenance of effective schools.

Edmunds (1979) defined process variables as factors that act to sustain a productive school climate. Four process variables are identified:

Collaborative planning and collegial relationships. Teachers and administrators work together to implement change.

A sense of community. A feeling of belonging contributes to reduced alienation and increased student achievement.

Clear goals and high expectations. These are commonly shared. A focus on those tasks deemed most important allows the school to direct its resources and shape its functioning toward the realization of goals.

Order and discipline. These help to maintain the seriousness and purpose with which the school approaches its task.

Carter and Chatfield (1986, p. 224) report similar attributes present in effective elementary schools serving Mexican American, African American, and Asian students in California. Their

Table 8.1   Attributes of High Schools that Promote the Achievement of Language Minority Students

1. **Value is placed on the students' languages and cultures by:**
   - Treating students as individuals, not as members of a group
   - Learning about students' cultures
   - Learning students' languages
   - Hiring bilingual staff with cultural backgrounds similar to the students'
   - Encouraging students to develop their primary language skills
   - Allowing students to speak their primary languages
   - Offering advanced as well as lower division content courses in the students' primary languages
   - Instituting extra-curricular activities that will attract LM students

2. **High expectations of language minority students are made concrete by:**
   - Hiring minority staff in leadership positions to act as role models
   - Providing a special program to prepare LM students for college
   - Offering advanced and honors bilingual/content-ESL classes in the content areas
   - Making it possible for students to exit ESL programs quickly
   - Challenging students in class and providing guidance to help them meet the challenge
   - Providing counseling assistance (in the primary language if necessary) to help students apply to college and fill out scholarship and grant forms
   - Bringing in representatives of colleges and minority graduates who are in college to talk to students
   - Working with parents to gain their support for students going to college
   - Recognizing students for doing well

3. **School leaders make the education of language minority students a priority. These leaders:**
   - Hold high expectations for LM students
   - Are knowledgeable of instructional and curricular approaches to teaching LM students and communicate this knowledge to staff
   - Take a strong leadership role in strengthening curriculum and instruction for all students, including LM students
   - Are often bilingual minority group members themselves
   - Hire teachers who are bilingual and/or trained in methods for teaching LM students

4. **Staff development is explicitly designed to help teachers and staff serve language minority students more effectively. Schools and school districts:**
   - Offer incentives and compensation so that the school staff will take advantage of available staff development programs
   - Provide staff development for teachers and other school staff in:
     - effective instructional approaches to teaching LM students, e.g., cooperative learning methods, content-ESL, and reading and writing in the content areas
     - principles of second language acquisition
     - the cultural backgrounds and experiences of the students

Table 8.1 Attributes of High Schools that Promote the Achievement of Language Minority Students (cont'd)

— the languages of the students
— cross-cultural communication
— cross-cultural counseling

5. A variety of courses and programs for language minority students is offered.

- Include courses in English as a Second Language and primary language instruction (both literacy and advanced placement) and bilingual and content-ESL courses in content areas
- Make sure that the course offerings for LM students do not limit their choices or place them in low level classes. Offer advanced as well as basic courses taught through bilingual and content ESL methods
- Keep class size small (20–25) in order to maximize interaction
- Establish academic support programs that help LM students make the transition from ESL and bilingual classes to mainstream classes and prepare them to go to college

6. A counseling program gives special attention to language minority students through counselors who:

- Speak the students' languages and are of the same or similar cultural backgrounds
- Are informed about post-secondary educational opportunities for LM students
- Believe in, emphasize, and monitor the academic success of LM students

7. Parents of language minority students are encouraged to become involved in their children's education. Schools can provide and encourage:

- Staff who can speak the parents' languages
- On-campus ESL classes for parents
- Monthly parent nights
- Parent involvement with counselors in the planning of their children's course schedules
- Neighborhood meetings with school staff
- Early morning meetings with parents
- Telephone contacts to check on absent students

8. School staff members share a strong commitment to empowering language minority students through education. This commitment is made concrete through staff who:

- Give extra time to work with LM students
- Take part in a political process that challenges the status quo
- Request training of various sorts to help them become more effective
- Reach out to students in ways that go beyond their job requirements, for example, by sponsoring extra-curricular activities
- Participate in community activities in which they act as advocates for Latinos and other minorities

Source: Lucas et al. (1990), "Promoting the Success of Latino Minority Students," *Harvard Educational Review, 60(3),* 315–334. Used with permission.

analyses suggest that processes, not structures, of pedagogy, administrative arrangements, and classroom organization are most closely linked to effectiveness. Carter and Chatfield describe an effective school for language minority students as a well-functioning total system producing a school social climate that promotes positive outcomes.

They broke their analysis into two parts, focusing on

1. Specific characteristics crucial to the development of effective schooling and thus to a positive school climate, such as: a safe and orderly school environment; positive leadership, usually from the formal leaders (administrators, principals, curriculum specialists). Also important was common agreement on a strong academic orientation—that is, clearly stated academic goals, objectives, and plans; and well-functioning methods to monitor school input and student outcomes.
2. A positive school social climate, which includes: high staff expectations for children and the instructional program; a strong demand for academic performance; denial of the cultural-deprivation argument and the stereotypes that support it; high staff morale, consisting of strong internal support, consensus building, job satisfaction, sense of personal efficacy, sense that the system works, sense of ownership, well-defined roles and responsibilities, and beliefs and practices that resources are best expended on people rather than on educational software and hardware.

Much like Edmunds (1979), Purkey and Smith (1985), Carter and Chatfield (1986), and Lucas, Henze, and Donato (1990) examined the attributes of high schools that selectively promoted achievement of linguistically and culturally diverse students. Table 8.1 identifies eight of these attributes.

The features identified significantly resonate with the findings of other studies of effective schools.

The research described above offers us a quick set of checklists for assessing what "good" schools should be like. Whereas these examinations are based on "what is," other educational reformers have pointed us in the direction of "what ought to be." Berman (1992) offers us a view which portrays the ideal schooling transformation. Table 8.2 outlines the elements of this transformation.

Transforming

Schools

Schools are asked to transform into institutions which actively engage learners in a diverse community. They must be cognizant of the fluidity of human development, focused on a thematically integrated curriculum, responsive to performance-

Table 8.2   Schooling Transformation: What Is Versus What Ought To Be

CURRENT SYSTEM: School as learning environment	NEW SCHOOL DESIGN: School as community of learners
Passive. Instruction relies on teacher as dispenser of known knowledge and student as consumer and is based on abstract modes of learning.	**Engaged.** Instruction relies on guided inquiry and conversations with teacher as mentor providing assistance to enable students to perform authentic tasks that they could not otherwise do by themselves; teachers create multiple learning activities and "group" for diverse learning styles, and students engage in self-regulated performance activities with clear goals and measures of performance.
Age-based groups and tracking. Classes and students are grouped by "ability" and/or tracks at age levels.	**Developmental.** Students would be organized in (cognitive and affective) developmentally appropriate groupings, rather than age-specific grades, and classes would be heterogeneous within development groups; students would work in smaller, fluid groups within classes, and act as coaches as well as performers.
Abstract curriculum. Curriculum based on abstract categorizations and driven by college entry requirements and standardized tests.	**Thematic and integrated curriculum.** Curriculum designed by teachers and students together and based on themes and projects that relate to student experiences and interests.
Unclear and/or irrelevant standards. Standards largely defined by college course entry requirements and vary greatly and idiosyncratically for students.	**Performance-based standards and assessments.** Standards defined and redefined by the broader community with a focus on authentic outcomes and indicators.
Affectively neutral. Psuedo "business" environment, professionals charged with producing academic goals.	**Affectively Engaged.** Professional "care" for the students, to celebrate and embrace them, and for the intellectual well-being of the institution.

Source: Paul Berman and Associates, *The Status of Bilingual Education in California.* Berkeley: 1992. Used with permission.

based standards and assessments, and staffed with highly professional and caring personnel. Although this is a tall order, such an envisioned transformation drives home the point that the schools of the future will not only need to do a better job but will need to change radically.

Effective Instructional Practices

Instructional reform is a necessary element of radical change in our schools. Given the notion that schools, like families, directly or indirectly socialize children as much as they formally teach (Spindler, 1955), the development of academic competence may

Socialization

be considered related to academic socialization (Trueba, 1987). Recent ethnographic studies and case studies (Au and Jordan, 1981; Diaz et al., 1986; Duran, 1983; Erickson, 1986; Moll, 1988; Tharp and Gallimore, 1988; Trueba, 1988) have reported a significant relationship between instruction that is congruent with a student's culture and children's academic success.

For example, Gallimore and Tharp (1989) have carefully described the educational program developed for native Hawaiians. These programs utilize gender-relevant cooperative education procedures which match the gender roles in this population: boys and girls work together in small groups. Similar cooperative education structures are utilized effectively in Navaho classrooms: boys are grouped together and girls are grouped together (Tharp, 1989). Moll (1988) has also described successful cooperative

Successful

Techniques

techniques used with Hispanic students in southwestern U.S. schools. He concludes that such cooperative social structures directly "match" specific Hispanic family values and practices. Other sociolinguistic studies have shown that the language of the classroom—or academic discourse—is a highly specialized code that students need to learn and "is not simply a transparent medium through which the academic curriculum is transmitted" (Mehan, 1979, p. 124). From this perspective, schooling involves not only cognitive development and the acquisition of knowledge but socialization as well (Spindler, 1974, 1982).

Interaction of

Factors

The understanding that cognitive development and socialization are paired leads to several important implications for the education of culturally and linguistically diverse children. Language and culture, and their accompanying values, are acquired in the home and community environment. Children come to school with some knowledge about language, how it works and is used, and learn higher-level cognitive and metalinguistic skills as they engage in socially meaningful activities. Children's development and learning is best understood as the interaction of linguistic, sociocultural, and cognitive factors.

These conclusions can be directly supported by recent research that documents instructually effective practices with linguistically and culturally diverse students in selected school sites around the United States (Cummins, 1986; Carter and Chatfield, 1986; García, 1988; Moll, 1988; Lucas et al., 1990; Pease-Alvarez and García, 1991; Tikunoff, 1983). These descriptive studies identified specific schools and classrooms which served linguistically and culturally diverse students well. Using the case study approach, these studies looked at instructional practices in preschool, elementary school, and high school classrooms. Researchers interviewed teachers, principals, parents, and students and conducted specific classroom observations which assessed the "dynamics" of the instructional process. We examine two of these studies below.

The SBIF Study

The previous chapter described the Significant Bilingual Instructional Features (SBIF) study performed by Tikunoff (1983) in order to identify attributes of exemplary teaching approaches. The SBIF findings can be divided into two parts: instructional features common to language minority and majority classrooms and instructional features unique to language minority classrooms. As we saw in Chapter 7, this study of fifty-eight "effective" classrooms identified the following set of instructional features:

SBIF Findings

1. Task outcomes were clearly specified for students.
2. "Active teaching" behaviors were utilized extensively to (a) maintain students' engagement in tasks by pacing instruction appropriately and promoting involvement, (b) monitor students' progress, and (c) provide immediate feedback to students.

Effective instructional features specific to limited-English-proficient students of Hispanic background included the use of two languages, special activities for teaching a second language, and instructional practices that took advantage of the students' culture.

Becoming a Responsive Teacher

8.1 An Effective Teacher's Reflections, in Her Own Voice

Cup of coffee in one hand and my journal in the other, I sit down to write my reflections. It is 7:30 a.m. and my bilingual first-grade class will start in half an hour. I flip to yesterday's page and recall how well our learning logs are going and how unsure I had been about their use. I also jot a short comment about how well Sammy is approximating in his phonetic guesses in reading and writing, something I also was not sure about just 24 hours ago. In fact, just eight years ago I was unsure about a lot of my teaching because of the paradigm shift that I was going through. That isn't true now because of the knowledge and practice I have acquired through professional reading, peer discussion groups, risk-taking, time, and reflection.

Today, April 2, 1993, I look around and I see a classroom filled with print: print that is chosen for its functional use; print that often reflects what we are currently learning and hope to learn; print that belongs to children in process of becoming literate community members. Today the children are immersed in a print-filled classroom that identifies our theme, dinosaurs. The brainstorm charts include the titles "What we know" and "What we want to learn" about dinosaurs. One vocabulary chart in particular will be used to classify dinosaur words or put them in ABC order. In the book corner there is a minimum of 100 books, with at least 20 authored by the children. Lists around the room remind us of our schedules, what we need to order, or who will be visiting our classrooms. I stop and look at a chart that lists the books we have already read during our dinosaur theme. We also have noted whether they inform us with scientific facts or teach us about literature. The condition of immersion supports children's reading and writing as well as collections of their knowledge.

The student-centered feeling in my classroom comes from children bringing themselves and their world into our collaborative learning. Their language, background, experiences, and interests, what they know and what they want to learn, are continually shared. On the first day of school we shared what we wanted to learn in first grade and why. These themes then became the curriculum and my role became one of orchestrating grade-level objectives, instructional strategies, and the content of the theme.

When my students write in interactive journals they highlight for me this condition of student-centeredness. They share their lives, what they know or are not sure about. Children write about the visit they had with their grandparents or what they hope Mommy will buy for them on Saturday or why the doctor can't help their little sister get better. I respond to each child about his or her written entry with both written and oral discourse. We read together my response and the child then responds orally to my questions or comments. A student-centered condition reflects that children have ownership of their learning.

As an instructional strategy, interactive journals allow me to demonstrate literacy on a very individual basis. I demonstrate that oral language is meaningful, that written language uses a phonetic system and that what they write (initially strings of letters) is important to me. During interactive journal writing, I sit next to each child and we read, write, speak, and listen to each other. Demonstration informs children as to how I do it and informs me as to how they do. Through thinking aloud during my demonstrations I try to communicate why and how they might make better approximations in their learning.

Approximation is a condition that allows children to take risks in all areas of literacy. I see approximations in their writing pieces that are in their learning logs, journal entries, and narrative first drafts. I hear approximations in their reading and personal response to literature as well as in their oral discussions about their learning. These approximations include the quality of being close to as well as knowing what is almost exact. These approximations help to inform my instruction so that I am able to plan for optimal learning.

I have organized my classroom in four distinct areas. These areas call for children to actively participate in social organizations that promote specific types of engagement. The main area of the classroom places children in desks that are in foursomes, allowing children to actively participate in cooperative structures quickly. It also produces lots of talk. The discourse that is shared might be about the content of the theme or about constructing meaning from one language to another.

Near the front of the room is a small area where I teach to four small groups, one group each half hour. The active participation that occurs during this strategy comes in part from the nature of the text we use for literacy lessons: whole texts. This morning I will be teaching about sequencing within a wordless book strategy. Even the wordless book has a complete story to be told, and therefore it supports the students as they construct with me a written text to accompany the story in pictures. Another lesson I will teach today begins with a whole poem which the children learned through repeated choral reading. During this shared reading lesson I will focus on rhyming words and their smaller parts, called short vowels.

Wholeness is a condition that also lies within theme work and literature conversations. A theme cycle begins with the whole class sharing thematic knowledge, moving into smaller groups to share and gain specific information, and returning to the whole to share new learning and initiate a new theme cycle. Within a literature conversation, I or a student reads the whole book, then in small groups or pairs we share personal connections as well as our thoughts on literature elements such as plot and setting.

Across the room, eight to ten children are able to sit around a long rectangular table and participate in the writing process. Children choose their own topics, share what they are writing, and ask for support in content and mechanics from each other at the writing table. Around the room there are centers that are organized by theme, ABC awareness, bilingual use, listening and/or art. Two children work at each center in pairs. These pairs were created so that children could demonstrate to each other language, knowledge, social skills, and/or work habits. Active participation as a condition occurs more often when the condition of choice is also present.

Choice happens in my classroom individually and collaboratively. In both interactive journals and during the author's cycle children choose topic, amount, genre and even language (Spanish or English) of their written work. During DEAR ["Drop Everything and Read"] Time, children choose what book or books they will read. In theme work they often choose what they will research and what group they will join. At the listening center children choose what form (such as story map, word web, or character profile) they will use to share their connections to the book with the rest of the class.

When children see the authentic purpose for the choices they are making they become more involved in their learning. The purpose must go beyond the classroom and beyond covering the skills of first grade. Again, the organization of my classroom supports children in real-life uses of language and literacy: children engage in talk in large groups, small groups (teacher-directed), groups of four (peer talk at the desk groups), and one-on-one (centers). The organization also helps them in the real life task of selecting which kind of talk is most functional. If students choose to author a book about their younger brother and his adventures, they realize they will go through the same process that real authors do. The narrative text will call for teaching and learning opportunities but the authenticity lies in the sharing of the published book with an audience. Much of the written work that my children write is shared with others for response.

Response helps children to understand their work better through the reflections of others. These reflections assist children in their oral and written performance. In the Author's Chair phase of writing, my children read their first draft to an audience that understands that they are to listen for story line or informational facts. If students in the audience are unable to construct meaning during Author's Chair, they need to ask the author for support and then assist him or her with words or ideas that support meaning. During editing, both peers and I will help with mechanics, such as spelling or punctuation. This type of response helps to create the condition of community.

The community of co-learners that my students and I belong to has common interests and commitment to working together. I often find this condition hard to describe but it is one you can feel and observe in a very short time. What is often mentioned by visitors to our classroom is the ownership that the children have of their classroom, how they participate in its management, and their interest in sharing their community with others.

As I sit here and complete my reflections, I am surprised that I have not mentioned the condition called expectations. In fact, this condition is the one I bring to my classroom and can be the most important one for my children. It is also the one condition that teachers control through what they believe their children are

Becoming a Responsive Teacher *(continued)*

able to do. Can all the children learn to read and write in my classroom? Yes, and so they will. Once, a long time ago, I expected that only one group of children in my classroom would read at grade level, that another group would almost achieve that level, and that the third group would just get through one small book. Expectations or lack of expectations are often influenced by social and economic factors that we note about our children (such as being poor, having no books at home, or no one to help at home). Our lack of understanding the linguistic or cultural diversity that our children bring to our classrooms also influences the expectations that we set for our children. This condition is also of interest because my peers set expectations for themselves as I do each school year. I have never failed to meet the expectations I have set for myself and would guess that very few have failed to meet theirs. Yet, I often hear about how expectations had to be lowered so that students could feel successful in learning. Holding high expectations for all learners not only calls for trust in the learner but also for creating conditions for optimal learning in every classroom.

It's 7:55 a.m., my coffee is cold, and the children will arrive in five minutes. As I look through my written reflections, I wonder what my colleagues think about these conditions creating optimal learning for all children?

Source: Erminda García, Alianza School, Watsonville, CA. Used by permission of the author.

Meeting the Challenge

1. According to this teacher, what are the conditions that create optimal learning for all children? Identify as many as you can, using the teacher's own wording.
2. If you could sit and talk with this teacher for a while, what questions would you ask? Describe what you think would be your areas of agreement or disagreement regarding the methods and goals of education.
3. Experiment with interactive journal writing in class. Go back through this book and select a topic that you still have questions about. Write a page or two of reflection as a journal entry. Now exchange journals with a classmate, write a response, and exchange journals once again.

Use of
Language

The SBIF study reported that English was used approximately 60 percent of the time, and the native language (L1) or a combination of L1 and the second language (L2) was used the rest of the time. The percentage of English used increased with grade level. The two languages were often combined in a particular way.

1. Instructors alternated between the students' native language and English whenever necessary to ensure clarity. They switched languages but rarely translated directly from one language to another.
2. Students developed English language skills during ongoing instruction in the regular classroom rather than in a separate ESL classroom.

Language
Switching

Of interest above is the finding that bilingual instruction was characterized by the use of both the native language and English in classroom interactions. This language switching seemed to directly assist in clarifying instructional discourse. Wong-Fillmore and Valadez (1985) have suggested that language switching may be detrimental to second-language acquisition if too much translation is encouraged. Milk (1986) reports in a study which focused on the use of a concurrent bilingual instructional model that a nontranslation concurrent approach yielded functional language switching discourse patterns similar to those reported for separation instructional models. Students in the study followed a language choice rule ("Speak to the speaker in the language [in which] you are addressed") in a discourse situation which included 47.5 percent Spanish use and 57.5 percent English use. Such data suggest further that instructional discourse should concentrate on clarity, and that clarity can be enhanced through the use of the students' native language.

The SBIF study also reports that incorporating aspects of the LEP students' home culture can promote engagement in instructional tasks and contribute to a feeling of trust between children and their teachers. The SBIF researchers found three ways in which home and community culture was incorporated into classroom life: (a) cultural referents in both verbal and nonverbal forms were used to communicate instructional and institutional demands; (b) instruction was organized to build upon rules of discourse from the home culture; and (c) values and norms of the home culture were respected equally with those of the school.

The García Studies

In recent research which focused on Mexican American elementary school children, García (1988) reported several related instructional strategies utilized in "effective" schools. Students at these schools, which were nominated for the study by teachers of language minority students, scored at or above the national average on standardized measures of academic achievement in Spanish and/or English. This research characterized instruction in the effective classrooms as follows:

1. Students were instructed primarily in small groups, and academic-related discourse was encouraged between students throughout the day. Teachers rarely utilized large-group instruction or more individualized (e.g., mimeographed worksheets) instructional activities. The most common activity across classes involved small groups of students working on assigned academic tasks with intermittent assistance by the teacher.
2. Teachers tended to initiate instruction in a way often reported in the literature (Mehan, 1979; Morine-Dershimer, 1985) and to elicit student responses at relatively lower cognitive and linguistic levels. They then allowed students to control the discourse and to invite participation from peers. These invited interactions often occurred at higher cognitive and linguistic levels.

Of particular relevance are intensive case studies of elementary and middle schools (García, 1988, 1992; Moll, 1988; Pease-Alvarez and García, 1991). The results of these studies are summarized in the next section according to several instructional categories that were empirically relevant. Much like attributes discussed earlier in Chapter 7, the attributes described are not to be construed as necessary for effective instruction of linguistically and culturally diverse students. Instead, they are offered as an example of how instructional environments can be structured to serve diversity.

High levels of communication. In the classrooms studied, functional communication between teacher and students and among fellow students was emphasized more than might be expected in a regular classroom. Teachers were constantly checking with students to verify the clarity of assignments and the students' roles in those assignments. Classrooms were characterized by a high, sometimes even noisy, level of communication emphasizing student collaboration on small-group projects organized

| Informal |
| Setting |

around "learning centers." This organization minimized individualized work tasks, such as worksheet exercises, and provided a very informal familylike social setting in which the teacher either worked with a small group of students (never larger than eight and as small as one) or traveled about the room assisting individuals or small groups of students as they worked on their projects. Large-group instruction was rare, usually confined to start-up activities in the morning.

Integrated and thematic curriculum. Significantly, the instruction of basic skills and academic content was consistently organized around thematic units. In the majority of classrooms studied, the students actually selected the themes in consultation with the teacher, either through direct voting or some related negotiation process. The teacher's responsibility was to ensure that the instruction revolving around the chosen themes covered the school district's content- and skill-related goals and objectives for that grade level. The theme approach allowed teachers to integrate academic content with the development of basic skills. The major thrust in these classrooms was the appropriation of knowledge centered around chosen themes, with the understanding that students would necessarily develop basic skills as a means to appropriate this knowledge. Students became "experts" in thematic domains while also acquiring the requisite academic skills.

Collaborative learning. Reported analysis of instructional events in literacy and math, along with analysis of actual literacy products (dialogue journals, learning logs, writing workshop publications, etc.) and math products (learning logs, homework, surveys, etc.), indicated that teachers in Latino language minority classrooms organized instruction in such a way that students were required to interact with each other utilizing collaborative learning techniques. It was during student-student interactions that most linguistic discourse of a higher cognitive order was observed (García, 1988, 1992). Students asked each other hard questions and challenged each other's answers more readily than they did in interactions with the teacher. Moreover, students were likely to seek assistance from other students and were successful in obtaining it.

Student

Discourse

Language and literacy. In classes with Spanish speakers, lower-grade teachers used both Spanish and English as the language of instruction, whereas upper-grade teachers utilized mostly

Table 8.3   Sheltered English Techniques in the Mainstream Class

1. **Increase wait time.**

   Give your students time to think and process the information before you rush in with answers. A student may know the answers, but need a little more processing time in order to say it in English.

2. **Respond to the message.**

   If a student has the answer correct and you can understand it, don't correct his or her grammar. The exact word and correct grammatical response will develop with time, especially with young children. Instead, repeat his or her answer, putting it into standard English, and let the student know that you are pleased with his or her response.

3. **Simplify your language.**

   Speak directly to the student, emphasizing important nouns and verbs, and using as few extra words as possible. Repetition and speaking louder doesn't help; rephrasing, accompanied by body language does.

4. **Don't force reticent students to speak.**

   Instead, give the students an opportunity to demonstrate his or her comprehension and knowledge through body actions, drawing pictures, manipulating objects, or pointing.

5. **Demonstrate; use manipulatives.**

   Whenever possible, accompany your message with gestures, pictures, and objects that help get the meaning across. Use a variety of different pictures or objects for the same idea. Give an immediate context for new words.

6. **Make use of all senses.**

   Give students a chance to touch things, to listen to sounds, even to smell and taste when possible. Talk about the words that describe these senses as the student physically experiences something. Write new words as well as say them.

7. **Pair or group students with native speakers.**

   Much of a child's language learning comes from interacting with his/her peers. Give your students tasks to complete that require interaction of each member of the group, but arrange it so that the student has linguistically easier tasks. Utilize cooperative learning techniques in a student-centered classroom.

Table 8.3   Sheltered English Techniques in the Mainstream Class (cont'd)

8. Adapt the materials.

Don't "water down" the content. Rather, make the concepts more accessible and comprehensible by adding pictures, charts, maps, time-lines, and diagrams, in addition to simplifying the language.

9. Increase your knowledge.

Learn as much as you can about the language and culture of your students. Go to movies, read books, look at pictures of the countries. Keep the similarities and differences in mind and then check your knowledge by asking your students whether they agree with your impressions. Learn as much of the student's language as you can; even a few words help. Widen your own world view; think of alternate ways to reach the goals you have for your class.

10. Build on the student's prior knowledge.

Find out as much as you can about how and what a student learned in his or her country. Then try to make a connection between the ideas and concepts you are teaching and the student's previous knowledge or previous way of being taught. Encourage the students to point out differences and connect similarities.

11. Support the student's home language and culture; bring it into the classroom.

Your goal should be to encourage the students to keep their home languages as they also acquire English. Many children in this world grow up speaking more than one language; it's an advantage. Let students help bring about a multicultural perspective to the subjects you are teaching. Students might be able to bring in pictures, poems, dances, proverbs, or games. They might be able to demonstrate a new way to do a math problem or bring in a map that shows a different perspective than that given in your history or geography book. Encourage students to bring these items in as a part of the subject you are teaching, not just as a separate activity. Do whatever you can to help your fluent English-speaking students see all students as knowledgeable persons from a respected culture.

Source: P. Sullivan, *ESL in Context*. Corwin Press: 1992. Used with permission.

English. However, students were allowed to use either language. With regard to literacy development of Spanish-speaking students, observations revealed the following:

- Students progressed systematically from writing in the native language in the early grades to writing in English in the later grades.
- Students' writing in English emerged at or above their grade level of writing in Spanish.
- Students' writing in English was highly conventional, contained few spelling or grammatical errors, and showed systematic use of invented spelling.
- Students made the transformation from Spanish to English themselves, without any pressure from the teacher to do so.

Unfortunately, similar research with non-Latino students is limited. Sullivan (1992), however, has identified a set of important instructional adaptations of importance to teachers who serve linguistically and culturally diverse students in mainstream classrooms. Table 8.3 provides several techniques of **sheltered English,** which maximizes non-verbal instructional communication that combines content with English-language-learning goals.

Perceptions. Interviews with classroom teachers, principals, and parents from diverse cultural and linguistic backgrounds revealed an interesting set of perspectives regarding the education of students in the schools studied. Classroom teachers were highly committed to the educational success of their students.

Teachers

They perceived themselves as instructional innovators and attended to their own professional development. They had a demonstrated commitment to school-home communication and felt empowered to make things happen in their classrooms, even if they did not follow the district's guidelines to the letter. These instructors "adopted" their students. They had high academic expectations and refused to consider any of their students as intellectually disadvantaged.

Principals tended to be well informed and highly articulate about the curriculum and instructional strategies undertaken in their schools. They were also highly supportive of their instruc-

Principals

tional staff and took pride in staff accomplishments. They reported their support of teacher autonomy, although they were quite aware of pressure to conform strictly to district policies regarding the standardization of curriculum and the need for academic accountability (testing).

Becoming a Responsive Teacher

8.2 A Letter Home

A letter written by a student in a new program integrating linguistically and culturally diverse students with the general school population.

Dear Mom and Dad,

Please read all of the theme assignments for the last two quarters in my portfolio. The folder should be set up so that the pieces for the "Coming of Age in the 90s" theme are on the left, and the assignments for the "Gangs" theme are on the right. I would like you to read the writing for the activities I have done about these themes.

When you read my folder, I am asking that you take the time to answer, in a letter back to me, a few questions:

1. What assignment in my portfolio tells you the most about my schoolwork?
2. What do you see as strengths in my writing?
3. What do you see as the areas that need improvement?
4. What suggestions do you have that might aid my growth as a student?

Thank you very much for investing your time in my theme portfolio.

Sincerely,

Meeting the Challenge

1. In addition to the letter response requested above, what other ways can you think of that might increase parental involvement in children's education?
2. Explain why it is important for parents to understand the challenges their children face in school.

Parents expressed a high level of satisfaction with and appreciation for their children's educational experience in these schools. All indicated or implied that their academic success was vital to their children's future economic success. Parents of both Anglo-American students and culturally diverse students were quite involved in formal support activities. However, whereas Anglo-American parents were somewhat distrustful of the school's interest in doing what was best for their child, the parents of culturally diverse students expressed a high level of trust in the teaching and administrative staff.

Parents
▓▓▓▓▓▓▓▓▓▓

Conclusion

The research described in this chapter addressed some significant practical questions about effective academic environments for linguistically and culturally diverse students:

Did native language instruction play a role?
The schools in these studies considered native language instruction key in the early grades (K–3).

Was there one best curriculum?
No common curriculum was identified in these studies. However, a well-trained instructional staff implementing an integrated student-centered curriculum with literacy pervasive in all aspects of instruction was consistently observed across grade levels. Basal readers were utilized sparingly and usually as resource material.

What instructional strategies were effective?
Teachers consistently organized instruction so as to ensure collaborative learning in heterogeneous small groups. Group academic activities required a high degree of student-student interaction. Individual instructional activity was limited, as was individual competition as an ingredient of classroom motivation.

Who were the key players in this effective schooling drama?
School administrators and parents played important roles, but teachers were the key. They gained the confidence of their peers and supervisors. They worked to organize instruction, create new instructional environments, assess effectiveness, and advocate for their students. They were proud of their students but consistently demanding. They rejected any notion of academic, linguistic, cultural, or intellectual inferiority in their students.

These features of effective classrooms for linguistically and culturally diverse students support, above all, the establishment of an interactive, student-centered learning context. In other words, effective instructional staff recognize that academic learning has its roots in processes of social interaction. The practices identified here as effective have also been affirmed by recent educational intervention research aimed at restructuring education for these students (Rivera and Zehler, 1990). The convergence of findings from this new empirical research generates the following set of specific guidelines:

- Any curriculum, including one for diverse children, must address all categories of learning goals (cognitive and academic, advanced as well as basic). We should not lower our expectations for these students; they, too, need to be intellectually challenged.

- The more linguistically and culturally diverse the children, the more closely teachers must relate academic content to a child's own environment and experience.

- The more diverse the children, the more integrated the curriculum should be. That is, multiple content areas (e.g., math, science, social studies) and language learning activities should be centered around a single theme. Children should have opportunities to study a topic in depth and to apply a variety of skills acquired in home, community, and school contexts.

- The more diverse the children, the greater the need for active rather than passive endeavors, particularly informal social activities such as group projects, in which students are allowed flexibility in their participation with the teacher and other students.

- The more diverse the children, the more important it is to offer them opportunities to apply what they are learning in a meaningful context. Curriculum can be made meaningful in a number of creative ways. Science and math skills can be effectively applied, for example, through hands-on, interactive activities that allow students to explore issues of significance in their lives, such as an investigation of the quality of the local water supply.

In conclusion, information derived from recent research indicates that linguistically and culturally diverse students can be served effectively. These students can achieve academically at levels at or above the national norm. Instructional strategies that serve these students best acknowledge, respect, and build upon the language and culture of the home. Teachers play the most critical role in students' academic success, and students become important partners with teachers in the teaching and learning enterprise. Although much more research is required, we are not without a knowledge base that can make a difference.

SUMMARY OF MAJOR IDEAS

1. As American educator John Dewey claimed, knowledge is not a thing to be dispensed but a process of construction and reconstruction that allows us to live and to grow. Schooling practices in the United States must begin to reflect this understanding of knowledge and to adapt to new populations of students and new societal expectations. If not, the educational vulnerability of culturally diverse students, with their accompanying loss in employment competence, will continue.

2. Some theorists claim that educational failure can be explained by a "clash" between the student's home and school cultures. Others claim that academic underachievement is caused by educators' failure to use principles of teaching and learning that have been proved to "work" with students. Both of these theoretical perspectives are useful in identifying instructional practices that might enhance education for culturally diverse students.

3. Research indicates that effective schools focus on making improvements according to the following organizational and structural variables: autonomy in school site management, instructional leadership from the principal, curriculum that considers students' cultural and linguistic attributes, staff development, parent support and involvement, recognition of student success, and district support. Effective schools also attend to the following process variables: collaborative planning and collegial relationships, a sense of community, clear goals and high expectations, and order and discipline.

4. Proponents of education reform claim that U.S. schools generally are environments that encourage passive learning, age-based groupings and tracking, abstract curriculum, unclear and irrelevant standards, and neutral affect. These reformers state that schools must be transformed to constitute a community of learners that emphasizes active engage-

ment, developmentally appropriate heterogeneous groupings, thematic and integrated curriculum, performance-based standards and assessments, and care for students.

5. For children, development and learning occur as a result of interactions among linguistic, sociocultural, and cognitive factors. Effective instructional practices for culturally diverse students take the social experiences of children into consideration.

6. Research into instructional practices has shown that high levels of communication between teacher and students can be especially effective, as can the use of a thematic curriculum and collaborative, small-group instruction. Students who work together in small groups tend to participate in linguistic discourse of a higher cognitive order. LEP students are more successful if both the native language and English are used for instruction.

EXTENDING YOUR EXPERIENCE

1. Much of the research cited in this text indicates that culturally and linguistically diverse children learn higher-level cognitive skills best in a social context—by talking and writing, reading and listening. What do the results of this research imply for the way classrooms are organized? For the role of teachers?

2. Explain the difference between active and passive learning activities. Give an example of a passive learning task typical of a traditional, teacher-centered classroom, and then describe a way to transform it into an active, student-centered activity.

3. Plan an integrated curriculum for a school of linguistically and culturally diverse children. Together with a few of your classmates, decide on the grade levels and demographic make-up of your students. Each one of you could design a single facet of the curriculum and then, acting as a collaborative team of teachers, assemble these facets into a whole. Specify the learning materials you will use, such as books, music, physical objects, resource people, and so on. Remember the importance of student-student interaction, and try to apply some of the research findings discussed throughout this text. Present your curriculum plan to the class.

4. Create a class book titled "Why Teach?" Ask each member of your class to contribute a single sheet of paper on which he

or she personally answers this question, in writing or in any other graphic form. Make sure your classmates use black ink, so their contributions are legible for duplicating. Bind enough copies for everyone in class, including your instructor, and distribute them.

RESOURCES FOR FURTHER STUDY

Carter, T. P., and Chatfield, M. L. (1986). Effective bilingual schools: Implications for policy and practice. *American Journal of Education, 5,* 200–234.

The authors describe the relationship between bilingual programs and effective schools. They argue that all students, including limited-English-proficient students, can succeed in an academic environment that is always striving to improve learning. This approach must be planned, organized, and sustained, and the guidelines for improvement must be part of the school's structure in order to be effective. Actions that promote support across departments, including bilingual programs, produce high levels of student achievement.

Diaz, S., Moll, L. C., and Mehan, H. (1986). Sociocultural resources in instruction: A context-specific approach. In *Beyond language: Social and cultural factors in schooling language minority students* (pp. 197–230). Sacramento: Bilingual Education Office, California State Department of Education.

This chapter is part of a publication written to better understand the factors that influence the education of minority students. The authors point out that before entering school, all children are capable of language acquisition and cognitive development. They suggest an ethnographic process as a means of addressing how children's learning differentiates upon entering school—in particular that of minority students. The process suggests interventions for correcting discrepancies. The authors give examples of instances in which both teachers and students can adapt their behavior toward becoming academically successful without giving up their culture.

Purkey, S. C., and Smith, M. S. (1983). Effective Schools: A review. *Elementary School Journal, 83,* 52–78.

This article presents an extensive review of literature and case studies which focus on ways of making schools more effective. The authors offer a series of characteristics to use to improve the learning environment and make it more conducive to knowledge transmission. Schools, they argue, are not solitary entities but rather an integral part of a social system with diverse cultures. For change to occur, educators must reexamine institutions and priorities to provide the best education possible for all students. Additional questions and issues are raised to further the discussion of promoting effective schools.

Slavin, R., Karweit, N., and Madden, N. (1989). *Effective programs for students at risk.* Needham Heights, Mass. Allyn and Bacon.

This volume reviews a large amount of research on effective programs for students at risk for school failure. The conclusion centers around two themes: (1) the type of program offered and (2) the prevention methods used to avoid implementating remedy programs for those students who are failing. The authors argue that school programs and curriculum should exist to help students catch up or improve their academic standing. Major changes are needed to enable the educational system to offer at-risk students a chance to succeed. Fundamental changes in the organization of schools, curriculum, and delivery of knowledge must be initiated to ensure that all students receive a good education.

Tharp, R. G. (1989). Psychocultural variables and k constants: Effects on teaching and learning in schools. *American Psychologist, 44,* 349–359.

The literate and cognitive activities in schooling are deeply connected to the psychocultural teachings and learning processes developed in the student's home and community. Psychocultural variables are also responsible for the sharp differences in school achievement shown by members of different cultural groups. All cultures bring different variables to the academic field, and schools must not only recognize but also embrace these variables to promote diversity and academic growth. The author offers some recommendations as to how schools can adapt and how the environment of the classroom may be improved. The author also suggests research questions that must be answered to advance school reform.

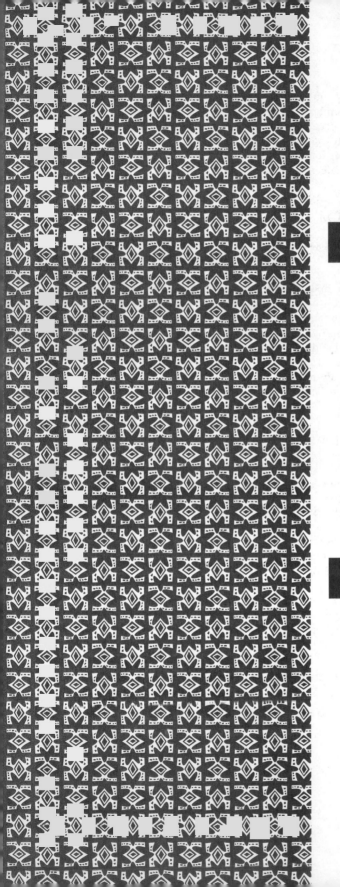

EPILOGUE:

CLOSING

CONTEXTS

In mid-June of 1992, Isabelle Castellon, Frank and Linola Lincoln, Manuel and Gloria Cabrera, and Nu Lin Tran met their first university professor. The occasion was the graduation of their respective daughters, Aretha Lincoln and Selene Tran, and sons, Jorge Mario Cabrera and Jesús Castellon, from the University of California. This occasion marked a significant event in the lives of each of these individuals but was equally significant for the country as a whole.

The accomplishments of these students represent the aspiration of many families in the United States. For linguistically and culturally diverse families, however, it is not so common an accomplishment. On several occasions our nation has acted to rectify this situation—through *Brown* v. *Board of Education*, the Equal Education Opportunity Act, the Bilingual Education Act, to name a few—but these actions can easily become engulfed by the enormity and complexity of the issues and the available data. Let's face it. Education has become embroiled in conflicts about race, politics, economics, power struggles, population shifts, competitiveness with other countries, and much more (Sarason, 1992). Aretha, Jorge Mario, Selene, Jesús, and their families should serve as our anchors in this ocean of statistical summaries and endless charts, tables, and analyses—including the ones in this book. We are concerned with real students, their families, and their communities.

A renewed concern has arisen in the last decade about the educational underachievement of culturally diverse students (Science, 1992). A broad set of analysts have reached virtual consensus that correcting this academic underachievement is in the best interest of our country. The schooling years represent one of society's best opportunities to fully prepare the next generation of citizens—those who will lead its institutions and shape future generations. In a nation where the population of culturally diverse students continues to rise, this opportunity is particularly significant.

However, the schooling years also represent a vulnerable period of human development. Young people are especially vulnerable as they construct their identities, values, and career choices. They must learn how to develop independence, build friendships, acquire new intellectual skills, solidify personal values, focus on career aspirations, and form more intense intimate relationships, and the school is not always organized to functionally assist in these processes. The traditional mission of the school has mainly been to transmit knowledge to students.

Moreover, the school presumes that families will send a child who has been prepared for learning and nurtured at home. The disjuncture between the traditional mission of the school and the circumstances of our students may explain why our educational system is so troubled.

This disjuncture is more severe for linguistically and culturally diverse students. The data are very clear in this regard. Their K–12 education does not prepare them as well as other groups. They have less firsthand knowledge about careers available to them. The language, norms, and values of their communities are dramatically different from those at the school. Categorical treatment based on their memberships in certain ethnic/racial, class, and gender groups are an added burden to negotiate in constructing their identities and achieving their academic and life goals.

This book has examined efforts mounted by the U.S. schools to serve a larger number of culturally diverse students. Research into these efforts has considered the culture of the students, their families, and their communities, and the culture of the school. The task is to organize and utilize our human, intellectual, and physical resources in order to allow these complex, intertwined cultures to meet constructively. Although the task is a difficult one, one presupposition can keep it focused:

- Educational programs should be constituted for all students. These programs should be caring, ethical, and socially responsible. They should take place in intellectual communities where knowledge is constructed and transmitted through relationships established between family members, teachers, administrators, support staff, and other students. In these educational environments, unity through diversity will be achieved.

We have discussed diversity extensively throughout these chapters and examined its challenges within educational contexts. In closing, I want to discuss two more contexts for understanding the perspective in this book. As you know, we ought not separate a text from its context.

First of all, as educators, we have three diverse personas. We are professional educators and scholars, we are citizens, and we are deeply caring individuals who advocate for children. It is the child advocate in us that speaks most harshly of the many ways in which diversity is not cherished in this society. Second, the social context this book enters features three myths in the public debate regarding diversity:

1. *Promoting diversity will divide us.* Strangely, this myth assumes that we are somehow presently united. In fact, our society is more segregated today than at any other time. It is society that sustains an economy in which huge gaps in median family income are plainly visible. It is a society with palpable fault lines in our urban centers—New York, Miami, Detroit, Chicago, San Francisco, Los Angeles—and in rural areas of Appalachia and on American Indian reservations. Some have argued that to embrace diversity is to unify in the face of division. The educator as child advocate agrees!

2. *An emphasis on diversity will lead to our doing things right as well as doing the right things.* This myth holds that equity, fairness, excellence, and reason will characterize our embracing of diversity, and that all previous "wrongs" perpetuated by the "devils" of division will be righted. It is important to be frank: an emphasis on diversity will not usher in an environment in which educational, economic, and social opportunities which have not been afforded members of this society will be excused away in the name of diversity. We must maintain the integrity of the meaning of *diversity*. A newfound respect for diversity, within and among us, will not be enough. We will need to work through the specific meanings of diversity as they relate to our educational practice.

3. *An emphasis on diversity will be easy.* It is not and never has been easy, this respect for diversity. The early Hebrew scholars debated "us versus them"—the Hom and the Goy. The Greek philosophers Plato and Aristotle differed vehemently on this issue. Plato argued that likeness minimizes political favoritism, and Aristotle argued that diversity promotes inventiveness and creativity. The Italian theologian Saint Thomas Aquinas professed that likeness ensures unity, and the Protestant reformer Martin Luther opted to promote diversity in reverence to God. Today, within our borders, proponents of the "English Only" movement are passionately concerned that multilingualism will cause the downfall of the United States. Meanwhile, indigenous people mourn the loss of their languages and cultures. The educator as scholar would remind us that embracing diversity with unity will not be easy. She understands that many people have tried and none have been particularly successful. The educator as professional encourages us to try again. The educator as child advocate insists on it.

There is an old Spanish language proverb which reminds us that "del árbol caído todos hacen leña"—roughly translated, "from a fallen tree, all will make firewood." When a magnificent living redwood loses the diverse contexts in which it thrives— the sun, the water, the clean air, the wind—then it will die, no matter how magnificent it might have been. It dries, changes its character, and can easily be gathered and burned. That burning destroys forever what it was and destroys almost all evidence that it ever existed. Like that tree, without the diverse elements which nurture us, we are likely to wither, die, and disappear. No educator wants any part of that future.

GLOSSARY

acculturation The process by which the members of a society are taught the elements of the society's culture.

act psychology A model for human cognitive processes that focus on the assertion that the mental functions perceiving, remembering, and organizing—ultimately knowing— are all acts of consumption.

affect A term used in psychology to refer to people's feelings and emotions as distinguished from their thoughts and actions.

Americanization *Assimilation* as it is practiced in the United States. See *assimilation.*

assimilation An approach to acculturation that seeks to merge small ethnic and linguistically diverse communities into a single dominant national institutional structure and culture.

bilingualism The ability to speak two languages with equal fluency.

Black English The most-studied nonstandard American English dialect. Although the roots of Black English lie in African Creole and English, it has its own distinct syntactic, phonological, semantic, and vocabulary rules.

burnout Physical or emotional exhaustion, most often caused by a great deal of stress experienced over a long period of time.

code switching The production of mixed language utterances.

cohort rates report A report, compiled over a given time period, that describes what happens to a single group of students.

communication A combination of verbal and nonverbal systems that enables humans to encode meaning and transmit it to others.

connoisseur model A method of teacher assessment that allows experienced and knowledgeable educators to train and judge other educators.

constructionist perspective The belief that for humans, knowing is a result of continual building and rebuilding.

contextualized language Language that conveys meaning using physical cues such as gestures, intonation, and other concrete representations characteristic of face-to-face communication.

culture concept A term defined by Edward Tylor in 1871 as "that complex whole which includes knowledge, belief, art, law, morals, custom, and other capabilities and habits acquired by man as a member of society."

cultural systems approach The approach to education that considers the organization of a society, specifically the roles and status assigned to cultural groups within a society, to be a major determinant of educational underachievement. Also known as *structural inequality theory, institutional racism, the perceived labor market explanation,* and *secondary cultural systems theory.*

culture A system of values, beliefs, notions about acceptable and unacceptable behavior, and other socially constructed ideas characteristic of a society of a subgroup within a society.

curriculum The area of schooling that addresses the content of instruction.

decontextualized language Language that relies on abstract linguistic and cognitive cues that are independent of the communicative context.

dialect A regional variation of language characterized by distinct grammar, vocabulary, and pronunciation.

direct instruction A teaching strategy wherein the teacher transmits knowledge to students through modeling and step-by-step instructions.

disposition An individual's usual temperament and frame of mind.

distributive model of culture A model that implies that each individual's portion of the culture differs in some ways from that of any other individual.

double immersion A program whose goal is to produce a student population that is bilingual and bicultural.

ecology The study of the relationships between an organism and its environment.

ethnic A general term used to refer to groups of people who are differentiated by race, religion, nationality, and region of origin.

ethnic images A term used to designate general beliefs that people have about the characteristics and attributes of a cultural group.

event rates report A report, compiled within a single year, that gives the percentage of students who left high school without finishing work toward a diploma.

grammar The system of rules implicit in a language that allows words to be arranged with some regularity of structure.

group-oriented concept of culture A view of culture as a set of attributes that are shared by all the members of a group.

individual-oriented concept of culture A view of culture as a set of attributes made available to members of a group, but that may not be shared by all members.

inservice preparation Professional training for teachers who are already working in a classroom.

institutional racism See **cultural systems approach.**

instructional conversation See **instructional discourse.**

instructional discourse A teaching strategy that emphasizes discussion in the classroom. Also called **instructional conversation.**

intelligence The ability of an individual's mind to acquire and apply knowledge.

language The use by human beings of voice sounds, written symbols, and hand signals to communicate thoughts and feelings. For the purposes of this text, *language* is a complex interaction of many variables, including: the verbal signal, the signal sender, the manner and context in which the signal is sent, the signal receiver, and previous experiences the sender and the receiver may have had with similar signals.

language minority student A student characterized by substantive participation in a non-English-speaking social environment, who has acquired the normal communicative abilities of that social environment and is exposed to an English-speaking environment on a regular basis only during the formal school process.

language pragmatics The rules of a language, as well as cultural notions about what is considered appropriate and effective use of the language.

magnet school A school whose purpose is to attract a highly diverse set of students around a thematically designed curriculum that is multilingual and multicultural.

May 25 memorandum A memorandum issued by the U.S. Department of Health, Education and Welfare in 1970, which clarified the mandate of the 1964 Civil Rights Act with respect to non-English-speaking populations of students.

meta analysis A method of analyzing and summarizing large numbers of research studies.

metalinguistic awareness The conscious awareness of how one uses language.

minority A group that is subordinate to another dominant group and that is subject to a negative power relationship.

modal grade level The academic level considered normal for students of a particular age.

multicultural education A curriculum whose content educates students on the contributions of more than one culture.

multilingualism The ability to speak three or more languages with equal fluency.

participant-structured demand In education, the demands of instruction that are imposed on children by the organization of the learning environment itself.

participant structures In communication, the rules that govern who speaks when.

perceived labor market explanation See **cultural systems approach.**

personality The pattern of character, behavioral, mental, and emotional traits of an individual. In education, the personality is a structure that reconciles a child's interpreted experiences with his or her emotional states.

phonology The study of speech sounds.

profession A job characterized by (a) acquisition of knowledge obtained through formal education and (b) an orientation toward serving the needs of the public, with an emphasis on ethical and altruistic concern for the client.

psychometrics The measurement of psychological attributes.

scaffolding An educational practice that provides support for children as they move between disparate home and school cultures.

schema A mental framework for perceiving the world.

secondary cultural systems theory See *cultural systems approach.*

second-language acquisition A process of language development whereby a child acquires first one language and then is exposed to and required to learn a second language.

Sheltered English A varied set of instructional techniques that recognize that the student is not a primary speaker of English and the teacher is not proficient in the student's primary language. These techniques maximize non-verbal instructional communication (e.g. using visual/demonstration strategies) that combine content (e.g. math, science, and social studies) and English-language-learning goals.

socialization The process through which prescriptions (ideas about what one should do) and prohibitions (ideas about what one should not do) are transmitted to members of the social group.

Social distance The relationship between two cultures, determined in part by the relative status of the two cultures.

sociocultural theory An international intellectual movement that brings together the disciplines of psychology, semiotics, education, sociology, and anthropology.

Standard English The version of English that has the grammar, vocabulary, and pronunciation considered appropriate for most occasions of public discourse and for written communication.

status rates report A report, compiled at any point in time, that gives the percentage of the population of a given age range who either have not finished high school or are not enrolled.

structural inequality theory See *cultural systems approach.*

syntax The feature of a grammatical system having to do with word order.

transitional bilingual education The program that provides language minority students of Spanish-speaking backgrounds with a transition from early-grade instruction with Spanish emphasis to later-grade instruction with English emphasis, and eventually to English-only instruction.

vocabulary The sum of words understood and used by an individual in any language group.

REFERENCES

Abi-Nader, J. (1990). A house for my mother: Motivating Hispanic high school students. *Anthropology and Education Quarterly 21*(1), 41–58.

Alder, M. (1982). *The paideia proposal: An educational manifesto.* New York: Macmillan.

Allport, G. (1954). *The nature of prejudice.* Reading, Mass: Addison-Wesley.

Altus, W. (1945). Racial and bilingual group differences in predictability on mean aptitude test scores in an Army Special Training Center. *Psychological Bulletin, 42,* 310–320.

———— (1948). A note on group differences in intelligence and the type of test employed. *Journal of Consulting Psychology, 12,* 194–196.

Appleton, C. (1983). *Cultural pluralism in education: Theoretical foundations.* New York: Longman.

Au, K. (1979). Using the experience-text-relationship method with minority children. *Reading Teacher, 32,* 677–679.

Au, K., and Jordan, C. (1981). Teaching reading to Hawaiian children: Finding a culturally appropriate solution. In H. Trueba, G. Guthrie, and K. Au (Eds.), *Culture and the bilingual classroom: Studies in classroom ethnography* (pp. 139–152). Rowley, Mass.: Newbury House.

August, D., and Garcia, E. (1988). *Language minority education in the United States: Research, policy and practice.* Chicago, Ill.: Charles C. Thomas.

Baden, B., and Maehr, M. (1986). Conforming culture with culture: A perspective for designing schools for children of diverse sociocultural backgrounds. In R. Feldman (Ed.), *The social psychology of education* (pp. 189–309). Cambridge: Harvard University Press.

Baetens Beardsmore, H. (1982). *Bilingualism: Basic principles.* Clevedon, Great Britain: Tieto Ltd.

Banks, J. (1981). *Multiethnic education: Theory and practice.* Boston, Mass.: Allyn and Bacon.

———— (1984). *Teaching strategies for ethnic studies.* Boston, Mass.: Allyn and Bacon.

Beauf, J. (1977). Development of ethnic awareness in Native American children. *Developmental Psychology, 13,* 244–256.

Bell, D., Kasschau, P., and Zellman, G. (1976). *Delivering services to elderly members of minority groups: A critical review of the literature.* Santa Monica, Calif.: Rand Corporation.

Ben-Zeev, S. (1977). The influence of bilingualism on cognitive strategy and cognitive development. *Child Development, 48,* 1009–1018.

Berk, R. A. (Ed.) (1986). *Performance assessment: Methods and applications.* Baltimore, Md.: Johns Hopkins University Press.

Berman, P. (1992). *The status of bilingual education in California.* Berkeley, Calif.: Paul Berman and Associates.

Bernstein, B. (1971). A sociolinguistic approach to socialization with some reference to educability. In B. Berstein (Ed.), *Class, codes and control: Theoretical studies towards a sociology of language.* London: Routledge and Kegan Paul.

Bloom, B. (1984). The search for methods of group instruction as effective as one-to-one tutoring. *Educational Leadership, 41*(8), 4–17.

Boggs, S. T. (1972). The meaning of questions and narratives to Hawaiian children. In Cazden, C., John, V., and Hymes, D. (Eds.), *Functions of language in the classroom.* New York: Teachers College Press.

————— (1985). *Speaking, relating and learning: A study of Hawaiian children at home and school.* Norwood, N.J.: Ablex.

Bok, D. (1990). *Universities and the future of America.* Durham, N.C.: Duke University Press.

Boykin, A. W. (1983). The academic performance of Afro-American children. In J. T. Spence (Ed.), *Achievement and achievement motives: Psychological and sociological approaches.* San Francisco: W. H. Freeman and Co.

————— (1986). The triple quandary and the schooling of Afro-American children. In U. Neisser (Ed.), *The school achievement of minority children* (pp. 57–92). New York: New Perspectives.

Brophy, J., and Good, T. (1986). Teacher behavior and student achievement. In M. Wittrock (Ed.), *Handbook of research on teaching* (3rd ed., pp. 328–xx). New York: Macmillan.

Brown vs. *Board of Education,* 347 US 483, 1954: 686.

Calderon, M. (1991). Trainer of trainers: Professional development for diversity. In Office of Bilingual Education and Minority Language Affaris (Eds.), *Proceedings of the First National Research Symposium on Limited English Proficient Students.* Washington, D.C.: U. S. Department of Education.

California Commission on Teacher Credentialing (1991). *Teacher credentialing in California: A special report.* Sacramento, Calif.: California Commission on Teacher Credentialing.

Carter, T. P. (1968). The negative self-concept of Mexican-American students. *School and Society, 96,* 217–219.

Carter, T. P., and Chatfield, M. L. (1986). Effective bilingual schools: Implications for policy and practice. *American Journal of Education, 5* (1), 200–234.

Cavasos, E. (1990, November). *An executive initiative for Hispanic education.* Testimony before U.S. House of Representatives, Committee on Education and Labor.

Cazden, C. B. (1988). *Classroom discourse: The language of teaching and learning.* Portsmouth, N.H.: Heinemann Press.

Cherry, L. J. (1981). Teacher-student interaction and teacher's expectations of students communicative competence. In O. Garnica and M. King (Eds.), *Language, children and society.* (pp. 246–261). New York: Pergamon Press.

Christian, T. and Livermore, G. (1970). A comparison of Anglo-American and Spanish-American children on the WISC. *Journal of Social Psychology, 81,* 9–14.

Chu, H., and Levy, J. (1988). Multicultural skills for bilingual teachers. *NABE Journal, 12*(2), 17–36.

Clark, R. M. (1983). *Family life and school achievement: Why poor black children succeed or fail.* Chicago: University of Chicago Press.

Clark, K. B., and Clark, M. P. (1939). Segregation as a factor in the racial identification of Negro preschool children. *Journal of Experimental Education, 8,* 161–163.

Clasen, D. R., and Brown, B. B. (1985). The multidimensionality of peer pressure in adolescence. *Journal of Youth and Adolescence, 14*(6), 451–468.

Clement, D., and Harding, J. (1978). Social distinctions and emergent student groups in a desegregated school. *Anthropology and Education Quarterly 9*(4), 272–283.

Colangelo, N., Foxley, C. H., and Dustin, D. (*Eds.*) (1982). *The human relations experience.* Monterey, Calif.: Brooks/Cole.

Coleman, J. S. (1963). *The adolescent society: The social life of the teenager and its impact on education.* New York: The Free Press.

Collier, J. P. (1985). University models for ESL and bilingual teacher training. In National Clearinghouse for Bilingual Education (Ed.), *Issues in English language development.* Rosslyn, Va.: Editor.

Committee for Economic Development (1991). *Children in need. Investment strategies for the educationally disadvantaged.* New York: Author.

Coons, J. E., Clune III, W., and Sugarman, S. D. (1970). *Private wealth and public education.* Cambridge, Mass.: Harvard University Press.

Cooper, C. R., Baker, H., Polichar, D., and Welsh, M. (1991). *Ethnic perspectives on individuality and connectedness in adolescents' relationships with family and peers.* Paper presented at the meeting of the Society for Research in Adolescence, Alexandria, Va.

Corder, S. P. (1967). The significance of learner's errors. *International Review of Applied Linguistics in Language Teaching.*

Cuellar, J. B. (1980). A model of Chicano culture for bilingual education. In R. Padilla (Ed.), *Ethnoperspectives in Bilingual Education Research,* vol. II: Theory in Bilingual Education. Ypsilanti, Mich.: Dept. of Foreign Languages and Bilingual Studies, Eastern Michigan University.

Cummins, J. (1979). Linguistic interdependence and the educational development of bilingual children. *Review of Educational Research, 19,* 222–251.

————— (1981). The role of primary language developments in promoting educational success for language minority students. In *Schooling and language minority students: A theoretical framework* (pp. 3–50). Los Angeles: Evaluation, Dissemination, and Assessment Center.

————— (1984). *Bilingualism and special education.* San Diego: College Hill Press.

————— (1986). *Empowering minority students: A framework for intervention.* Harvard Educational Review, *56*(1), 18–35.

————— (1989). *Empowering minority students.* Sacramento, Calif.: CABE.

————— (1991). Interdependence of first- and second-language proficiency in bilingual children. In Bialystok, E. (Ed.), *Language processing in bilingual children.* New York: Cambridge University Press.

Darcy, N. T. (1953). A review of the literature of the effects of bilingualism upon the measurement of intelligence. *Journal of Genetic Psychology, 82,* 21–57.

————— (1963). Bilingualism and the measurement of intelligence: Review of a decade of research. *Journal of Genetic Psychology, 103,* 259–282.

Destefano, J. (1972). Social variation in language: Implications for teaching reading to black ghetto children. In J. A. Figurel (Ed.), *Better reading in urban schools* (pp. 18–24). Newark, Del.: International Reading Association.

Development Associates (1984). *Final report descriptive study phase of the national longitudinal evaluation of the effectiveness of services for language minority limited English proficient students.* Arlington, Va.: Author.

Dewey, J. (1916). *Democracy and education: An introduction to the philosophy of education.* New York: Macmillan.

————— (1921). *Reconstuction and philosophy.* London: University of London Press.

Diaz, R. M. (1983). The impact of bilingualism on cognitive development. In E. W. Gordon (Ed.), *Review of research in education* (vol. 10, pp. 23–54). Washington, D.C.: American Educational Research Association.

——— (1985). Bilingual cognitive development: Addressing these gaps in current research. *Child Development, 56,* 1376–1388.

Diaz, R. M., and Klinger, C. (1991). Towards an explanatory model of the interaction between bilingualism and cognitive development. In E. Bialystock (Ed.), *Language processing in bilingual children.* New York: Cambridge University Press.

Diaz, S., Moll, L. C., and Mehan, H. (1986). Sociocultural resources in instruction: A context-specific approach. In *Beyond language: Social and cultural factors in schooling language minority students* (pp. 197–230). Sacramento: Bilingual Education Office, California State Department of Education.

Dolson, D. (1984). *The influence of various home bilingual environments on the academic achievement, language development, and psychosocial adjustment of fifth and sixth grade Hispanic students.* Unpublished doctoral dissertation, University of San Francisco.

Donald, M. (1991). *Origins of the modern mind: Three stages in the evolution of culture and cognition.* Cambridge, Mass.: Harvard University Press.

Dulay, H., and Burt, M. (1974). *Natural sequence in child second language acquisition.* Working papers on bilingualism. Toronto: The Ontario Institute for Studies in Education.

Duquette, G. (1991). Cultural processing and minority language children with needs and special needs. In G. Duquette and L. Malave (Eds.), *Language, culture and cognition.* Philadelphia: Multilingual Matters, Ltd.

Duran, R. (1983). *Hispanics' education and background: Predictors of college achievement.* New York: College Entrance Examination Board.

——— (1986). *Improving Hispanics' educational outcomes: Learning and instruction.* Unpublished manuscript. Graduate School of Education, University of California, Santa Barbara.

Dwyer, C. (1991). Language, culture and writing (working paper 13). Berkeley, Calif.: Center for the Study of Writing, University of California.

Dyson, A. H. (1983). The role of oral language in early writing processes. *Research in the Teaching of English, 17,* 1–30.

Eckert, P. (1989). *Jocks and burnouts: Social categories and identity in the high school.* New York: Teachers College Press.

Eder, D. (1982). Difference in communication styles across ability groups. In L. C. Wilkinson (Ed.), *Communicating in the classroom*. New York: Academic Press.

Edmonds, R. (1979). Some schools work and more can. *Social Policy, 9*(5), 28–32.

———— (1979). Effective schools for the urban poor. *Educational Leadership, 37*, 20–24.

Elam, S. (1972). Acculturation and learning problems of Puerto Rican children. In F. Corrdasco and E. Bucchini (Eds.), *The Puerto Rican community and its children on the mainland*. Metuchen, N.J.: Scarecrow Press.

Erickson, F. (1986). Qualitative methods in research on teaching. In M. C. Wittrock (Ed.), *Handbook of research on teaching* (pp. 119–158). New York: Macmillan.

———— (1987). Transformation and school success: The politics and culture of educational achievement. *Anthropology and Education Quarterly 18*(4), 335–355.

Ervin-Tripp, S. M. (1974). Is second language learning like the first? *TESOL Quarterly, 8*(2), 111–127.

Feldman, C., and Shen, M. (1971). Some language-related cognitive advantages of bilingual five-year-olds. *Journal of Genetic Psychology, 118*, 235–234.

Feldt, L. S., and Brennan, R. C. (1989). Reliability. In R. L. Linn (Ed.), *Educational Measurement* (3rd ed., pp. 105–146), New York: American Council on Education and Macmillan.

Fernandez, R., and Shu, G. (1988). School dropouts: New approaches to an enduring problem. *Education and Urban Society, 20*, 363–386.

Ferreiro, E. (1988, April). *Emergent literacy*. Paper presented at the annual convention of the American Educational Research Association. New Orleans, La.

Ferreiro, E., and Teberosky, A. (1982). *Literacy before schooling*. Exeter, N.H.: Heinemann.

Fiere, P. (1970). *Pedagogy of the oppressed*. New York: Seabury Press.

Fishman, J. (1989). Bias and anti-intellectualism: The frenzied fiction of 'English only.' In *Language and Ethnicity in Minority Sociolinguistic Perspective*. London: Multilingual Matters Ltd.

Fordham, S. (1988). Racelessness as a factor in black students' school success: Pragmatic strategy or pyrrhic victory? *Harvard Educational Review, 58*(1), 54–83.

Frase, M. (1989). *Dropout rates in the United States: 1988* (Analysis Report). Washington, D.C.: Superintendent of Documents, U.S. Government Printing Office.

Friedson, E. (1986). *Professional powers.* Chicago, Ill.: University of Chicago Press.

Galambos, S. J., and Hakuta, K. (1988). Subject-specific and task-specific characteristics of metalinguistic awareness in bilingual children. *Applied Psycholinguistics, 9,* 141–162.

Gallas, K. (1991). Arts as epistemology: Enabling children to know what they know. *Harvard Educational Review, 61,* 40–50.

Gallimore, R., and Tharp, R. G. (1989). *Challenging cultural minds.* London: Cambridge University Press.

García, E. (1983). *Bilingualism in early childhood.* Albuquerque: University of New Mexico Press.

———— (1986). Bilingual development and the education of bilingual children during early childhood. *American Journal of Education, 95,* 96–121.

———— (1988). Effective schooling for language minority students. In National Clearing House for Bilingual Education (Ed.), *New Focus.* Arlington, Va.: National Clearing House for Bilingual Education.

———— (1989). Instructional discourse in "effective" Hispanic classrooms. In R. Jacobson and C. Faltis (Eds.), *Language distribution issues in bilingual schooling* (pp. 104–120). Clevedon, England: Multilingual Matters, Ltd.

———— (1991). Bilingualism, second language acquisition in academic contexts. In A. Ambert (Ed.), *Bilingual education and English-as-a-second language: A research annual* (pp. 181–217). New York: Garland.

———— (1991a). *Characteristics of effective teachers for language minority students: A review.* Education Report #1, National Center for Research on Cultural Diversity and Second Language Learning.

———— (1991b). Attributes of effective language minority teachers: An empirical study. *Journal of Education, 173,* 130–141.

———— (1992). Hispanic children: Theoretical, empirical and related policy issues. *Educational Psychology Review, 4,* 69–93.

———— (1992). Effective instruction for language minority students: The teacher. *Journal of Education, 173* (2), 130–141.

García, E. and Gonzales, G. (1984). Spanish and Spanish-English development in the Hispanic child. In S. V. Martinez and R. H. Mendoza (Eds.), *Chicano psychology.* New York: Academic Press.

García, E., Maez, L., and Gonzalez, G. (1983). Language switching in bilingual children: A national perspective. In E.

García (Ed.), *The Mexican-American child: Language, cognition and social development.* (pp. 56–73). Tempe: Arizona State University.

García, R. (1979). *Teaching in a pluralistic society.* New York: Harper and Row.

Gardner, H. (1985). *Frames of mind: The theory of multiple intelligences.* New York: Basic Books.

Gardner, R. C., and Lambert, E. (1972). *Attitudes and motivation in second language learning.* Rowley, Mass.: Newbury House.

Garth, T., Elson, T., and Morton, M. (1936). The administration of non-language intelligence tests to Mexicans. *Journal of Abnormal and Social Psychology, 31,* 53–58.

Gay, G. (1975). Organizing and designing culturally pluristic curriculum. *Educational Leadership, 33,* 176–183.

Genishi, C. (1981). Code switching in Chicano six-year-olds. In R. Duran (Ed.), *Latino language and communicative behavior.* (pp. 133–152) Norwood, N.J.: Ablex Publishing Corporation.

Genishi, C., and Dyson, A. H. (1984). *Language assessment in the early years.* Norwood, N.J.: Ablex.

Gibson, M. A. (1987). The school performance of immigrant minorities: A comparative view. *Anthropology and Education Quarterly 18* (4), 262–275.

Gibson, M. A., and Ogbu, J. U. (1991). *Minority status and schooling.* New York: Garland.

Giroux, H. A., and McLaren, P. (1986). Teacher education and the politics of engagement: The case for democratic schooling. *Harvard Review, 56,* 213–238.

Gleason, J. B. (1988). *The development of language.* Columbus, Ohio: Merrill Publishing Company.

Goldenberg, C. (1992). *Instructional conversations and their classroom application: Education practice report #2.* National Center for Research on Cultural Diversity and Second Language Learning, University of California, Santa Cruz.

Goldenberg, C, and Gallimore, R. (1991). *Teaching and learning in a new key: The instructional conversation.* Paper presented at the annual meeting of the American Educational Research Association, Chicago, Ill.

———— (1990, September). *Meeting the language arts challenge for language-minority children: Teaching and learning in a new key.* Progress Report for 1989–90 to Presidential Grants for School Improvement Committee, University of California Office of the President.

Goldenberg, C., and Patthey-Chavez, G. (1991). *Discourse processes in instructional conversations: Interactions between teacher and transition students.* Manuscript submitted for publication.

Goldman, S., and Trueba, H. (Eds.) (1987). *Becoming literate in English as a second language: Advances in research and theory.* Norwood, N.J.: Ablex Corp.

Golnick, D. M., and Chinn, P. C. (1986). *Multicultural education in a pluristic society.* New York: Maxwell Macmillian International Press.

Gonzalez, G. (1970). The acquisition of Spanish grammar by native Spanish speakers. Unpublished doctoral dissertation, University of Texas.

———— (1990). *Chicano education in the segregation era: 1915–1945.* Philadelphia: The Balch Institute.

———— (1991). Spanish language acquisition research among Mexican American children. *Early Childhood Research Quarterly, 6,* 411–426.

Goodenough, W. H. (1981). *Culture, language, and society* (2nd ed.). Menlo Park, Calif.: Benjamin/Cummings Publishing Co.

Goodlad, J. (1984). *A place called school.* New York: McGraw-Hill.

Goodman, Y. (1980). The roots of literacy. In M. P. Douglass (Ed.), *Reading: A humanizing experience.* (pp. 286–301). Claremont: Claremont Graduate School.

Grant, C. (1991). Educational research and teacher training for successfully teaching LEP students. In office of Bilingual Education and Minority Language Affairs (Ed.), Proceedings of the Second National Research Symposium on Limited English Proficient Student Issues. Washington, D.C.: U.S. Department of Education.

Grant, C. A., and Sleeter, C. (1987). An analysis of multicultural education in the U.S. *Harvard Educational Review, 57,* 421–444.

Guerra, M. H. (1979). Bilingualism and biculturalism: Assets for Chicanos. In A. Trejo (Ed.) *The Chicanos: As we see ourselves* (pp. 129–136). Tucson: University of Arizona Press.

Hakuta, K. (1974). A preliminary report on the development of grammatical morphemes in a Japanese girl learning English as a second language. *Working Papers in Bilingualism.* Toronto: The Ontario Institute for Studies in Education, *3,* 294–316.

———— (1986). *Mirror of language: The debate on bilingualism.* New York: Basic Books.

Hakuta, K., Diaz, R., and Ferdman, M. (1986). *Bilingualism and cognitive development: Three perspectives and methodological implications.* Los Angeles: CLEAR.

Hakuta, K., and García E. (1989). Bilingualism and bilingual education. *American Psychologist, 44*(2), 374–379.

Hakuta, K., and Snow, C. (1986, January). *The role of research in policy decisions about bilingual education.* Washington, D.C.: Testimony before the U.S. House of Representatives, Education and Labor Committee.

Hall, N. (1987). *The emergence of literacy.* Portsmouth, N.H.: Heinemann Educational Books, Inc.

Halliday, M. A. K. (1973). *Explorations in the functions of language.* London, England: Edward Arnold.

Hamers, J. F., and Blanc, M. (1989). *Bilinguality and bilingualism.* New York: Cambridge University Press.

Harrison, J. (1985). Functions of language attitudes in school settings. *Language in Society, 22,* 1–21.

Heath, S. B. (1981). Towards an ethnohistory of writing in American education. In M. Farr-Whitman (Ed.), *Variation in writing: Functional and linguistic-cultural differences, Vol. 1 of Writing: The nature, development and teaching of written communication.* (pp. 225–246). 2 Vols. Hillsdale, N.J.: Lawrence Erlbaum,.

———— (1982). Questioning at school and at home: A comparative study. In G. D. Spindler (Ed.), *Doing the ethnography of schooling: Educational anthropology in action* (pp. 102–131). New York: Holt, Rinehart and Winston.

———— (1983). *Ways with words.* Cambridge, England: Cambridge University Press.

———— (1986). Sociocultural contexts of language development. In Evaluation, Dissemination, and Assessment Center, *Beyond language: Social and cultural factors in schooling language minority students.* Los Angeles: California State University.

Henze, R., Regan, K., Vanett, L., and Power, M. (1990). *An exploratory study of the effectiveness of the lower Kuskokwin school district's bilingual program.* Paper prepared for The Lower Kuskokwin School District, Oakland, Calif.

Hetherington, E. M., and Parke, R.D. (Eds.) (1988). *Contemporary reading in child psychology* (3rd ed.). New York: McGraw-Hill.

Hoffman, D. M. (1988). Cross-cultural adaptation and learning: Iranians and Americans at school. In H. Trueba and C. Delgado-Gaitian (Eds.), *School and society: Learning content through culture.* New York: Praeger Publishers.

Huerta, A. (1977) The development of codeswitching in a young bilingual. *Working Papers in Sociolinguistics, 21.*

Irujo, S. (1988). An introduction to intercultural differences and similarities in nonverbal communication. In Wurzel, J. (Ed.), *Toward multiculturalism.* Yarmouth, Maine: Intercultural Press.

Jackman, M. R. (1973). Education and prejudice or education and response-set. *American Sociological Review 38,* 327–339.

Jaynes, G. D., and Williams, R. M., Jr. (Eds.). (1989). *A common destiny: Blacks and American society.* Washington, D.C.: National Academy Press.

Jencks, C., Smith, M., Acland, H., Bane, M., Cohen, D., Gintis, H., Hynes, B., and Micelson, S. (1972). *Inequality: A reassessment of the effects of family and schooling in America.* New York: Basic Books.

Johnson, D., and Johnson, R. (1981). Effects of cooperative and individualistic learning experiences on interethnic interaction. *Journal of Educational Psychology 73*(3),444–449.

Johnson, D. L., Teigen, K. and Davila, R. (1983). Anxiety and social restriction: A study of children in Mexico, Norway, and the United States. *Journal of Cross-Cultural Psychology, 14,* 439–454.

Joyce, B., Murphy, C., Showers, B., and Murphy, J. (1989). School renewal as cultural change. *Educational Leadership,* 47(3), 70–77.

Kagan, S. (1983). Social orientation among Mexican American children: A challenge to traditional classroom structures. In E. Garcia (Ed.), *The Mexican American child.* Tempe: Arizona State University.

———— (1984). Interpreting Chicano cooperativeness: Methodological and theorethical considerations in Chicano psychology. In E. Garcia, (Ed.), *The Mexican American child.* Tempe: Arizona State University.

———— (1986). Cooperative learning and sociocultural factors in schooling. In *Beyond language: Social and cultural factors in schooling language minority students.* Los Angeles: Evaluation, Dissemination, and Assessment Center, California State University.

Kagan, S., Knight, G. P., Martinez, S., and Espinosa-Santana, P. (1981). Conflict resolution style among Mexican children: Examining urbanization and ecology effects. *Journal of Cross-Cultural Psychology, 12,* 222–232.

Kanter, D. L., and Mirvis, P. H. (1989). *The cynical Americans: Living and working in an age of discontent and disillusion.* San Francisco: Jossey-Bass.

Kaufman, P., and Frase, M. J. (1990). *Dropout rates in the United States: 1989.* Washington, D.C.: National Center for Education Statistics.

Keefe, S. E. (1979, summer). Urbanization, acculturation, and extended family ties: Mexican Americans in cities. *American Ethnologist, 349–362.*

Keefe, S. E. and Padilla, A. M. (1987). *Chicano ethnicity.* Albuquerque: New Mexico Press.

Keefe, S. E., Padilla, A. M., and Carlos, M. L. (1979). The Mexican American extended family as an emotional support system. *Human Organization, 38,* 144–152.

Kessler, C. and Quinn, M. E. (1987). Language minority children's linguistic and cognitive creativity. *Journal of Multilingual and Multicultural Development, 8*(1), 173–185.

Knight, G. P., and Kagan, S. (1979). Development of prosocial and competitive behaviors in Anglo American and Mexican American children. *Child Development, 48,* 1385–1394.

Kozol, J. (1991). *Savage inequalities: Children in America's schools.* New York: Crown.

Krashen, S. D. (1981). Bilingual education and second language acquisition theory. In California State Department of Education (Ed.), *Schooling and language minority students.* Dissemination and Assessment Center, California State University, Los Angeles, 3–50.

——— (1985). *The input hypothesis: Issues and implications.* New York: Longman.

Kroeber, A. L., and Kluckhohn, C. (1963). *Culture: A critical review of concepts and definitions.* New York: Vintage Books.

Labov, W. (1972). The logic of nonstandard English. In W. Labov (Ed.), *Language in the inner city: Studies in black English vernacular.* Philadelphia: University of Pennsylvania Press.

Laosa, L. M. (1982). School, occupation, culture and family: The impact of parental schooling on the parent-child relationship. *Journal of Educational Psychology, 74.*

Larkin, R. W. (1979). *Suburban youth in cultural crisis.* New York: Oxford University Press.

Lave, J. (1988). *Cognition in practice: Mind mathematics and culture in everyday life.* Cambridge, UK: Cambridge University Press.

Lee, L. C. (1991, Winter). The opening of the American mind: Educating leaders for a multicultural society. *Human Ecology Forum,* pp. 2–5.

Leopold, W. F. (1939). *Speech development of a bilingual child: A linguist's record. Vol. I, Vocabulary growth in the first two years.* Evanston, Ill.: Northwestern University Press.

Levin, H. M. (1986). *Educational reform for disadvantaged students: An emerging crisis.* Washington, D.C.: National Education Association.

Levin, I. (1988). *Accelerated schools for at-risk students.* (CPRE Research Report Series RR-010). New Brunswick, N.J.: Rutgers University Center for Policy Research in Education.

Lindholm and Christiansen. (1990). pp. 3–15.

Lucas, T. (1987). *Black English discourse in urban contexts.* Doctoral dissertation. Georgetown University, Washington, D.C.

Lucas, T., Henze, R., and Donato, R. (1990). Promoting the success of Latino language minority students: An exploratory study of six high schools. *Harvard Educational Review, 60,* 315–334.

MacNab, G. (1979). Cognition and bilingualism: A re-analysis of studies. *Linguistics, 17,* 231–255.

Manuel, H., and Hughes, L. (1932). The intelligence and drawing ability of young Mexican children. *Journal of Applied Psychology, 16,* 382–387.

Matute-Bianchi, E. (1990). *A report to the Santa Clara County School District: Hispanics in the schools.* Santa Clara, Calif.: Santa Clara County School District.

McClintock, C. G. (1972). Social motivation: A set of propositions. *Behavioral Science, 17,* 438–454.

———— (1974). Development of social motives in Anglo American and Mexican children. *Journal of Personality and Social Psychology, 29,* 348–354.

McClintock, E., Bayard, M., and McClintock, C. G. (1983). The socialization of social motives in Mexican-American families. In E. Garcia (Ed.), *The Mexican American Child* (pp. 143–162). Tempe: Arizona State University.

McDermott, R. P. (1987). The exploration of minority school failure, again. *Anthropology and Education Quarterly 18*(4), 361–364.

McGahie, W. C. (1991). Professional competence evaluation. *Educational Researcher, 20*(1), 3–9.

Mead, M. (1937). *Cooperation and competition among primitive people.* New York: McGraw.

———— (1939). *Culture of the islander.* New York: Academic Press.

Mehan, H. (1979). *Learning lessons: Social organizations in the classrooms.* Cambridge, Mass.: Harvard University Press.

———— (1985). *Handicapping the handicapped.* Stanford, Calif.: Stanford University Press.

Melmed, P. J. (1971). Black English phonology: The question of reading interference. Philadelphia: *Monographs of the Language-Behavior Research Laboratory.*

Milk, R. D. (1986). The issue of language separation in bilingual methodology. In E. Garcia and B. Flores (Eds.), *Language and literacy in bilingual education* (pp. 67–86). Tempe: Arizona State University.

Moll, L. (1988). Educating Latino students. *Language Arts, 64,* 315–324.

Moll, L., and Diaz, S. (1986). Bilingual communication and reading. *Elementary School Journal,* in press.

Morine-Dershimer, G. (1985). *Talking, listening and learning in elementary classrooms.* New York: Longman.

Nanda, S. (1990). *Cultural anthropology.* New York: D. Van Nostrand.

National Association of State Directors of Teacher Education and Certification. (1984). *NASDTEC Certification Standards.* Washington, D.C.: Author.

National Center for Education Statistics. (1991). *The Condition of Education,* Vols. 1 and 2, Washington, D.C.: United States Department of Education.

National Center for the Study of Children in Poverty. (1990). *Five million children: A statistical profile of our poorest young citizens.* National Center for Children in Poverty. New York: Columbia University.

National Commission on Children. (1991). *Beyond rhetoric. A new American agenda for children and families: Final report of the National Commission on Children.* Washington, D.C.: Author.

New Jersey State Board of Education Handbook. (1991). *Guidelines for Development of Program Plan and Evaluation Summary.* Bilingual/ESL Programs and English Language Services, Fiscal Year 1991. New Jersey State Department of Education.

Nieto, S. (1979). Curriculum decision-making: The Puerto Rican family and the bilingual child. Unpublished doctoral dissertation, University of Massachusetts, Amherst.

Nine Curt, C. J. (1984). *Nonverbal communication.* Cambridge, Mass.: Evaluation, Dissemination, and Assessment Center.

Oakes, J. (1984). *Keeping Track.* New Haven, Conn.: Yale University Press.

———— (1988). Tracking: Can schools take a different route? *National Education Association School Journal, 63,* 131–154.

———— (1990). *Multiplying inequalities: The effects of race, social class, and tracking on opportunities to learn mathematics and science.* Santa Monica, Calif.: Rand Corp.

————— (1991). *Lost talent: The underparticipation of women, minorities, and disabled persons in science.* Santa Monica, Calif.: Rand Corp.

Oakes, J., and Lipton, M. (1992, February). Detracking schools: Early lessons from the field. *Phi Delta Kappan.*

Ochs, E., Taylor, C., Rudolph, D., and Smith, R. C. (1989). *Narrative activity as a medium for theory-building.* Unpublished manuscript, University of Southern California.

Ogbu, J. (1983). Minority status and schooling in plural societies. *Comparative Education Review 27*(22), 168–190.

————— (1982). Socialization: A cultural ecological approach. In K. M. Borman (Ed.), *The social life of children in a changing society,* 253–267.

————— (1986). The consequences of the American caste system. In Ulric Neisser (Ed.), *The school achievement of minority children: new perspectives.* Hillsdale, N.J.: Erlbaum.

————— (1987a). *Minority education and caste: The American system in cross-cultural perspective.* New York: Academic Press.

————— (1987b). Variability in minority school performance: A problem in search of an explanation. *Anthropology and Education Quarterly, 18*(4), 312–334.

————— (1988). Class stratification, racial stratification and schooling. In L. Weiss (Ed.). *Class, race and gender in American education,* Albany, N.Y.: State University of New York Press.

Ogbu, J., and Matute-Bianchi, M. E. (1986). Understanding sociocultural factors: Knowledge, identity and school adjustment. In Bilingual Education Office, California State Department of Education (Ed.), *Beyond language: Social and cultural factors in schooling language minority students.* Los Angeles, Calif.: Evaluation, Dissemination, and Assessment Center, California State University.

Olsen, L. (1988). *Crossing the schoolhouse border: Immigrant students and the California public schools.* San Francisco, Calif.: California Tomorrow Policy Research.

O'Malley, M. J. (1981). *Children's and services study: Language minority children with limited English proficiency in the United States.* Rosslyn, Va.: National Clearinghouse for Bilingual Education.

Ovando, C. and Collier, V. (1985). *Bilingual and ESL classrooms: Teaching in multicultural contexts.* New York: McGraw-Hill.

Padilla, A. M. and Liebman, E. (1975). Language acquisition in the bilingual child. *The Bilingual Review/La Revista BilinguÅe, 2,* 34–55.

Paley, V. (1981). *Wally's stories.* Cambridge: Harvard University Press.

———— (1986). *Mollie is three: Growing up in school.* Chicago, Ill.: The University of Chicago Press.

Paul, B. (1965). Anthropological perspectives on medicine and public health. In J. K. Skipper, Jr. and R. C. Leonard (Eds.), *Social interaction and patient care.* Philadelphia: J. B. Lippincott.

Peal, E., and Lambert, W. E. (1962). The relation of bilingualism to intelligence. *Psychological Monographs: General and Applied, 76*(546), 1–23.

Pearl, A. (1991). Democratic education: Myth or reality. In R. Valencia (Ed.), *Chicano school failure and success* (pp. 101–118). New York: Falmer Press.

Pease-Alvarez, C., and García, E. (in press). Effective instruction for language minority students: An early childhood case study. *Early Childhood Research Quarterly.*

Pease-Alvarez, L., Espinoza, P., and García, E. (1991). Effective schooling in preschool settings: A case study of LEP students in early childhood. *Early Childhood Research Quarterly,* 153–164.

Pelto, P., and Pelto, G. H. (1975). Intra-cultural variation: Some theoretical issues. *American Ethnologist, 2,* (1), 1–45.

Perry, J. (1975). Notes toward a multicultural curriculum. *English Journal, 64.*

Phelan, P., Davidson, L. A., and Cao, T. H. (1991). *Students' multiple worlds: Navigating the borders of family, peer, and school cultures.* U.S. Department of Education, Cooperative Agreement #OERI-G0087C235.

Phillips, S. U. (1972). Participation structures and communication incompetence: Warm Springs children in community and classroom. In C. Cazden, D. Hymes, and W. J. Johns (Eds.), *Functions of language in the classroom.* (pp. 161–189). New York: Teachers College Press.

Phillips, S. U. (1984). *The invisible culture.* New York: Longman.

———— (1983). *The invisible culture: Communication in classroom and community on the Warm Springs Indian reservation.* New York: Longman.

Purkey, S. C., and Smith, M. S. (1983). Effective schools: A review. *Elementary School Journal, 83,* 52–78.

Ramirez, A. (1985). *Bilingualism through schooling.* Albany, N.Y.: State University of New York Press.

Ramirez, J. D., and Merino, B. J. (1990). Classroom talk in English immersion, early-exit and late-exit transitional bilingual education programs. In R. Jacobson and C. Faltis

(Eds.), *Language distribution issues in bilingual schooling.*
(pp. 61–103). Clevedon, England: Multilingual Matters.

Ramirez, J. D., Yuen, S. D., Ramey, D. R., and Pasta, D. J.
(1991). *Final report: Longitudinal study of structured English
immersion strategy, early-exit and late-exit transitional bilingual
education programs for language-minority children.* San Mateo,
Calif.: Aguirre International.

Ramirez, M., and Castaneda, A. (1974). *Cultural democracy,
bi-cognitive development and education.* New York: Academic
Press.

Reyhner, J. (1989). Changes in American Indian education: A
historical retrospective for educators in the United States. In
ERIC Digest, EDO-RC-89-1, Clearinghouse on Rural Education and Small Schools, Charleston, W.Va.: Appalachia
Educational Laboratory.

Reynolds, A., and Elias, P. (1991). *What is good teaching: A
review of the literature.* Princeton, N.J.: Educational Testing
Service.

Rivera-Medina, E. J. (1984). The Puerto Rican return migrant
student: A challenge to educators. *Educational Research
Quarterly, 8,* 82–91.

Rivera and Zehler (1990). *Collaboration on teaching and learning: Findings from the innovative approaches research project.*
Arlington, Va.: Development Associates.

Rodriguez, C. E. (1989). *Puerto Ricans born in the U.S.A.*
Winchester, Mass.: Unwin Hyman, Inc.

Rogoff, B. (1990). *Apprenticeship in thinking: Cognitive development in social context.* Oxford: Oxford University Press.

Rose, M. (1989). *Lives on the boundary.* New York: The Free
Press.

Rosenshine, B. (1986). Synthesis of research on explicit teaching. *Educational Leadership, 43,* 60–69.

Rueda, R., and Mehan, H. (1987). Metacognition and passing.
Anthropology and Education Quarterly, 17(3), 145–165.

Rutter, M., Maughan, B., Mortimore, P., and Ouston, J.
(1979). *Fifteen thousand hours: Secondary schools and their effects
on children.* Cambridge: Harvard University Press.

Sarason, S. B. (1990). *The predictable failure of educational reform:
Can we change course before it's too late?* San Francisco: Jossey-
Bass Publishers.

———— (1992). *Letter to a serious education president.* Newbury
Park, Calif.: Corwin Press.

Schuman, H., and Harding, J. (1964). Prejudice and the
norm of rationality. *Sociometry, 27,* 353–371.

Schuman, H., Steeh, C., and Bobo, L. (1985) *Racial attitudes in America: Trends and interpretations.* Cambridge: Cambridge University Press.

Schumann, J. H. (1976). Affective factors and the problem of age in second language acquisition. *Language Learning, 25,* 209–239.

Schwartz, T. (1978). Where is the culture? Personality as the distributive locus of culture. In G. Spinder (Ed.), *The making of psychological anthropology.* Berkeley, Calif.: University of California Press.

Science Magazine Editors. (1992). Minorities in science: The pipeline problem. *Science, 258,* 1057–1276.

Scollon, R., and Scollon, S. (1981). *Narrative literacy and face in interethnic communication.* Norwood, N.J.: Ablex.

Scribner, S., and Cole, M. (1981). *The psychology of literacy.* Cambridge: Harvard University Press.

Seginer, R. (1989). *Adolescent sisters: the relationship between younger and older sisters among Israeli Arabs.* Paper presented at the meeting of the International Society for the Study of Behavioral Development, Jyvaskyla, Finland.

Seliger, H. W. (1977). Does practice make perfect? A study of interactional patterns and L2 competence. *Language Learning, 27*(2), 263–278.

Sharan, S. (1980). Cooperative learning in small groups: Recent methods and effects on achievement, attitudes, and ethnic relations. *Review of Education Research 50*(2), 241–271.

Sheldon, W. (1924). The intelligence of Mexican children. *School and Society, 19,* 139–142.

Shimberg, B. (1983). What is competence? How can it be assessed? In M. R. Stern (Ed.), *Power and conflict in continuing professional education* (pp. 17–37). Belmont, Calif.: Wadsworth.

Skinner, B. F. (1957). *Verbal behavior.* Englewood Cliffs, N.J.: Prentice-Hall.

Skrabanek, R. L. (1970). Language maintenance among Mexican Americans. *International Journal of Comparative Sociology, 11,* 272–282.

Skutnabb-Kangas, T. (1979). *Language in the process of cultural assimilation and structural incorporation of linguistic minorities.* Rosslyn, Va.: National Clearinghouse for Bilingual Education.

Slavin, R. E. (1988). Cooperative learning and student achievement. In R. E. Slavin (Ed.), *School and classroom organization.* Hillsdale, N.J.: Erlbaum.

———— (1989). The pet and the pendulum. Fadism in education and how to stop it. *Phi Delta Kappan, 70.*

Slavin, R., Karweit, N., and Madden, N. (1989). *Effective programs for students at risk.* Needham Heights, Mass.: Allyn and Bacon.

Sleeter, C. E., and Grant, C. A. (1987). An analysis on multicultural education in the U.S. *Harvard Educational Review, 57,* (4).

Smith, F. (1971). *Understanding reading.* New York: Holt, Rinehart and Winston.

Smith, T. W. (1990). *Ethnic images.* (*GSS Topical Report No. 19*). National Opinion Research Center, University of Chicago.

Smith, T. W., and Sheatsley, P. B. (1984). American attitudes towards race relations. *Public Opinion, 7,* 14–15, 50–53.

Snow, C. E., Barnes, W. S., Chandler, J. , Goodman, I. F., and Hempfill, L. (1991). *Unfulfilled expectations: Home and school influence on literacy.* Cambridge, Mass.: Harvard University Press.

Sorenson, A. P. (1967). Multilingualism in the Northwest Amazon. *American Anthropologist, 69,* 67–68.

Spencer, D. (1988). Transitional bilingual education and the socialization of immigrants. *Harvard Educational Review, 58(2).*

Spencer, M. B. (1988). Self-concept development. In D. T. Slaughter (Ed.), *Black children and poverty: A developmental perspective* (pp. 103–116). San Francisco: Jossey-Bass.

Spencer, M. B., and Horowitz, F. D. (1973). Effects of systematic social and token reinforcement on the modification of racial and color concept attitudes in black and in white preschool children. *Developmental Psychology, 9,* 246–254.

Spindler, G. (1955). *Anthropology and education.* Stanford: Stanford University Press.

———— (1974). *Education and cultural process: Toward an anthropology of education.* New York: Holt, Rinehart and Winston.

———— (1982). *Doing the ethnography of schooling: Educational anthropology in action.* New York: Holt, Rinehart and Winston.

———— (1987). *Education and cultural process: Anthropological approaches.* Prospect Heights, Ill.: Waveland Press.

Spiro, M. E. (1951). Culture and personality: The natural history of a false dichotomy. *Psychiatry, 14,* 19–46.

Sternberg, R. J., and Wagner, R. K. (Eds.) (1986). *Practical intelligence.* New York: Cambridge University Press.

Suarez-Orozco, M. M. (1985, May). *Opportunity, family dynamics and school achievement: The sociocultural context of motivation* *among recent immigrants from Central America.* Paper read at the University of California Symposium on Linguistics, Minorities and Education, Tahoe City, Calif.

———— (1987). Becoming somebody: Central American immigrants in U. S. inner-city schools. *Anthropology and Education Quarterly, 18,* 287–299.

———— (1989). *Central American refugees in U.S. high schools: A psycho-social study of motivation and achievement.* Stanford: Stanford University Press.

Sue, S., and Okazaki, S. (1990). Asian-American educational achievements: A phenomenon in search of an explanation. *American Psychologist, 45,* (8), 913–920.

Sue, S., and Padilla, A. (1986). Ethnic minority issues in the United States: Challenges for the educational system. In *Beyond language: social and cultural factors in schooling language minority students.* Sacramento, Calif.: Bilingual Education Office. California State Department of Education.

Sullivan, P. (1992). *ESL in context.* Newbary Park, Calif.: Corwin Press.

Tharp, R. G. (1989). Psychocultural variables and k constants: Effects on teaching and learning in schools. *American Psychologist, 44,* 349–359.

Tharp, R. G., and Gallimore, R. (1988). *Rousing minds to life: Teaching, learning and schooling in social context.* Cambridge: Cambridge University Press.

———— (1989). *Challenging cultural minds.* London: Cambridge University Press.

The College Board and the Western Interstate Commission for Higher Education (1991). *The road to college: Educational progress by race and ethnicity.* New York: The College Board.

Thomas, S. V. and Park, B. (1921). *Culture and personality* (2nd ed.). New York: Random House.

Thornton, S. (1981). *The issue of dialect in academic achievement.* Unpublished doctoral dissertation, University of California, Berkeley.

Tikunoff, W. J. (1983). *Compatibility of the SBIF features with other research on instruction of LEP students.* San Francisco: Far West Laboratory (SBIF-83-4.8/10).

Trueba, H. T. (1987). *Success or failure? Learning and the language minority student.* Scranton, Pa.: Harper and Row.

———— (1988). *Rethinking learning disabilities: Cultural knowledge in literacy acquisition.* Unpublished manuscript. Office for Research on Educational Equity. Graduate School of Education, Santa Barbara, University of California.

———— (1988). Peer socialization among minority students: A high school dropout prevention program. In H. Trueba and C. Delgado-Gaitan (Eds.), *Schools and society: Learning content through culture.* New York: Praeger Publishers.

Trueba, H. T., Moll, L. C., Diaz, S., and Diaz, R. (1982). *Improving the functional writing of bilingual secondary students.* Washington, D.C.: National Institute of Education.

Trujillo, F. X. (1989). *The teacher.* Poem prepared for the Celebration of the Teacher, Sacramento, Calif.

Ueda, R. (1987). *Avenues to adulthood: The origins of the high school and social mobility in an American suburb.* Cambridge: Cambridge University Press.

U.S. Congress. (1984). *Equal Educational Opportunities and Transportation of Students Act of 1974,* 294(f).20 U.S.L.

———— (1965). Senate Committee on Labor and Public Welfare. Subcommittee on Education. *Elementary and secondary education act of 1965.* Washington, D.C. United States Government Printing Office.

U.S. General Accounting Office. (1987, March). *Research evidence on bilingual education.* Washington, D.C.: U.S. General Accounting Office, GAO/PEMD-87-12BR.

U.S. v. Texas. 647F. 2d 69 (9th Cir. 1981).

Valadez, C. M. (1986). *The acquisition of English syntax by Spanish-English bilingual children.* Doctoral dissertation, Stanford University.

Valencia, R. (1991). *Chicano school failure and success.* New York: The Falmer Press.

Valsiner, J. (1989). How can developmental psychology become "Culture Inclusive"? In J. Valsiner (Ed.), *Child development in cultural context* (pp. 1–8).

Varenne, H. (1982). Jocks and freaks: The symbolic structure of the expression of social interaction among American senior high school students. In G. Spindler (Ed.), *Doing the ethnography of schooling: Educational anthropology in action.* New York: Holt, Rinehart and Winston.

Veltman, C. (1988). *The future of the Spanish language in the United States.* New York: Hispanic Policy Project.

Villegas, A. M. (1991). *Culturally responsive pedagogy for the 1990's and beyond.* Princeton, N.J.: Educational Testing Service.

Vogt, L., Jordan, C., and Tharp, R. (1987). Explaining school failure, producing school success: Two cases. *Anthropology and Education Quarterly, 18*(4), 276–286.

Waggoner, D. (1984). The need for bilingual education: Estimates from the 1980 census. *NABE Journal, 8,* 1–14.

———— (1991). *Language minority census newsletter.* Washington, D.C.: Waggoner Incorporated.

Walberg, H. (1986). What works in a nation still at risk. *Educational Leadership 44*(1), 7–11.

———— (1986). Synthesis of research on teaching. In M. Wittrock (Ed.), *Handbook of research on teaching* (3rd ed., pp. 15–32). New York: Macmillan.

Walker, C. L. (1987). Hispanic achievements: Old views and new perspectives. In H. Trueba (Ed.), *Success or Failure? Learning and the language minority student.* (pp. 15–32). Cambridge, Mass.: Newbury House.

Wallace, A. F. C. (1970). *Culture and personality* (2nd ed.). New York: Random House.

Walsh, R. (October 12, 1990). Minority students in Santa Clara County continue to deteriorate academically. *San Francisco Examiner,* B1–4.

Weis, L. (1988). *Class, race and gender in American education.* Albany, N.Y.: State University of New York Press.

Wertsch, J. V. (1985). *Vygotsky and the social formation of mind.* Cambridge, Mass.: Harvard Press.

Wiesner, T. S., Gallimore, R., and Jordan, C. (1988). Unpackaging cultural effects on classroom learning. Native Hawaiian peer assistance and child-generated activity. *Anthropology and Education Quarterly, 19*(4).

Wilson, W. J. (1987). *The truly disadvantaged: The inner city, the underclass, and public policy.* Chicago, Ill.: University of Chicago Press.

Wong-Fillmore, L. (1976). *The second time around: Cognitive and social strategies in second language acquisition.* Ph.D. dissertation, Stanford University.

———— (1991). When learning a second language means losing the first. *Early Childhood Research Quarterly, 6,* 323–346.

Wong-Fillmore, L., and Valadez, C. (1985). Teaching bilingual learners. In M. S. Wittrock (Ed.), *Handbook on research on teaching* (3rd ed., pp. 648–685). Washington, D.C.: American Educational Research Association.

Wong-Fillmore, L., Ammon, M. S., and McLaughlin, B. (1985). *Learning English through bilingual instruction* (NIE Final Report #400-360-0030). Rosslyn, Va.: National Clearinghouse for Bilingual Education.

Zentella, A. C. (1981). Ta bien you could answer me en cualquier idioma: Puerto Rican code switching in bilingual classrooms. In R. Duran (Ed.), *Latino language and communicative behavior.* (pp. 109–112). Norwood, N.J.: Ablex Publishing Corp.

INDEX

achievement, 23–24; dropout rate,
16–17; funding for education, 18, 20–23
Elementary and Secondary Act (1965),
81, 98
Empowerment, 92, 95
English as Second Language, 37, 124–126,
230
English, nonstandard, 134–135
English speakers, 138
English, standard, 131
Enrollment, public school, 11–13
Environment: passive language, 129–130,
139; self-concept and, 196
Equal Educational Opportunities and
Transportation Act (1974), 82, 98
Equity, educational, 80–82, 89, 97
Errors, language acquisition, 118, 125–126
Escalante, Jaime, 65
ESL. *See* English as Second Language
Ethnic image, 193–197, 215
Ethnicity, 151, 155, 195
Ethnic studies, 211: ability grouping,
210–214; bridge building, 208–210;
educational implications of, 207
European students, 35
Event rates report, 17, 40
Examinations, professional, 223
Expectations, for students, 55, 242,
254–256, 258, 274–275
Experience, extending, 41–42, 71–72,
100–101, 139–140, 176, 216–217,
246–248, 277–278

Fairness, 21, 40
Family: alienation, 50–51; income, 11,
13–14; influence on students, 185;
language heritage and, 50; role in
socialization, 188–194; stability, 11;
violence, 11
Feedback, 254
"Female" professions, 48
Fiere, Paulo, 92
Filipino students, 32
First language, 119–120, 149
Five Million Children, 14
Florida, 35, 49
Folk theory, 201, 203
Follow Through, 86

Formulaic expressions, 120
French–English bilinguals, 156
Funding, 18–23, 40, 81

Gallas, Karen, 170
Ganas, 65
García studies, 268–274
Gender discrimination, 48
Gender–relevant education, 260
Gender-separate culture, 191
Generalization, 119
General Social Survey, 194
German-English bilinguals, 156
Global marketplace, 47, 69
Goals, need for, 255, 258
Goodenough Intelligence Test, 151
Grammar, 111–112, 138
Group membership, 202
Group-oriented culture concept, 52–55,
69–70, 80

Haiti, 9–10
Hawaiian children, 114, 123
Head Start, 86
Health, child, 11
Heath, Shirley Brice, 62
Hebrew-English bilinguals, 157
High-input generators, 122
High school education, 47
Hill, Ken (Dr.), 79–80
Hispanic families, 192–193
Hispanic students, 11–14, 17–18, 32, 34,
39, 49, 164, 168–169
Home language loss, 50. *See also* Language,
use of native
Home-school communication, 66
Home-school culture mismatch, 62, 91, 99,
128, 139, 146, 148, 168, 174–175, 253,
276, 282
Human relations, 86–87

Idioverse, 56
Illinois, 49, 226
Images, 193
Imitation, 119
Immersion programs, 87–88, 98
Immigrants, 7–10, 26–27, 39, 77–78,
84–85, 97, 198, 203, 205–207